CRITICAL READING
WORKBOOK

SAT®

ies™ Test Preparation
Integrated Educational Services

ADVANCED PRACTICE SERIES

ILEX
Educational Publishers

Created by
Arianna Astuni, President IES
Khalid Khashoggi, CEO IES

Editorial
Christopher Carbonell, Executive Editor
Patrick Kennedy, Senior Editor
Caitlin Hoynes-O'Connor, Editor

Design
Kim Brown, Creative Director
Ana Grigoriu, Book Cover Designer

Authors
Arianna Astuni
Christopher Carbonell
Joseph Carlough
Chris Holliday
Caitlin Hoynes-O'Connor
Patrick Kennedy
Khalid Khashoggi
Sarah Khashoggi
Paul King
John Manna
Annie Shi

Published by ILEX Publications

24 Wernik Place

Metuchen, NJ 08840

www.ILEXpublications.com

© ILEX Publications, 2014

ON BEHALF OF

Integrated Educational Services, Inc.

355 Main Street

Metuchen, NJ 08840

www.ies2400.com

We would like to thank the ILEX Publications team as well as the teachers and students at IES2400 who have contributed to the creation of this book. We would also like to thank our Chief Marketing Officer, Sonia Choi, for her invaluable input.

The SAT is a registered trademark of the College Board, which was not involved in the production of, and does not endorse, this product.

ISBN: 978-0-9913883-6-3

QUESTIONS OR COMMENTS? Email us at info@ilexpublications.com

TABLE OF CONTENTS

TRY ALL OF OUR ADVANCED PRACTICE SERIES BOOKS

If you like this easy-to-use workbook, check out our other great volumes. The *SAT Grammar Workbook* is part of the *IES Advanced Practice Series*, which currently includes a *Reading Comprehension Workbook*, a *Math Workbook*, a *Grammar Workbook*, and the soon to be released *New 2016 SAT Workbook*. Please visit www.ILEXpublications.com to order these resources, or find our complete line of SAT workbooks on Amazon.com.

anomalous - unusual or different
discourse - modes of teaching (discussion)

PRACTICE TEST 1

anomalous - unusual or different

Practice Test 1

SECTION 1
Time–25 minutes
24 Questions

Directions: For each question in this section, select the best answer from among the choices given and fill in the corresponding circle on the answer sheet.

Each sentence below has one or two blanks, each blank indicating that something has been omitted. Beneath the sentence are five words or sets of words labeled A through E. Choose the word or set of words that, when inserted in the sentence, best fits the meaning of the sentence as a whole.

Example:

Jimmy opened his gas station in the ------- because he wanted to be in the middle of a metropolis.

(A) country
(B) suburbs
(C) periphery
(D) environment
(E) city

---

1. Rather than ------- his mother, Bernard decided to clean his room before she got home, therefore ------- her tirade.

   (A) frustrate . . ensuring
   (B) provoke . . avoiding
   (C) exult . . dodging
   (D) encourage . . eschewing
   (E) enervate . . securing

2. Jules was a ------- businessman, one who showed keen judgment when ------- potential investments.

   (A) incompetent . . evaluating
   (B) savvy . . contradicting
   (C) astute . . excoriating
   (D) inane . . investigating
   (E) shrewd . . assessing

3. Eunice was born into poverty, but after graduating from college she improved her ------- in life by achieving success and fortune.

   (A) lot   (B) task   (C) talent
       (D) saga   (E) goal

4. As humanitarians, Mother Teresa and Norman Borlaug both sought to ------- human suffering by performing acts of compassion and personal sacrifice.

   (A) alleviate   (B) exacerbate   (C) revive
       (D) indulge   (E) encapsulate

5. Under normal circumstances, rescue work can be -------: moreover, during inclement weather, it is often -------.

   (A) dangerous . . intemperate
   (B) challenging . . perilous
   (C) stimulating . . fatal
   (D) boring . . exciting
   (E) selfless . . altruistic

6. While often exhausted after a long day of work, our father would frequently be infused with ------- when we suggested that he join us for a hike in the woods behind our house.

   (A) conviviality   (B) temerity   (C) vitality
       (D) fatigue   (E) athleticism

7. The world of science has witnessed a sudden ------- applications for research grants for the study of marine ecology: historically at the ------- of environmental awareness, this field has only recently gained prominence.

   (A) recrimination of . . trough
   (B) fascination with . . nadir
   (C) retraction of . . bottom
   (D) spate of . . peak
   (E) surge in . . periphery

8. James Packard was not of aristocratic rank when he married into the British royal family; he was the first ------- to do so.

   (A) charlatan   (B) commoner   (C) maverick
       (D) jingoist   (E) speculator

GO ON TO THE NEXT PAGE

The passages below are followed by questions based on their content; questions following a pair of related passages may also be based on the relationship between the paired passages. Answer the questions on the basis of what is <u>stated</u> or <u>implied</u> in the passages and in any introductory material that may be provided.

Questions 9-12 are based on the following passages.

Passage 1

If one were to turn back the geological clock by 200 million years, one would find that all the continents on today's Earth were once contiguous: they
Line formed a single supercontinent known as Pangaea. But
5 turn the geological clock forward, and today's separated continents will once again collide. Geologists are widely convinced that a new supercontinent, known as "Amasia," will be formed 100 million years from now. This time, Europe and North America will touch
10 borders somewhere in the Arctic Circle, while Southern Hemisphere landmasses such as South America and Australia will move north.

Passage 2

The possibility of a new supercontinent, commonly referred to as "Amasia," is a prospect that
15 fires the imagination. Naturally, none of us will live to see this new landmass. Even so, we can speculate about where such geological upheaval will leave the species and civilizations that are here hundreds and millions of years on. Perhaps all intelligent life will
20 fuse together in a single super-civilization. Perhaps the animals of the Eastern and Western Hemispheres will be pitted all-against-all in a worldwide contest for survival. But I am most intrigued by the prospect of a new super-ocean on the other side of the globe. What
25 unforeseen new forms of life will emerge to claim this giant world of water as their own?

9.   Both passages express the view that Amasia is

(A) a little-known theory
(B) an inevitable outcome
(C) a harshly contended topic
(D) a chimerical hypothesis
(E) a conjectural notion

10. Unlike the author of Passage 1, the author of Passage 2 considers all of the following EXCEPT:

(A) the conjoining of land masses
(B) the repercussions of a change
(C) the interactions of species
(D) the proposals of geologists
(E) the fate of human society

11. Compared to the tone of Passage 2, the tone of Passage 1 is more

(A) informative
(B) meditative
(C) quizzical
(D) laudatory
(E) accusatory

12. Which best describes the relationships between the two passages?

(A) Passage 1 considers a hypothesis that is discussed imaginatively in Passage 2.
(B) Passage 1 proposes a likelihood that is then substantiated in Passage 2.
(C) Passage 1 explains the origins of a past event in a manner that Passage 2 contradicts.
(D) Passage 1 supports a claim with evidence that is shown to be incomplete in Passage 2.
(E) Passage 1 takes an experimental approach to a concept that is presented lyrically in Passage 2.

GO ON TO THE NEXT PAGE

1　　1　　1　　1　　1　　1

Unauthorized copying or
reuse of any part of this
page is illegal.

Questions 13-24 are based on the following passage.

This passage discusses famous lyricist-and-composer duos, and describes how these pairs influenced the world of musical theatre.

Both on Broadway and in London's West End, the majority of theaters are, to this day, offering musicals to the public. For the ordinary theatergoer, the twenty-first century might seem to be a golden
5　age for such shows. The aficionado, however, may have some reservations. Whenever experts examine what is actually being offered under the banner of "musical comedy," they find that the product is either a stage version of a popular film
10　or a collection of "greatest hits" from some long-disbanded pop group. Even worse, it could be an offering from Andrew Lloyd Webber, who replaces musical wit with repetitive, cacophonous chords of noise, and who abandons the energetic but
15　carefully-interpreted roles usually played by singers and dancers in favor of the spectacular movement of stage machinery to create spurious "emotional" effects. This is not what the sophisticated follower of this genre considers a "musical."
20　A true musical has a storyline that makes reference to the period in which it is written, often affectionately poking fun at contemporary politics, culture, and attitudes. Certainly, musicals are directed at audiences that are not necessarily familiar with the
25　more classical approach of opera or ballet; nonetheless, these shows proffer songs and dance sequences in order to help advance the plot, explain a character's motivations, or comment on a situation. The storyline, dialogue, and lyrics often possess a sense of irony and
30　wit that embodies the times. If we accept this definition of a musical, then it would seem that John Gay's *The Beggars' Opera*, written way back in 1728, was the very first example of this genre of entertainment. However, Gay's composition seems to have been
35　a relatively isolated piece: it was not until over a hundred years later that Jacques Offenbach composed a series of witty and popular light operas. There is little doubt that Offenbach's success in Paris encouraged the emergence in England of the light comic operas of
40　W. S. Gilbert and Arthur Sullivan, which mark the real beginnings of the modern musical.
Gilbert and Sullivan came together from different backgrounds to foster a new and lasting form of theater. Sullivan was a proficient musician, regarded
45　during his lifetime as one of Britain's most promising composers. Gilbert, on the other hand, began as a naval surgeon but became a writer of clever and funny short stories and verse. Gilbert's famous technique was to use what he called the "topsy-turvy"
50　method, portraying society in apparently outrageous situations not normally expected in the real world and doing so in a deadpan style: this juxtaposition

gave his work a veneer of objectivity as well as a wealth of surprising humor. Gilbert and Sullivan were
55　introduced to one another by the theatrical impresario and producer Richard D'Oyly Carte, who wanted to develop the possibilities of Parisian light opera within the English tradition. The union Carte engineered between Gilbert and Sullivan was a stroke of genius:
60　for the first time in musical theater, composer and lyricist worked collaboratively and not separately, so that music and word fused together.
The influence of Gilbert and Sullivan was enormous not only in London, but also, more
65　importantly, in the United States. Very few composers of musicals have demonstrated an ability to create lyrics that not only fit the rhythms of the music but also echo the emotions and psychological implications within the instrumentation. The Americans adopted
70　the essence of what Gilbert and Sullivan had achieved together and began to follow suit. Even Cole Porter, who could write individual songs to perfection, turned to various lyricists with whom he could forge a rapport in order to bring his musicals to life. The great
75　American musicals of the early and middle twentieth century were almost exclusively hammered out, often brilliantly, by talented collaborative pairs, who melded music and word to create perfect harmony for their audiences. (Irving Berlin and Steven Sondheim were
80　anomalies, the only creators of classic musicals who managed to achieve remarkable success individually.) Today, the mid-century musicals of Richard Rodgers and Oscar Hammerstein are often regarded as "schmaltzy" and "saccharine," derided by supposedly
85　sophisticated critics. However, if we examine *Carousel*, the second show Rodgers and Hammerstein wrote together, we can only wonder at the ease with which dialogue moves into song and at the apt use of dance to reveal the joys, the memories, and the fears
90　of the characters. Songs are used to bring out the characters' thoughts: although the music in isolation may contribute a simple tune and the lyrics in isolation can be decried as sentimental, when combined on stage, they produce a mood and an intensity that
95　overwhelm the audience's emotions. I challenge anyone to listen to the finale number, "As You Walk Through a Storm", without shedding a tear.
Powerful musicals make us feel that we have been involved in something that has helped us to
100　accept the state of the world a little more cheerfully. It is that quality in musicals that seems to have disappeared, to be replaced by something rather tawdry and second-hand. As Cole Porter and P. G. Wodehouse wrote in one of their musicals:

GO ON TO THE NEXT PAGE

105　　*"Good authors too, who once knew better words*
Now only write four-letter words,
Writing prose. Anything goes."

Indeed. In today's "musicals," anything does go.

13. The author's primary purpose in writing this passage is to

(A) describe the works of contemporary playwrights and how these authors maintain popularity

(B) analyze what seems to be a decline in the emotional and social impact of musical theater

(C) argue in favor of his own unique method of creating popular and meaningful theater

(D) contradict a common attitude among critics that musicals today are increasingly complicated

(E) repudiate the concept of a lyricist working with a composer to create musical theater

14. The author's contrast between the "ordinary theatergoer" (line 3) and the "aficionado" (line 5) primarily

(A) juxtaposes great musicals to determine how producers can succeed financially

(B) explains the merits of both popular and classical musical theater

(C) indicates differences in quality between contemporary musicals and earlier productions

(D) reveals the wide range of popular forms of musical theater available today

(E) exposes a source of growing conflict between experts on musicals and more casual viewers

15. Based on information presented in the first paragraph, the "aficionado" (line 5) enjoys musicals that feature

(A) balanced numbers of solo and duet songs

(B) special effects and high production values

(C) loud and raucous orchestral music

(D) stage adaptations of popular cinematic hits

(E) lively roles that are full of meaning

16. The author uses quotation marks around "musical comedy" (line 8), "greatest hits" (line 10), "emotional" (line 17), and "musical" (line 19) to convey an attitude of

(A) confusion

(B) amazement

(C) cynicism

(D) elitism

(E) corruption

17. In context of the second paragraph, the author's definition of a "true musical" (line 20) most strongly supports which of the following arguments?

(A) True musicals are still more popular among theatergoers than plays based on movies.

(B) Musical accompaniment exists solely to increase the production value of modern musicals.

(C) Writers of musicals avoid controversy when deciding on the subject matter of their works.

(D) Theater is rewarding when it is both entertaining and historically relevant.

(E) Musical theatre will continue to grow more sophisticated as the centuries progress.

18. According to the passage, the author is most likely to argue that Gilbert's "topsy-turvy" (line 49) method of storytelling

(A) provides satirical commentary alongside engaging entertainment

(B) muddles the intended message of the lyricist by twisting the facts of reality

(C) avoids angering the audience because it incites melancholy responses

(D) announces the playwright's intentions explicitly by creating an alternative world

(E) amounts to an accurate representation of situations that occur in everyday life

19. According to the passage, the author believes that Carte's most important contribution to the inception of the modern musical was that his "stroke of genius" (line 59)

(A) convinced both Gilbert and Sullivan to abandon their past careers to work on musicals

(B) encouraged a tradition of pairing writers and composers to produce meaningful musicals

(C) invited a wider audience into the theater with simpler themes in order to increase revenue

(D) subverted the older traditions of operatic epics, which had become stale and unpopular

(E) enriched the world of theater by mixing real world scenarios with ludicrous situations

GO ON TO THE NEXT PAGE ⟶

20. The author's parenthetical statement in lines 79-81 ("Irving Berlin . . . individually") provides the reader with examples of which of the following?

(A) Composers who could not find a profitable place in the world of musicals
(B) Brilliant playwrights whose work did not catch popular attention
(C) Famous writers of musicals who did not consistently pair with collaborators
(D) Lyricists who found acclaim despite their indifference to contemporary social issues
(E) Actors who eventually became famous producers of musicals

21. The author's characterization of Rodgers and Hammerstein's modern "critics" (line 85) implies that these critics

(A) erroneously dismiss the pair's musicals based on their sentimental nature
(B) actively cultivate a refined opinion of musicals written in the last century
(C) properly respect the time and effort that went into combining word and song in these shows
(D) reverently wonder at the technological advances brought on by big-budget stage productions
(E) disparage the musical duo for their cavalier attitude toward the standards of musical theater

22. The author's description of Rodgers and Hammerstein's *Carousel* (line 86) in the fourth paragraph reveals the idea that

(A) the complex choreography of *Carousel* provides specific cues to the audience that are missing in audio recordings
(B) the character-revealing songs in *Carousel* make the musical especially appropriate for film and ballet adaptation
(C) the emotional impact of a musical is explained by the intensity of the audience's experience
(D) the simpler productions of Rodgers and Hammerstein's earlier works have a greater value than the later, more elaborate musicals
(E) the ease of transition between dialogue and lyrics is unique to Rodgers and Hammerstein's works and is missing in earlier musicals

23. The author mentions "As You Walk Through a Storm" (lines 96-97) as an example of

(A) a strongly written set of lyrics that lost much of its power due to a lack of harmony in the music
(B) a song that seemed compelling in theory but whose components never cohered properly in performance
(C) a unique song that has never been matched in emotional force by another musical composition
(D) a piece that was originally intended for a musical but eventually gained popularity among the general public
(E) a representative piece from a musical whose depth cannot be evaluated based on its lyrics alone

24. "Powerful musicals" (line 98), according to the entire passage, would be most analogous to which of the following?

(A) Novels that present a fatalistic view of the modern world
(B) Wholesome and nostalgic films with strong moral directives that represent idealized lifestyles
(C) Essays that analyze human experiences common to a wide variety of cultures
(D) Television dramas that present realistic situations using both witty dialogue and scenes of powerful emotion
(E) Dance performances that employ philosophical abstractions to represent that which is surreal and unattainable

STOP

If you finish before time is called, you may check your work on this section only.
Do not turn to any other section in the test.

2   2   2   Unauthorized copying or
                            reuse of any part of this   2   2   2
                            page is illegal.

SECTION 2
Time–25 minutes
24 Questions

Directions: For each question in this section, select the best answer from among the choices given and fill in the corresponding circle on the answer sheet.

Each sentence below has one or two blanks, each blank indicating that something has been omitted. Beneath the sentence are five words or sets of words labeled A through E. Choose the word or set of words that, when inserted in the sentence, <u>best</u> fits the meaning of the sentence as a whole.

Example:

Jimmy opened his gas station in the ------- because he wanted to be in the middle of a metropolis.

(A) country
(B) suburbs
(C) periphery
(D) environment
(E) city

---

1. The road from New York to Boston is ------- by so many ------- that it is considered unusable by most motorists.

    (A) beset . . inconveniences
    (B) characterized . . efficiencies
    (C) refined . . attractions
    (D) supported . . interferences
    (E) connected . . municipalities

2. When Jason, the waiter at the restaurant where Samantha dined, ------- her complaints, she became so ------- that she decided never to eat there again.

    (A) acknowledged . . annoyed
    (B) aggravated . . depressed
    (C) eliminated . . angry
    (D) fueled . . satisfied
    (E) ignored . . disillusioned

3. It was difficult to follow the teacher's instructions because of the many ------- in his lecture, which constantly pursued unusual new digressions.

    (A) stopgaps   (B) tangents   (C) prevarications
    (D) traces   (E) consequences

4. Although the Svalbard Islands are located in the icy waters of the Arctic Ocean, the climate of this archipelago is unexpectedly -------.

    (A) glacial   (B) balmy   (C) soporific
    (D) arid   (E) inhospitable

5. Without giving explicit -------, Harriet expressed ------- approval by nodding her head.

    (A) confirmation . . tacit
    (B) consent . . candid
    (C) support . . exhaustive
    (D) prohibition . . implicit
    (E) obstruction . . indirect

GO ON TO THE NEXT PAGE

11

Practice Test 1

The passages below are followed by questions based on their content. Answer the questions on the basis of what is <u>stated</u> or <u>implied</u> in the passages and in any introductory material that may be provided.

Questions 6-7 are based on the following passage.

Although of Japanese descent, Kazuo Ishiguro was raised in England, and thus attained a unique perspective on British culture and society. Yet the
Line displacement of immigration is not explored in
5 particularly great depth in his books. For instance, in *The Remains of the Day*, Ishiguro uses flashbacks to explore the profound dynamics of a World War II-era romance between a butler and a housekeeper. Another Ishiguro masterpiece, *Never Let Me Go*, is a science
10 fiction parable about clones who accept their ephemeral existences as doomed-to-die organ donors. Many critics wonder if Ishiguro would have anything pertinent to say about contemporary British culture. But if anything, his novels transcend time and place to offer a
15 global understanding of the human condition.

6. The passage is primarily concerned with

  (A) the difficulty of portraying contemporary society in fiction
  (B) the reception of books that describe World War II
  (C) the unique and specific insights of a modern novelist
  (D) the controversy surrounding a contemporary author's reputation
  (E) the influence of cultural exchange on a single writer's prose style

7. The book examples mentioned in lines 5-11 ("For instance . . . donors") primarily suggest that

  (A) Ishiguro has little interest in exploring any single milieu in great depth
  (B) Ishiguro's stories are directed at readers with extensive knowledge of history
  (C) Ishiguro's ideology made him more progressive than his contemporaries
  (D) Ishiguro's books are not exclusively concerned with immigration issues
  (E) Ishiguro consistently focuses on the motifs of self-acceptance and self-fulfillment

Questions 8-9 are based on the following passage.

"Growing up Italian-American" is not a topic that seems to warrant TV specials or critical theory bestsellers. Socially, it is just not a big deal. But let me
Line tell you, behind this face that seems to meld into any
5 ethnic group, I am tainted by my Italian ancestry. I cringe like a dog when a hand comes near my face—so strongly have I been conditioned to expect that my cheeks will be pinched until my blood vessels pop. I am an English teacher, but I still hear nothing wrong
10 when my uncles pronounce "three" without the "h." I do quick translations in my head before ordering "gravy" or "manicot" and I use funeral prayer cards to mark pages the way most people would use a normal bookmark.

8. According to the passage, "Growing up Italian-American" can best be described as

  (A) a lightly humorous ordeal with few meaningful repercussions
  (B) a seemingly quotidian subject with surprisingly deep implications
  (C) a means of analyzing widely-neglected cultural differences
  (D) a rarely-discussed topic that should be a source of greater interest
  (E) a source of ironies that make the narrator's daily life confusing

9. The statements in lines 8-14 of the passage ("I am . . . bookmark") primarily serve to

  (A) show how the author remains optimistic in distressing circumstances
  (B) cast doubt on how well Italian-Americans can adapt to new conditions
  (C) humorously digress from the primary argument of the passage
  (D) identify causes of vexation that are widely misunderstood
  (E) demonstrate how the author's heritage plays a role in everyday life

GO ON TO THE NEXT PAGE

Questions 10-17 are based on the following passage.

This passage is adapted from an autobiographical essay written by an author whose parents immigrated to the United States. Here, the author discusses the phenomenon of first-generation immigrant children.

Today, when you walk into a supermarket, above the normal humming of the air conditioning, the harsh scraping of shopping cart wheels, and the
Line lilting songs on the radio, you can hear occasional
5 snippets of dialogue from places all over the world. When you turn into the cereal aisle, maybe you'll walk past a cheerful greeting from India. Roll your cart past the dairy section and you'll hear easy banter from China. As you meander through the store, you'll
10 pass a smile from Russia, a question from Kenya, and perhaps an apology from Mexico. By the time you've paid for your groceries and are taking out your keys for the car ride home, you'll have tasted a crumb from every slice of the world pie.
15 America isn't known as the melting pot for nothing. Since its first colonization in the fifteenth century, the New World has attracted all types of people, from the tight-lipped Puritans who settled in New England to the debt-laden criminals who were
20 sent to Georgia. However, today America's diversity has risen far beyond the sole distinction of religion. With immigrants flocking to the country from every corner of the world, America's melting pot now contains more ingredients than anyone can count, and
25 these ingredients are slowly but steadily melding with the original stew.
While the influx of ethnic diversities may color America into a country vastly different from what it once was, America is also changing the tone of
30 its newest additions. Known as first-generation Americans, these children of immigrants have centuries of their home cultures pumping through their veins, yet these relative newcomers are struggling against what is innate and are trying to
35 comprehend what is shaping them on the outside. These children are caught between two worlds: that of their well-remembered ancestors and that of an alluring American culture. In this situation, first-generation Americans are pushed and pulled until
40 they are simply stretched in every direction.
I grew up in an extremely diverse community. In my high school, three Chinese students were given the top grades, the best concert seats at Carnegie Hall, and the surest promises of successful futures.
45 One became a lawyer, the other two doctors—they all will be able to live good, comfortable lives, and they will be good at everything that they try.
But if you take a closer look into the lives of these children, and children like them, a different
50 story may unfold. With parents who had to risk all in order to get an education and have the

opportunity to find a new life in America, these children face enormous expectations. In the eyes of many immigrant parents, a person without an
55 education is a person without a future. And yet, the burden of getting the best grades isn't the only burden that these first-generation Americans carry.
Perhaps Amy Tan, author of *The Joy Luck Club* (a novel featuring four Chinese immigrant mothers
60 and their American-born daughters) puts it best. As one of the daughters remarks about her mother, "I think how to explain this, recalling the words Harold and I have used with each other in the past… But these are words she could never understand." For
65 first-generation Americans, the biggest struggle is deciding on a cultural identity. These children are born American, are members of distant cultures, are educated in American schools, and are instructed at home in the values of their ancestors. So are they
70 American? Or do they belong to their heritage?
Many first-generation Americans, despite being born and raised here, still need to take ESL (English as a Second Language) classes in grade school in order to keep up with their peers. Growing up with
75 two languages on the tips of their tongues may seem like an advantage to some, but it is really another sign that these students possess two minds squashed into one body. They may speak English with their friends, play the same games, and talk about the
80 same topics, but after they step off the bus back home, they walk through doors into very different worlds. Within the walls they call home, they speak the language of their parents, eat the food of their country, and adhere to standards of behavior that
85 would please their ancestors.
Having two different cultural identities isn't always a burden, though. Certainly, pride in your cultural heritage is never something to be disparaged. Multi-cultural fairs and minority organizations are
90 becoming increasingly popular all across the United States. Also, with American businesses growing past our country's borders, a bilingual background can give you a critical edge when it comes to job interviews. As Tan notes, once again in the voice of
95 one of her characters, "I wanted my children to have the best combination: American circumstances and Chinese character."
That's the ideal result of the theory, anyway. The reality? It's true that first-generation Americans have
100 many advantages that seem to float them to the top of the pot, but first they have to balance the two cultures that are trying to shape them. They may live in America, but there will always be the nagging doubt that they are not truly American. Nevertheless, when
105 that wave of anxiety has passed, a new story begins, maybe even one that can be told perfectly in many languages.

GO ON TO THE NEXT PAGE

10. The passage is primarily concerned with

   (A) the struggle to coordinate two disparate cultures in one's life
   (B) the importance of assimilating a new culture and its customs
   (C) the adversities faced by immigrant families with young children
   (D) analyzing what it takes to succeed in an ever-changing America
   (E) comparing the author's experiences to those of a well-known writer

11. The sentence in which the phrase "a crumb from every slice of the world pie" appears (lines 13-14) indicates that the author considers the supermarket to be

   (A) rife with unique cultures
   (B) a socially disorienting place
   (C) a market for foreign cuisine
   (D) psychologically upsetting
   (E) filled with cultural bias

12. In line 27, the word "color" most nearly means

   (A) tarnish
   (B) shade
   (C) tone
   (D) change
   (E) separate

13. The statement "a different story may unfold" (lines 49-50) refers to

   (A) the difference in point of view between a parent and a child
   (B) the adversities faced by immigrant parents as they try to assimilate
   (C) the poor academic performance of many immigrant children
   (D) the prospects for success that attract people from around the world to America
   (E) the pressures that are brought to bear on the children of immigrants

14. Which best describes the function of the statement in lines 48-50 ("But if . . . unfold")?

   (A) It describes a particularly dangerous way of looking at a certain problem.
   (B) It underscores an argument about how recent immigrants relate to American consumerism.
   (C) It illustrates how immigrant children deal with peer pressure.
   (D) It compares the parents' success with the children's adversities.
   (E) It transitions to a discussion of the tensions faced by a particular group.

15. It can be inferred from lines 71-85 that having "two minds squashed into one body" (lines 77-78) is most similar to the situation of

   (A) a young musician who craves to write his own songs, but is only allowed to play the classics by order of his instructor
   (B) a stage actor who practices colloquial slang with one theater group, but resorts to traditional Shakespearean verse with another theater group
   (C) a swimmer who spends all of his time practicing in a pool, but cannot overcome the pull of the tide when he swims his first race in the ocean
   (D) an exchange student from France who teaches his host family a few simple phrases in his native language
   (E) a first-generation Chinese American student who visits South Korea and finds that he has little in common with the students there

16. The question in lines 98-99 ("The reality?") functions primarily to

   (A) dispute the source of a previous statement
   (B) change the discussion from hypothetical to factual
   (C) hint at what the reader should be feeling
   (D) imply that the truth is not always tangible
   (E) refer to the high quality of a certain lifestyle

17. The overall tone of the passage is

   (A) diffident
   (B) melancholy
   (C) apologetic
   (D) reflective
   (E) flippant

GO ON TO THE NEXT PAGE

Questions 18-24 are based on the following passage.

The following passage is adapted from a 2013 essay in which the author describes a common French shopping experience.

For me, shopping is a necessity, and something to be accomplished in as short a time as possible: for the French, it is an art to be learned, taken seriously,
Line and pursued with a critical enthusiasm. I need bread
5 for breakfast? My reaction is to dash into the nearest *boulangerie**, give my order, pay, and leave. I warn you now: it is a mistake to attempt a quick excursion like that in the local shops of rural France. There is a ritual that must be followed.
10   As an Englishman, I understand the necessity of queuing in an orderly line should the shop be busy. No Frenchman—or woman—has ever believed that standing in line is necessary. French shoppers group themselves in sets of two or three, blocking
15 the passage between the counter and the door, and then settle down for a discussion—but only after first shaking hands or kissing one another on both cheeks. Hands gesture vigorously, heads nod or shake; each participant makes a perfectly constructed speech.
20 Interruptions are not permitted, but interjections of agreement are allowed to punctuate the progress of the argument. In a debate, this would be wonderful. In a shop, it is infuriating, for the shopkeeper would not dream of stepping in to move the customers along.
25   After a time the debate pauses, and one of the participants moves forward to be served; however, he or she does so not to present an order, but to segue into the next part of the discussion. This is the elaborate greeting between shopkeeper and
30 customer. A mere "Good morning!" is insufficient. The opening remark begins with a greeting, certainly, but is followed by an inquiry about the shopkeeper's health, a brief discussion of the weather, a rebuke over the difficulties of parking the car, and sundry
35 other matters. Eventually, the shopkeeper will ask about the requirements of the customer. This phase of the discussion could be compared to an aria at the Grand Opera; the customer launches into an elaborate recitation of what was bought in the shop
40 last time, how these items looked before preparation, how the preparation was achieved, and how the food tasted once prepared and served—here there is a small detour as the presentation to the guests and the guests' reactions are sketched out. One is reminded
45 of a Rossini opera, especially when the aria develops into a duet: the shopkeeper takes the contralto or baritone line and provides counterpoints to the customer, who is in much the same position as a principal soprano or tenor. I love *The Barber of Seville*
50 and *La Cenerentola* in the opera house, but I find it tedious when all I want from the *boulangerie* are three croissants to accompany my morning coffee.

This overview of the meal is followed by a serious passage in which the qualities of different
55 breads are discussed. It is true to say that any *boulangerie* in France will have a dazzling selection of boules and baguettes of various shapes, widths, and lengths; the shopkeeper is willing to cut large items in half or to slice the loaf to measure while the
60 customers—including the rest of the people in the shop—wait. To me, bread is bread. To a Frenchman, requesting bread is an exploration of complex tastes and health-giving properties.
The sequence moves to the finale. The various
65 items are popped into small brown bags, wrapped in squares of paper that are never large enough to cover the items, and popped into plastic bags which are then tied at the neck with little red tags, all with a smile and a quick calculation of the total price. Just
70 as you think the scene is drawing to a close, we move into a dazzling coda in which the customer realizes that payment is necessary and now begins to hunt for a purse or a wallet. Usually, this takes a good deal of patting of pockets, then diving into deep shopping
75 bags to find the handbag, which has to be opened so that another little search sequence can begin. There are two variations to this further routine. The first involves handing over a card that has to be placed into its little machine and waiting while the owner
80 remembers the code. The second involves writing a check. Never in my life have I thought of paying by check for an item that costs four Euros or less, but this is the norm in France and the rest of us must wait whilst the customer hunts for the checkbook, searches
85 for the ballpoint pen, asks what the date is, and finally signs and hands the check over.
The shopkeeper helps the customer to pick up and pack what has been bought and wishes the customer good morning. The shopkeeper will not
90 move onto the next customer until the previous customer has moved away from the counter; the shopkeeper waits longer, though, until the customer inevitably pops back in to make a comment or ask a question, and then sets off towards the shop door
95 but soon pauses, naturally, to join in the group discussions. About half an hour later, I receive my croissants and leave the shop. By the time I get home, I have already wolfed them down. I pause. Should I go back for more? *Non, Non, Non*!

* *"Boulangerie"* is a French term meaning "bakery."

18. The overall tone of the passage is one of

(A) sardonic humor
(B) unmitigated sadness
(C) jocular optimism
(D) recurring disbelief
(E) respectful impartiality

GO ON TO THE NEXT PAGE

19. The primary purpose of the passage is to

(A) express frustration with a foreign custom
(B) introduce the many varieties of French baked goods
(C) show how foreigners react to unknown protocols
(D) create a work of fantasy-like fiction based on an everyday experience
(E) compare buying bread to singing in an opera

20. The narrator states "For me . . . enthusiasm" (lines 1-4) in order to

(A) justify his idiosyncratic shopping behavior
(B) explain a discrepancy in culinary tastes
(C) introduce contrasting cultural attitudes
(D) criticize an entire social group for its lack of respected traditions
(E) support a controversial viewpoint

21. The author's references to *The Barber of Seville* (line 49) and *La Centerola* (line 50) serve to

(A) change the passage into a diatribe against modern marketing
(B) apply lighthearted humor to a dark situation
(C) add vital information about the setting
(D) wittily extend an earlier comparison
(E) introduce the concept of a *boulangerie* to a foreign reader

22. According to the author, the "finale" described in lines 64-86 is

(A) exaggerated and ignorant
(B) time-consuming and costly
(C) slow and humiliating
(D) humorous and outdated
(E) multi-faceted and trifling

23. In context, the word "norm" in line 83 most nearly means

(A) practice
(B) morality
(C) respect
(D) teaching
(E) yearning

24. The author uses which of the following to make his point?

(A) Historical comparison
(B) Extended analogy
(C) Scientific fact
(D) Objective analysis
(E) Slapstick humor

STOP
If you finish before time is called, you may check your work on this section only.
Do not turn to any other section in the test.

SECTION 3
Time–20 minutes
19 Questions

Directions: For each question in this section, select the best answer from among the choices given and fill in the corresponding circle on the answer sheet.

Each sentence below has one or two blanks, each blank indicating that something has been omitted. Beneath the sentence are five words or sets of words labeled A through E. Choose the word or set of words that, when inserted in the sentence, best fits the meaning of the sentence as a whole.

Example:

Jimmy opened his gas station in the ------- because he wanted to be in the middle of a metropolis.

(A) country
(B) suburbs
(C) periphery
(D) environment
(E) city   Ⓐ Ⓑ Ⓒ Ⓓ ●

1. Some scholars assert that the discovery of cheese was ------- because, although accidental, this event led to a food source both delicious and nutritious.

   (A) rewarding   (B) inevitable   (C) ingenious
      (D) fortuitous   (E) spontaneous

2. Some species of spider are more ------- than others, able to thrive under the most extreme weather conditions, while others are more ------- and therefore more prone to death at the slightest variation in temperature.

   (A) dependent . . fragile
   (B) resilient . . delicate
   (C) robust . . poisonous
   (D) venomous . . deadly
   (E) vulnerable . . endangered

3. Delicious when cooked, efficient when processed into energy, and appealing when dried as a decoration, corn truly has a ------- of different uses.

   (A) myriad   (B) deficit   (C) profundity
      (D) concession   (E) prohibition

4. In time, layers of sediment will transform into metamorphic rock through the joint influences of high temperature and tectonic pressure, a process described by geologists as simultaneously ------- and -------.

   (A) chemical . . chronological
   (B) integral . . elective
   (C) sequential . . derivative
   (D) thermal . . dynamic
   (E) spontaneous . . cyclical

5. The biggest selling point for the company's furniture is the ------- of its assembly instructions: the verbal directions are so clear that any graphic inserts are merely -------.

   (A) effectiveness . . invaluable
   (B) eloquence . . edifying
   (C) lucidity . . superfluous
   (D) ambiguity . . extraneous
   (E) complexity . . decorative

6. In anticipation of the much-touted new version of the iPhone, vendors have ------- existing versions of the product, which customers no longer wish to purchase.

   (A) stunted   (B) flaunted   (C) sidelined
      (D) scrutinized   (E) pillaged

GO ON TO THE NEXT PAGE

Practice Test 1

The two passages below are followed by questions based on their content and on the relationship between the two passages. Answer the questions on the basis of what is <u>stated</u> or <u>implied</u> in the passages and in any introductory material that may be provided.

Questions 7-19 are based on the following passages.

The two passages below discuss the acquisition of language by infants. Passage 1 is adapted from a 2002 book on infant psychology. Passage 2 was written by a science journalist in 2004.

Passage 1

From the very moment we come into this world, we find ourselves adrift in a sea of language. If it were possible to look back on our first few moments
Line of life, we would likely recall a cacophony of
5 unknown sounds, spoken by our nearest relatives. These strange sounds, incomprehensible to us at first, miraculously begin to take on both shape and meaning. In time, we learn to associate the word "clock" with the round object with two hands that
10 hangs upon the wall, while "cloud" comes to stand for that white ball of cotton up in the sky. This process of language acquisition is so natural and organic that we scarcely notice its occurrence at all. By the age of seven or eight, most of us have
15 experienced such total language acquisition that, by the time we reach adulthood, we find it nearly impossible to conceive of a "world without language"—even though this was the very world into which we were born, kicking and screaming, and not
20 understanding a thing. We have simply become so accustomed to seeing our world through the veil of our mother tongue that the world as an "undivided canvas"—that is, the world as perceived by an infant —has been all but lost from memory.
25 As Henry David Thoreau once said, "You don't gain something but that you lose something." In acquiring language, we gain the convenience and the expediency of a shared and common lexicon, while losing the holistic view of the world that is one aspect
30 of infancy. This is because our language acts as a knife, splitting the world neatly into subjects and objects—"I" as opposed to "you," "this" as opposed to "that," "us" as opposed to "them." Thus, we come see the world as a random jumble of distinct and
35 separable objects, not because this is how the world truly is, but because this is the best response to the world that our language can muster—and it is an inadequate response at best. Is it a fact that my neighbor, the sun, and the air around us are all quite
40 distinct and separable things, when in fact the sun is at all times heating the air, which is in turn being inhaled by my neighbor, only to be absorbed by his lungs and circulated by his blood? When we truly consider the diverse and nuanced interrelationships in
45 the world around us, we begin to see that our

language is capable of describing things only piecemeal. Like a camera lens that captures only the brightest colors, leaving everything else out of the image, the invisible net of our language allows much
50 of our world's richness and subtlety to slip through.

Passage 2

"Oh, I wish I was young again when everything seemed so wonderful!" So wrote Betty Smith in her novel *A Tree Grows in Brooklyn*. Such wistful nostalgia for the past is quite common—who among
55 us doesn't occasionally pine for the carefree days of our childhood? But as mature adults, we understand that the past is the past, and that there is no going back. To long for the golden days of our youth is perhaps natural, but if this yearning is indulged for
60 too long it becomes an exercise in futility.
One would think that the scientists, being some of the brightest and most pragmatic individuals among us, would most especially agree with this sentiment. Yet in the field of psychology, there is a
65 small but vociferous group of researchers who seem to view our very first few moments of life as a kind of paradisaical state, as the very pinnacle of human experience—if only we could remember it. According to these "experts," it is only in the pure, unadulterated
70 consciousness of our infancy that we can experience the world as a unified whole, or "as it really is." As time passes, however, we are cursed with the fate of having to learn language in order to communicate with our fellows. It is on account of this process of
75 language acquisition, so the researchers claim, that our words come to surround us like the curved and crooked mirrors of a funhouse, distorting our ability to see anything clearly.
Such sentiments are neither new nor remarkable
80 in the field of psychology. Over a century ago, even Sigmund Freud himself commented on the infantile consciousness, which he referred to as the "oceanic state." "That feeling of oneness with the universe," wrote Freud, in his seminal text *Civilization and Its*
85 *Discontents*, "sounds . . . like another way taken by the ego of denying the dangers it sees threatening in the external world." According to Freud himself, the "oceanic state" is a case of the ego in denial—not unlike the state of mind of the current crop of
90 researchers, who denounce language as the cause of

GO ON TO THE NEXT PAGE

all our woes. In their very view on the matter, they deny some very basic facts of reality—namely, that if it were not for those language-using, "fallen" adults who nurtured us from the very first day of life, the
95 "oceanic state" that these researchers praise would hardly be sustainable at all. Therefore, it is the very growth *out* of an infantile consciousness and into a mature one that is necessary to sustain life. To wish otherwise, and to long for the days of our pre-linguistic
100 infancy, is to go against a very natural and ordered flow.

7. The phrases "splitting the world" (line 31) and "crooked mirrors of a funhouse" (line 77) describe language, respectively, as

  (A) divisive and distorting
  (B) evolving and growing
  (C) conciliating and elucidating
  (D) expedient and unique
  (E) nuanced and fragmented

8. The figurative language used in the first sentence of Passage 1 conveys a sense of

  (A) permanence
  (B) vastness
  (C) aimlessness
  (D) hopelessness
  (E) terror

9. The "clock" (line 9) and the "cloud" (line 10) are mentioned in order to

  (A) illustrate the type of vocabulary that is taught by parents to their children
  (B) refute the idea that all language is incomprehensible to infants
  (C) introduce a theory that is later developed more fully
  (D) highlight a pivotal moment in the history of language acquisition
  (E) give examples of distinct sounds that eventually take on meaning

10. In the first paragraph of Passage 1, the process of language acquisition is characterized as

  (A) strange and intricate
  (B) unlikely and profound
  (C) subtle and complete
  (D) unsurprising and mundane
  (E) systematic and routine

11. In context, the phrase "through the veil" (line 21) most nearly means

  (A) around the obstruction
  (B) based on the memory
  (C) with the pretension
  (D) under the influence
  (E) with the motivation

12. According to the second paragraph of Passage 1, the effect of language acquisition is most analogous to which of the following?

  (A) Distinct performances by several operatic singers are blended to generate a discordant and incoherent sound.
  (B) A lump of clay is progressively shaped and molded into a recognizable figure of a man.
  (C) A blurred image comes into focus through the lens of a camera.
  (D) A scenic photograph is turned into the image on a jigsaw puzzle, the pieces of which are then scattered at random.
  (E) A speech made in a foreign language is elucidated by an interpreter.

13. The "researchers" (line 65) would most likely view the "world without language" (lines 17-18) mentioned in Passage 1 as one that is

  (A) feasible and worthy of rediscovery
  (B) desirable and free of conflict
  (C) preposterous and detrimental to society
  (D) justifiably lost through the process of maturity
  (E) the source of all of humanity's psychological troubles

14. The "sentiment" mentioned in line 64 of Passage 2 most directly refers to the idea that

  (A) youth is the most fulfilling stage of life
  (B) language detracts from genuine emotion
  (C) nostalgia is frequently unproductive
  (D) scientific study is a route to enlightenment
  (E) infancy can be remembered distinctly and coherently

15. The author of Passage 2 uses quotations in line 69 in order to

  (A) define a term used often by specialists
  (B) question the objectivity of a group
  (C) establish distance from a viewpoint
  (D) use vocabulary in an unconventional way
  (E) convey hostility for established authority

GO ON TO THE NEXT PAGE ⟶

Practice Test 1

16. The "oceanic state" mentioned in lines 82-83 of Passage 2 is most UNLIKE:

(A) the "undivided canvas" (lines 22-23)
(B) the "paradisaical state" (line 67)
(C) the "curved and crooked mirrors" (lines 76-77)
(D) the "infantile consciousness" (lines 81-82)
(E) the "pre-linguistic infancy" (line 99-100)

17. In context, the word "crop" (line 89) most nearly means

(A) sample
(B) group
(C) development
(D) reduction
(E) culture

18. In context of the passage as a whole, the author of Passage 1 characterizes language as

(A) insufficient in capturing the complexity of life, whereas Passage 2 views it as essential to survival
(B) attained in an automatic and natural manner, whereas Passage 2 views it as an artificial acquisition
(C) tending to distort reality, whereas Passage 2 views it as a unifying and healing influence
(D) arduous and complex, whereas Passage 2 views it as simple and accessible
(E) subjective yet vividly descriptive, whereas Passage 2 views it as candid and factual

19. The author Passage 2 would most likely characterize the final sentence of Passage 1 as

(A) justifiably carefree
(B) suspiciously manipulative
(C) scientifically accurate
(D) excessively wistful
(E) aptly philosophical

STOP

If you finish before time is called, you may check your work on this section only.
Do not turn to any other section in the test.

POST TEST ANALYSIS

This post test analysis is important if you want to see an improvement on your next test. Each section has a set of possible reasons for errors. Place check marks next to the ones that pertain to you, and write your own on the blank lines provided. Use this form to better analyze your performance. **If you don't understand why you made errors, there is no way you can correct them!**

1. **SENTENCE COMPLETION:**

    Problems with the sentence:
    - ❑ Wasn't familiar with phrases, idioms, or words in the sentence
    - ❑ Missed the clues or tones
    - ❑ Put your OWN word in the blank rather than one from the sentence
    - ❑ Completely avoided marking
    - ❑ Other: _____

    _____

    Problems with the answers:
    - ❑ Did not use process of elimination
    - ❑ Did not ignore unknown words
    - ❑ Did not use prefix/root/suffix knowledge to figure out the meaning of the unknown words
    - ❑ Did not match the clues and tones of the answer with those of the sentence
    - ❑ Did not recognize vocabulary words
    - ❑ Did not check answer to see if it fit
    - ❑ Other: _____

    _____

    Leaving questions unanswered:
    - ❑ Did not try
    - ❑ Did not fill in the blank(s) with words
    - ❑ Ran out of time
    - ❑ Other: _____

    _____

2. **SHORT READING COMPREHENSION:**

    - ❑ Did not read entire paragraph
    - ❑ Did not see more than one point
    - ❑ Missed contrast clues
    - ❑ Did not pinpoint thesis
    - ❑ Did not identify similarities and differences in Double Short Reading Comp
    - ❑ Other: _____

    _____

3. **LONG READING COMPREHENSION:**

    - ❑ Did not understand the question, line reference, or answers
    - ❑ Spent too much time reading the passages
    - ❑ Did not underline the line reference
    - ❑ Read too much or too little
    - ❑ Did not answer the specific question; instead analyzed its main idea
    - ❑ Did not do process of elimination based on facts in the passage
    - ❑ Couldn't find the false words
    - ❑ Couldn't choose between two possible answers
    - ❑ Did not use tone to help eliminate answers
    - ❑ When stuck at 2 guessed instead of pulling additional fact
    - ❑ Couldn't finish in time
    - ❑ Other: _____

    _____

ANSWERS

ANSWER KEY

TEST 1

SECTION 1

#	Answer	LEVEL	#	Answer	LEVEL	#	Answer	LEVEL	#	Answer	LEVEL
1	B	(1)	7	E	(4)	13	B	(3)	19	B	(2)
2	E	(2)	8	B	(5)	14	C	(2)	20	C	(3)
3	A	(2)	9	E	(3)	15	E	(2)	21	A	(3)
4	A	(2)	10	D	(4)	16	D	(1)	22	D	(3)
5	B	(3)	11	A	(2)	17	D	(3)	23	E	(3)
6	C	(3)	12	A	(3)	18	A	(3)	24	D	(5)

SECTION 2

#	Answer	LEVEL	#	Answer	LEVEL	#	Answer	LEVEL	#	Answer	LEVEL
1	A	(1)	7	D	(3)	13	D	(2)	19	A	(2)
2	E	(3)	8	B	(5)	14	D	(3)	20	C	(3)
3	B	(3)	9	E	(3)	15	B	(3)	21	D	(3)
4	B	(4)	10	A	(2)	16	B	(3)	22	E	(4)
5	A	(5)	11	A	(2)	17	B	(2)	23	A	(3)
6	C	(2)	12	D	(1)	18	A	(3)	24	C	(4)

SECTION 3

#	Answer	LEVEL	#	Answer	LEVEL	#	Answer	LEVEL	#	Answer	LEVEL
1	D	(1)	6	C	(5)	11	D	(3)	16	C	(5)
2	B	(2)	7	A	(3)	12	D	(5)	17	B	(2)
3	A	(3)	8	B	(3)	13	B	(3)	18	A	(4)
4	D	(3)	9	E	(4)	14	C	(2)	19	D	(3)
5	C	(4)	10	C	(4)	15	C	(4)			

Difficulty levels range from 1 - 5 with 1 being the easiest and 5 being the hardest.
For answer explanations please visit www.ies2400.com/criticalreading

PRACTICE TEST 2

Practice Test 2

SECTION 1
Time–25 minutes
24 Questions

Directions: For each question in this section, select the best answer from among the choices given and fill in the corresponding circle on the answer sheet.

Each sentence below has one or two blanks, each blank indicating that something has been omitted. Beneath the sentence are five words or sets of words labeled A through E. Choose the word or set of words that, when inserted in the sentence, best fits the meaning of the sentence as a whole.

Example:

Jimmy opened his gas station in the ------- because he wanted to be in the middle of a metropolis.

(A) country
(B) suburbs
(C) periphery
(D) environment
(E) city

---

1. Because cats are primarily ------- hunters, they are rarely active after dawn and spend most of their daylight hours sleeping.

   (A) gloomy   (B) nocturnal   (C) phlegmatic
      (D) dangerous   (E) energetic

2. As public transportation continues to improve, the New York workforce will benefit from an increase in -------, which will facilitate greater efficiency than ever before.

   (A) equality   (B) mobility   (C) acumen
      (D) proximity   (E) variation

3. The teachings of Existentialism can have an incredibly ------- effect on a young mind, opening doors that one may not have known could open; however, this school of thought can also be -------, confusing young readers with its impenetrability.

   (A) edifying . . bewildering
   (B) mystifying . . incomprehensible
   (C) obfuscating . . unclear
   (D) illuminating . . interesting
   (E) complex . . enlightening

4. The host repeatedly ------- his guests, delighting them with songs and yarns.

   (A) berated   (B) regaled   (C) exonerated
      (D) placated   (E) praised

5. African artists customarily ------- the shortcuts afforded by advanced technology, such as the use of premixed paints, instead ------- traditional ways of mixing natural ingredients to make their own dyes.

   (A) abandon . . glamorizing
   (B) adopt . . implementing
   (C) analyze . . reviving
   (D) circumvent . . abhorring
   (E) shun . . embracing

GO ON TO THE NEXT PAGE

Practice Test 2

The passages below are followed by questions based on their content; questions following a pair of related passages may also be based on the relationship between the paired passages. Answer the questions on the basis of what is <u>stated</u> or <u>implied</u> in the passages and in any introductory material that may be provided.

Questions 6-9 are based on the following passages.

Passage 1

Japanese Internment was the systematic relocation of Japanese Americans to secluded camps within the U.S. in 1942. As the result of Roosevelt's Executive
Line Order 9066, local military commanders were given
5   power to designate "exclusion zones," thereby banning those of Japanese ancestry from the Pacific coast. Consequently, lawful Japanese-American citizens were displaced from their homes, many of which were lucrative farms. After Internment was declared unjust
10   40 years later, the U.S. paid a paltry twenty thousand dollars in reparation funds to each internment camp survivor. However, there was no compensation for the lost farms. Instead, these farms, which diminished in value due to coerced neglect, were sold cheaply
15   to non-Japanese Americans, who then tended the appropriated land to eventually make millions.

Passage 2

From my school's only window, I stared at the plastic tatters on the barbed wire and watched these fragments whip back and forth in the desert breeze.
20   This place, known as Heart Mountain, was where I spent part of my childhood, learning English, math, and different ways to be more American. Twenty families were "nestled" into my bunk. The frame of the structure had been warped by the desert weather; we
25   were packed like sardines in a broken can. For some semblance of a life, we would go to Bunk 29, where a second generation Japanese-American band played swing music under the watchful eye of a machine gun nested in a tower above. We weren't allowed to resist
30   this Internment. We just had to play along.

6. Which of the following best describes the relationship between the two passages?

(A) Passage 2 uses a single perspective to clarify some of the ambiguous observations in Passage 1.
(B) Passage 2 offers a less biased stance on a development that is deplored in Passage 1.
(C) Passage 2 provides a personal commentary on historical events analyzed in Passage 1.
(D) Passage 2 attempts to invalidate sociological research that is endorsed by Passage 1.
(E) Passage 2 employs a broader statistical view of private struggles that are mentioned in Passage 1.

7. The primary purpose of Passage 1 is to

(A) encourage renewed interest in the issue of reparations for Japanese-American Internment
(B) define a strong position on an issue that continues to elicit mixed reactions from commentators
(C) explain how economic trends worsened the disparities in wealth among American farmers
(D) indicate that the reparations for Internment were incommensurate with the real damage caused by the policy
(E) criticize the United States government for its unwillingness to acknowledge the suffering caused by Internment

8. Unlike Passage 1, Passage 2 employs which of the following?

(A) Hyperbole
(B) Visual description
(C) Paraphrasing
(D) Direct quotation
(E) Social satire

9. Both passages suggest that

(A) the experience of Internment had lasting effects on Japanese-American children
(B) Japanese Americans had trouble adapting to government-imposed limitations
(C) the Internment policy had negative repercussions for Japanese Americans
(D) Internment camps were notable for their squalid and crowded conditions
(E) Internment forced Japanese Americans to relinquish valued traditions

GO ON TO THE NEXT PAGE

1   1   1   Unauthorized copying or
reuse of any part of this
page is illegal.   1   1   1

Questions 10-15 are based on the following passage.

This passage was written by a specialist on ethical issues in medicine and biology.

Pedigree. The word alone elicits notions of distinction, aristocracy, and grandeur; even cats and dogs now assume ideal, "pedigreed" forms. Thousands
Line of years of domestication have given us remarkable
5 variations in the attributes of these animals, and some feline and canine qualities are now more sought after than others. Yet appearance and personality, two of the major considerations for breeding, can often only be stabilized through restrictive measures. In order
10 to maintain, say, even-tempered blue-eyed kittens, one must breed cats having these qualities to keep the wanted traits in circulation within a relatively small group. Repeating this process generation after generation delivers dependable results, and this
15 eradication of discrepancies in coat color, body size, and eye shape is why breeders regularly mate Siamese with Siamese and almost never mate Siamese with Persian.

Time-honored though they are, such inbreeding
20 practices entail major health concerns; animal welfare groups are trying to spread awareness of these problems, and to change the breeding system. These iconoclasts disdain the standards of perfection delineated by breed registries such as the American
25 Kennel Club. The goal is to prevent the creation of shortsighted and unhealthy extremes by protecting animal health before the relationship between man and animal becomes hopelessly skewed. Of course, pets and their owners foster bonds as companions, but
30 such bonds could be at risk if pet-owners begin to see their animals as perfectly-engineered objects, not as creatures that deserve sensitivity and kindness.

For example, a registry-qualifying German Shepherd looks nothing like the German Shepherds
35 typically seen at a dog park. These real-life specimens are long-bodied with low, bushy tails. But the most striking difference between the idealized Shepherd and the actual animal involves poise and stature. Continuous inbreeding to capture the "correct" posture
40 configuration has given the Shepherd hind leg bones that are bowed into a permanent hunch. A lap around the show track highlights the typical Shepherd's awkward stride, which hinders the dog's ability to perform intense acrobatics and is a far cry from the
45 progenitor Shepherd's steady gait.

German Shepherds are not the only animals that have suffered inbreeding-related afflictions. The hairless Sphynx cat has been bred for its suede-like touch but—because there is nothing to protect
50 this animal from the environment—is vulnerable to diseases such as skin cancer and regularly contracts respiratory infections. King Cavalier Charles Spaniels are toy breeds noted for the baby-like appearance

of their heads; unfortunately, a genetic disorder in
55 which the skull is too small to accommodate the brain, leading to seizures, has increased in incidence among these dogs. And despite the trademark hair ridge that breeders cultivate in Rhodesian Ridgebacks, the majority of puppies are born without this feature.
60 To keep good stock, breeders will naturally mate only Ridgebacks with the desired characteristics. The problem is that many of the pups that are born are prone to a condition called dermoid sinus, which involves the formation of a cyst on the spinal cord. If
65 this cyst cannot be drained, the pup's life is normally terminated.

Anti-inbreeding activists may be agitating for too much change too fast, but their ethics are fundamentally right. How much longer will breed
70 supersede quality of life for dogs and cats? Not long, let us hope. After all, excruciating fashions such as foot-binding in Imperial China and tight corsets in medieval Europe fell into near-complete disuse as the centuries progressed. If history repeats itself, maybe
75 the animals will also get a reprieve.

10. The statements in lines 9-18 ("In order . . . Persian") primarily serve to

    (A) argue that restrictive breeding only affects a small range of traits
    (B) explain why animals instinctively seek out similar mates
    (C) describe and account for a typical breeding method
    (D) indicate a practical solution to an ethical problem
    (E) undermine the claims of unconventional animal breeders

11. The tone of the statement in lines 28-32 ("Of course . . . kindness") can be best characterized as

    (A) deprecatory
    (B) hackneyed
    (C) apologetic
    (D) pugnacious
    (E) cautionary

GO ON TO THE NEXT PAGE

12. In the third paragraph, the author presents the German Shepherd as an animal that

(A) is popular among pet-owners despite unreasonable breeding expectations
(B) has been prized primarily for its aesthetically pleasing appearance
(C) has been bred in a way that harms its quality of life
(D) has been subjected to rigid regulation by the American Kennel Club
(E) was domesticated on account of its acrobatic abilities

13. The author uses quotation marks in line 39 in order to

(A) temporarily cast doubt on the thesis of the passage
(B) call attention to a mantra of animal rights activists
(C) suggest that traditional standards of beauty are being abandoned
(D) imply skepticism about the aptness of a particular term
(E) argue that the criteria for correct posture remain ambiguous

14. All of the following are examples of the concept explained in the fourth paragraph EXCEPT:

(A) a strain of lab chimpanzee with an abnormally weak respiratory system
(B) a durable tropical fruit that is cultivated to become soft and infertile
(C) a species of rare eel that becomes smaller after generations in an aquarium
(D) a mixed-breed dog that reaps health benefits from its mother's genes
(E) a parrot that is inbred to feature more colorful but less aerodynamic plumage

15. The final sentence of the passage is based on the unstated assumption that

(A) current outrage over the state of feline and canine inbreeding will soon influence inbreeding practices as whole
(B) the positive effects of animal inbreeding have been seldom acknowledged
(C) foot-binding and related practices were considered superfluous even when they were popular
(D) humans' concern for their own comfort will eventually extend to a concern for the comfort of other species
(E) breeders will soon realize that unhealthy animals are of interest to only a small minority of buyers

Practice Test 2

GO ON TO THE NEXT PAGE

Practice Test 2

Questions 16-24 are based on the following passage.

The following passage was written by a historian who studies contemporary culture. Here, the author considers the role of nature, particularly state-owned forests, in French society.

While many people are aware that France is a
country of rivers—the Seine, the Loire, the Rhone, the
Garonne—few people are aware that France is also a
Line country of woods and forests. Surprisingly, ten percent
5   of all the forests in Europe are to be found in France.
Unsurprisingly, the French are deeply attached to these
stretches of nature, and with good reason. Since 1556,
by a law that cannot be changed, the *forêts dominiales**
have belonged to the people of France for their needs
10   and use. The English may cherish rural walks among
the green woodlands of their country, but for the most
part their ancient woodlands have been urbanized (as
in the case of the New Forest in Hampshire, where
the smells and scents of the countryside have been
15   smothered by the stink of petrol and diesel fumes)
or industrialized by the Forestry Commission (as in
Northumberland, where serried ranks of fir cover the
landscape in blank anonymity). The real, ancient forest
that once covered England has been dissipated and
20   degraded. This is not so in France: the forests are not
regarded as expendable. This is not to say that they
have remained untouched for the last five hundred
years. The need for direct communication between
towns and cities has meant that roads and high speed
25   rail lines have been permitted, but these have not been
allowed to impose on the land, which is why transit
routes are so direct and straight, with the occasional
aires† where motorists may pause, sit at wooden tables
and benches, and wander a little into the untarnished
30   woods, before continuing the journey to the next town
and experiencing once again the staccato pace of
modern life.
They are calm, these woods with their glades
of wildflowers and ferns and their occasional swaths
35   of heathland: calm, but not without activity. Clouds
of butterflies celebrate among the shafts of sunlight
that pierce through the leafy branches of sturdy oak,
smooth beech, and silver birch. Birds, of course, nest
and flit and hunt; at dusk, owls sail past, silent and
40   deadly. Rabbit and hare, fox and badger are here. Sit
for a while on the gnarled roots of an ancient oak, and
you will soon become aware of the presence of deer.
Perhaps, if you are very still, you will be privileged
to see a stag stepping regally and silently through a
45   nearby clearing. I doubt you will have the chance to
see wild boar, but they are here, in the inner reaches of
the forest.
There is a human presence, of course. These
forests are not abandoned, but are tended by foresters.
50   Trees are felled to provide the logs for wood stoves,
still a major form of heating in the towns and villages

of rural France. One cubic meter of logs for a stove
will last a week, and a forester can often sell you
this quantity for about 50 euros. The foresters are
55   the gardeners of this ancient woodland, coppicing it
and replanting it, ensuring its survival; they are also
responsible for the culling and pruning necessary to
keep the woods alive. Between September and March,
hunting is permitted—if you have the correct papers
60   of permission, that is. French hunting is not like
English hunting: the French relish the pursuit, but not
necessarily the killing, of animals. Hounds are used for
scenting, not slaughter. The huntsmen here often seem
more relaxed than their English counterparts, and the
65   curled French hunting horn produces a sound much
more tuneful than the English bray. French hunting is
not a contest between man and animal: it is much more
of a social event on horseback. Of course, if you want
to join in the hunt, you have to belong to an established
70   group and must complete mountains of paperwork, in
a uniquely French bureaucratic fashion.
Regardless, at any time, without asking anyone's
permission, any citizen may enter a French forest
and pick the wild fruits and berries and mushrooms.
75   Any citizen can walk through the forest at any time,
alone or with family, with a dog, with whomever.
These forests belong to every citizen, as they have
for centuries. They are the national heritage or, as it is
called in French, *le patrimoine*.††

---

*   forêts dominiales: forest owned by the state

†   aires: rest stops

†† le patrimoine: national heritage

16. The first paragraph is primarily concerned with

(A) contrasting French and English attitudes
      toward their forests
(B) detailing the natural landscape of the French
      countryside
(C) advocating a revolutionary environmental
      policy
(D) describing a cherished relationship between a
      nation and its forests
(E) analyzing the present-day infrastructure of
      rural France

GO ON TO THE NEXT PAGE

Practice Test 2

17. The phrase "The English . . . country" in lines 10-11 serves primarily to

   (A) describe a popular English pastime
   (B) concede a point in an opposing argument
   (C) qualify the narrator's larger point about English forests
   (D) cast the English in a predominantly favorable light
   (E) highlight the controversial nature of English industry

18. The tone of the parenthetical statements in the first paragraph can best be described as

   (A) vindictive
   (B) presumptuous
   (C) rueful
   (D) equivocal
   (E) rhapsodic

19. It can be inferred from lines 23-27 ("The need . . . straight") that

   (A) winding roads are more detrimental to the surrounding ecosystem than straight roads
   (B) direct transit routes have needlessly disrupted the French natural landscape
   (C) the French have built their national infrastructure without in any way harming the environment
   (D) French roads are designed to minimize car emissions and other forms of pollution
   (E) French infrastructure is respected for its combination of durability and cost efficiency

20. The author mentions wildlife in the second paragraph in order to

   (A) criticize the wanton destruction of natural habitats
   (B) encourage new hiking and camping expeditions
   (C) refute a series of popular misconceptions
   (D) validate a new set of forestry practices
   (E) dispel the notion that the woods are uninhabited

21. In context, the word "activity" (line 35) most nearly means

   (A) movement
   (B) fervor
   (C) endeavor
   (D) diversion
   (E) anxiety

22. In context, "reaches" in line 46 most nearly means

   (A) outgrowths
   (B) efforts
   (C) explorations
   (D) depths
   (E) attainments

23. The author's attitude toward the "foresters" (line 49) is best characterized as

   (A) appreciation
   (B) camaraderie
   (C) jocularity
   (D) defensiveness
   (E) disbelief

24. The final paragraph of the passage functions to

   (A) catalog the most popular pastimes undertaken in French forests
   (B) suggest the prevalence of irresponsible behavior in the French woodlands
   (C) define a French term used in patriotic contexts
   (D) explain how bureaucratic measures have redefined French attitudes toward wildlife
   (E) emphasize a concept of ownership mentioned earlier in the passage

STOP

If you finish before time is called, you may check your work on this section only.
Do not turn to any other section in the test.

2   2   2   Unauthorized copying or
                                  reuse of any part of this
                                  page is illegal.   2   2   2

SECTION 2
Time–25 minutes
24 Questions

Directions: For each question in this section, select the best answer from among the choices given and fill in the corresponding circle on the answer sheet.

Each sentence below has one or two blanks, each blank indicating that something has been omitted. Beneath the sentence are five words or sets of words labeled A through E. Choose the word or set of words that, when inserted in the sentence, best fits the meaning of the sentence as a whole.

Example:

Jimmy opened his gas station in the ------- because he wanted to be in the middle of a metropolis.

(A) country
(B) suburbs
(C) periphery
(D) environment
(E) city

---

1. Lucy rushed to her daughter's side to ------- the distraught and trembling child.

    (A) avoid   (B) ease   (C) face
      (D) spoil   (E) surprise

2. Lauren Ambrose has attained a great number of ------- during her illustrious acting career, though acting as a lead in *Six Feet Under* is the most remarkable of these -------.

    (A) feats . . oversights
    (B) flops . . accomplishments
    (C) successes . . exploits
    (D) failures . . achievements
    (E) roles . . memorials

3. The President managed the crisis with poise and equanimity, thereby fueling his reputation for being -------.

    (A) pragmatic   (B) magnanimous
      (C) aggressive   (D) intelligent
        (E) composed

4. Nothing surprises scientists more than ------- behavior exhibited by animals whose ------- have already been thoroughly documented by biologists worldwide.

    (A) aggressive . . intentions
    (B) anomalous . . activities
    (C) irregular . . habitats
    (D) predictable . . patterns
    (E) typical . . idiosyncrasies

5. What is most needed is a ------- approach to politics and society, one that is centered on everyday contingencies rather than on lofty idealizations.

    (A) pragmatic   (B) exemplary   (C) proscribed
      (D) transient   (E) continental

6. Using stem cells to regenerate decaying organs at first seemed a ------- scientific practice, but has since become widely accepted by even formerly intolerant critics.

    (A) formidable   (B) groundbreaking   (C) taboo
      (D) tedious   (E) surreptitious

7. The carpenter ignored minor miscalculations in the sizing of his components, electing to proceed with the job in the hope that the overall outcome would be so ------- as to ------- his imperfections.

    (A) breathtaking . . camouflage
    (B) forgiving . . justify
    (C) holistic . . underscore
    (D) ostentatious . . mask
    (E) pedestrian . . invalidate

8. Many people consider meditation to be the ultimate form of relaxation, though scientists have found that exercise can have the same ------- effect, purging bad emotions.

    (A) symptomatic   (B) retroactive
      (C) enlightening   (D) remunerating
        (E) cathartic

GO ON TO THE NEXT PAGE

2   2   2   Unauthorized copying or   2   2   2
                                  reuse of any part of this
                                  page is illegal.

Each passage below is followed by questions based on its content. Answer the questions on the basis of what is <u>stated</u> or <u>implied</u> in the passages and in any introductory material that may be provided.

Questions 9-10 are based on the following passage.

What is it that explains the staying power of mad scientists? Readers past and present are fascinated by the Fausts and Frankensteins of this world, and if
Line recent entertainment is any indication, mad scientists
5 aren't going anywhere: the most acclaimed television series of recent times, *Breaking Bad*, features a main character who is both a brilliant chemist and a violent sociopath. Perhaps mad scientists so captivate us because they are villains of the most sophisticated
10 and dramatic kind. They have massive IQs and wreak equally massive havoc. Or perhaps these devious inquirers evoke something different in us: the awareness that every discovery, every benefit science brings, also brings the potential for distortion and
15 destruction.

9. The author cites the television show *Breaking Bad* in order to illustrate the idea that

    (A) characters such as mad scientists are the products of unstable artistic minds
    (B) mad scientists endure as protagonists because of their brilliance
    (C) television has prospered financially from relying on a proven character mode
    (D) a certain archetype will continue to be an enthralling element of culture
    (E) Faust and Frankenstein will serve as character blueprints for future mad scientists

10. The last sentence of the passage ("Or perhaps . . . destruction") primarily serves to

    (A) offer a solution to a problem
    (B) question an already proven point
    (C) provide an additional example
    (D) propose an alternative hypothesis
    (E) expose the fallacy of an opposing view

Questions 11-12 are based on the following passage.

Bran Castle, located in the Carpathian Mountains in Romania, stands high above the surrounding farmland. This edifice was originally built as a bulwark
Line against Ottoman conquest. Yet popular myth, spurred
5 on by Bram Stoker's vampire novel, transformed Bran Castle into Dracula's home. However fallacious, this new status has sparked a recent wave of tourism. It is said that the residents of nearby Bran village had until recently been completely oblivious to Dracula. But
10 as new tourists have flocked in, bringing the prospect of new income, the collective memory has changed. Ask any local farmer if Bran castle had been the home of Dracula and you will be entertained with tales of a grandma who sported a double puncture wound on her
15 neck.

11. The primary purpose of this passage is to

    (A) highlight the irony of a phenomenon
    (B) debunk the myth surrounding a structure
    (C) encourage the reader to visit a location
    (D) chronicle the history of a region
    (E) deride the tourism industry in a specific area

12. The farmer described in the final sentence is represented as

    (A) a detached observer
    (B) a willful collaborator
    (C) an immoral opportunist
    (D) a reliable source
    (E) an unsuspecting accomplice

GO ON TO THE NEXT PAGE

Practice Test 2

2   2   2   2   2   2

Unauthorized copying or reuse of any part of this page is illegal.

Practice Test 2

Questions 13-24 are based on the following passages.

The following two passages analyze the Theatre of the Absurd, an artistic and philosophical tendency that was especially prominent after World War II. Passage 1 is part of an article by a theatre historian; Passage 2 is adapted from an essay by a professor of literature.

Passage 1

The Theatre of the Absurd seized the attention of the public in the 1950s. During the decade, this artistic movement gained momentum with the London production of Samuel Beckett's play *Waiting for Godot*, and remained highly visible as plays such as Eugene Ionesco's *The Bald Prima Donna* and *The Killer* and Jean-Paul Sartre's *No Exit* were staged across Europe and the United States. Depending on their audiences, these plays were greeted as either "brilliant" or "baffling." Even today, there is no compromise: you either love them or hate them.

Drama scholar Martin Esslin once defined "The Theatre of the Absurd" as theatre "that expresses the idea that human existence has no meaning or purpose." As a result, all communication breaks down. The playwrights involved portray man's reaction to a world apparently without meaning, where man is a puppet controlled or menaced by invisible outside forces. This brand of theatre is closely related to the branch of philosophy we know as "Existentialism," which states that there is no reason, no grand reason at all, for our existence. We must just accept it.

Waiting for Godot, for instance, unfolds over two acts. Two tramps, Estragon and Vladimir, sit by the edge of a road. These two are apparently awaiting the arrival of someone called Godot. They are joined later by the pompous Pozzo and his companion Lucky, who is mostly silent and has a rope round his neck. Throughout, the characters talk at random. Then a boy enters to announce that Godot will not come today. End of Act One. Act Two repeats the sequence, with a few variations, though for many in the original audiences one act was enough.

"It has no plot, no climax, no dénouement, no beginning, no middle, no end. It has a situation, but barely. It jettisons everything by which we recognize theatre. A play, it asserts and proves, is basically a means of spending two hours in the dark without being bored, " wrote Kenneth Tynan, a leading twentieth-century theatre critic. Even the actors in early *Godot* productions called the play "Waiting for God Knows What," summing up in their own way the divisive nature of the Theatre of the Absurd.

Other critics were not merely accepting; they were almost ecstatic. As one commentator noted, "His (Beckett's) uncompromising rejection of an easy solution or cheap illusion of comfort ultimately has a liberating effect; such is the nature of Man that in the very act of facing up to the reality of his condition his dignity is enhanced. We can only be defeated by things by which we are taken unawares: what we know and have faced up to we can master."

Passage 2

The search for a meaning in life is an ongoing pursuit in literature. That the universe is indifferent to man has been a common assumption almost from the beginnings of recorded history. In their tragedies, the Greeks implied that if a man defies the gods by searching for his own answers, he is on his own. Later, in Christopher Marlowe's *Doctor Faustus*, the demon Mephistopheles delivers his judgment of the world: "Why, this is hell, nor am I out of it." The isolation, the terrifying disorientation of the solitary individual has been the very basis not only of theatre, but of all literature. Indeed, the novelist Thomas Hardy clearly expresses the insignificance of the individual in *The Return of the Native*. This masterful Victorian novel focuses on the character of Mrs. Yeobright and evokes her life on the bleak and isolated Egdon Heath. At one point, Mrs. Yeobright glimpses an unknown man on the distant horizon:

"The silent being who thus occupied himself seemed to be of no more account of life than an insect. He appeared as a mere parasite of the heath, fretting its surface in his daily labor as a moth frets a garment, entirely engrossed with its products, having no knowledge of anything but the fern, furze, heath, lichens, and moss."

Egdon Heath, in Hardy's novel, represents the universe; "the great inviolate place (that has) an ancient permanence that the sea cannot claim. Who can say of a particular sea that it is old? Distilled by the sun, kneaded by the moon, it is renewed in a year, in a day, or in an hour. The sea changed, the fields changed, the rivers, the villages, and the people changed, yet Egdon remained." There the universe, in all its intimidating permanence, is defined for you. Hardy understood that change in this world is superficial, that the basis of creation is immutable. And man within the universe?

For that we must turn to another Hardy novel, *The Mayor of Casterbridge*. Near the end, Hardy presents the dying wishes of Michael Henchard, the tragic Mayor of the title:

"That no man remember me"

GO ON TO THE NEXT PAGE

95   The basic tenets that lie behind twentieth-century
Absurdism are not new ideas. What is new, perhaps,
is that we are no longer provided with characters who
struggle and strive to find themselves, their place, their
purpose; we encounter only people who have given
100 up and simply accept that nothing can be done about
anything. Not that relatively recent authors such as
Jean-Paul Sartre and Samuel Beckett really care one
way or the other: they do not defend their ideas, they
just blankly present their beliefs.
105   But is acceptance an appropriate answer to the
human condition? Or is it just a cop-out? Surely,
literature is meant to motivate us to demand a meaning
to life. Look up at the stars at night. There is a meaning
somewhere out there. We have to find it.

13. The authors of both passages would most likely
     agree that

     (A) the Theatre of the Absurd caused a
         widespread decline in knowledge of the arts
     (B) modern literature exists solely to address
         difficult philosophical problems
     (C) whether purpose exists in human life is a
         potent topic for discourse
     (D) Jean-Paul Sartre and Samuel Beckett were
         sadly oblivious to current events
     (E) the controversy surrounding *Waiting for
         Godot* was largely unwarranted

14. The plays named in the first paragraph of
     Passage 1 are given as examples of

     (A) dramas that only theatre connoisseurs can
         appreciate
     (B) signs of plummeting standards of politeness
         and civility
     (C) manifestations of an emerging trend in
         modern theatre
     (D) narratives that few scholars have attempted to
         interpret
     (E) texts that continue to be misunderstood by
         many readers

15. Lines 8-11 ("Depending on . . . them") of
     Passage 1 emphasize the idea that

     (A) playwrights such as Samuel Beckett
         personally enjoyed controversy and
         argument
     (B) most of the staunchest opponents of the
         Theatre of the Absurd were American critics
     (C) the critical reception of the Theatre of the
         Absurd was based on a few overreactions by
         audiences
     (D) the techniques developed by the Theatre of
         the Absurd dominate theatre today
     (E) the Theatre of the Absurd incited polarized
         audience reactions

16. The statement in lines 19-22 ("This brand . . .
     existence") serves primarily to

     (A) align the Theatre of the Absurd with another
         school of modern thought
     (B) cite an expert on a particular branch of
         philosophy
     (C) undermine the reputation of popular school of
         modern thought
     (D) argue against the reader's presumed stance on
         iconoclastic writing
     (E) paraphrase the adversaries of the Theatre of
         the Absurd

17. The overall tone of Passage 1 can best be
     described as

     (A) histrionic
     (B) cajoling
     (C) informative
     (D) vitriolic
     (E) critical

18. The author of Passage 2 would most likely
     respond to the statement in line 22 ("We must . . .
     it") of Passage 1 with

     (A) enthusiasm
     (B) indifference
     (C) bemusement
     (D) sympathy
     (E) dissent

GO ON TO THE NEXT PAGE

Practice Test 2

Practice Test 2

19. The author of Passage 2 mentions the "Greeks" in line 57 most likely in order to

   (A) substantiate an earlier claim about a literary theme
   (B) demonstrate how Hardy was influenced by earlier literature
   (C) explain why readers today are fascinated by ancient cultures
   (D) pinpoint the first civilization to produce classic tragedies
   (E) indicate that aesthetic standards have declined over the centuries

20. Lines 96-101 ("What is . . . anything") imply that

   (A) proponents of Absurdism and Existentialism vehemently attacked writers who did not adhere to these philosophies
   (B) all the new artistic inclinations that appeared in the twentieth century were simply offshoots of a single earlier movement
   (C) the influence of ideologies such as Existentialism has been overestimated by researchers and historians
   (D) dramatic works that predate Absurdism depict characters who endeavor to find meaning in their lives
   (E) Jean-Paul Sartre and Samuel Beckett were completely indifferent to public responses to their writings

21. The final paragraph of Passage 2 functions primarily to

   (A) conclude an otherwise dour account with an upbeat personal anecdote
   (B) balance the author's earlier assertiveness with an instance of ambivalence
   (C) declare that further discussion of the meaning of life is superfluous
   (D) discourage readers from adopting ideologies mentioned earlier in the passage
   (E) accommodate readers who believe that life is without meaning

22. Passage 2 indicates that Jean-Paul Sartre and Samuel Beckett (line 102) would most likely respond to Kenneth Tynan's review in Passage 1 with

   (A) evident indifference
   (B) haughty dismissal
   (C) vituperative objection
   (D) explicit ingratitude
   (E) veiled optimism

23. Which contrast best describes how each passage treats Absurdist writing?

   (A) Passage 1 recapitulates major disagreements, whereas Passage 2 outlines an approach based on meaningful compromise.
   (B) Passage 1 surveys existing perspectives, whereas Passage 2 offers the author's personal evaluation.
   (C) Passage 1 records the history of a theatrical trend whereas Passage 2 mentions only a single playwright.
   (D) Passage 1 quotes experts extensively, whereas Passage 2 argues that earlier scholars have been egregiously misinformed.
   (E) Passage 1 praises the achievements of ancient literature, whereas Passage 2 shows how the Theatre of the Absurd rests on flawed assumptions.

24. Unlike the author of Passage 1, the author of Passage 2

   (A) provides a biographical profile of a classic author
   (B) urges readers not to adopt extreme or controversial views
   (C) addresses a historical precedent for a particular genre
   (D) relies on the testimonies of well-known art critics
   (E) names characters from specific novels

STOP

If you finish before time is called, you may check your work on this section only.
Do not turn to any other section in the test.

3   3   3   3   3   3

Unauthorized copying or reuse of any part of this page is illegal.

SECTION 3
Time–20 minutes
19 Questions

Directions: For each question in this section, select the best answer from among the choices given and fill in the corresponding circle on the answer sheet.

Each sentence below has one or two blanks, each blank indicating that something has been omitted. Beneath the sentence are five words or sets of words labeled A through E. Choose the word or set of words that, when inserted in the sentence, <u>best</u> fits the meaning of the sentence as a whole.

Example:

Jimmy opened his gas station in the ------- because he wanted to be in the middle of a metropolis.

(A) country
(B) suburbs
(C) periphery
(D) environment
(E) city

1. In light of threats to the environment from global warming, a prosperous future for our planet is by no means -------.

    (A) a blessing   (B) a challenge   (C) a given
       (C) an uncertainty   (E) an issue

2. Surprisingly, instead of causing her to become -------, the blatant opposition that she faced ------- her to promote her cause.

    (A) encouraged . . dejected
    (B) dismayed . . affronted
    (C) disheartened . . emboldened
    (D) inspired . . invigorated
    (E) conscientious . . incited

3. Maria felt ------- about her visit to the dentist long after she left his office and could hardly calm her nerves whenever she thought of what she had gone through.

    (A) apologetic   (B) vitriolic   (C) enervated
       (D) anxious   (E) perplexed

4. Although Henry James was seen as ------- when he wrote fiction, his compositions for the theatre were regarded as the work of a -------.

    (A) idiosyncratic . . conformist
    (B) unmatched . . rebel
    (C) inferior . . traditionalist
    (D) essential . . skeptic
    (E) avant-garde . . revolutionary

5. When we behave aggressively toward the innocent, our ------- is punished by a subsequent firing of remorse-inducing neurons in the brain.

    (A) abhorrence   (B) bellicosity
       (C) equivocation   (D) negligence
          (E) superiority

6. Heroes always prevail in Hollywood thrillers, yet the genre contains sufficient spectacle and excitement to make even a ------- ending to such a movie seem -------.

    (A) banal . . finite
    (B) dreadful . . frightening
    (C) predictable . . stimulating
    (D) foreseeable . . boring
    (E) bracing . . mundane

GO ON TO THE NEXT PAGE

Practice Test 2

Practice Test 2

The passage below is followed by questions based on its content. Answer the questions on the basis of what is <u>stated</u> or <u>implied</u> in the passage and in any introductory material that may be provided.

Questions 7-19 are based on the following passage.

The passage that follows is adapted from a work of historical fiction written in 2013.

William the Miller was neither the poorest nor the wickedest man in the village. However, if anyone inquired about the use he made of his miller's thumb
Line when he pressed it casually on the scales whilst
5 measuring out flour, he would grin and shrug his shoulders. "We all have a choice in life. Take it or leave it."

William's wife, Abigail, approved. She had been just eighteen when William had approached
10 her parents to ask their permission to court her. They had been delighted, and when he had offered her a place in his heart and a sparkling, jeweled bracelet, Abigail had been delighted too. Her disappointed other suitors had sulked a while, and her closest friends had
15 pointed out that William was twenty years older than she; nonetheless, she had defied these reservations and donned the gown with the latest fashionable sleeves and the steeple head-dress that came with her elevated new position in life. The tradesmen now gave
20 her precedence, no matter how long the queue, and, whenever she went to church, the other village women deferred to her and stood aside so she could enter first.

It was in church that she first noticed Absalom. He was a poor student, newly come to the town, and on
25 holy days he helped the priest by collecting the weekly tithe from the parishioners. He stood before Abigail with the plate, and she looked up from her devotions. His coat was patched but his eyes were of the deepest blue Abigail had ever encountered. She returned his
30 smile. He winked and moved on.

Waiting by the church door while William chatted with the priest, Abigail considered Absalom. He was about the same age as she, had a boyish smile and, from what she had observed before returning
35 to her prayer, he was hale and fit. She turned and eyed William critically as he lumbered up the aisle towards her. His hair was graying and he had put on much weight since their marriage. He looked a little tired, irritated even. No doubt he would sink into
40 a doze before the fire after supper. She sighed, and then caressed the gold bangle on her wrist, William's gift for her birthday. It had cost a lot of money and her acquaintances had admired it, envied it. She chuckled to herself at the memory. Well, she doubted
45 that Absalom could give his girl such a gift, although he did have other attractions, as she admitted. He certainly was a very handsome fellow.

"You saw that new young lad in church?" William's rough bass voice broke her reverie. She
50 looked at him, her cheeks burning.

"What new lad? Oh yes, he took the tithe. I hardly noticed him."

"You must have been the only female in the church that didn't! Even Goody Putnam gawped, and
55 she's eighty and toothless," William wheezed and spluttered in his glee. She looked around, her face scarlet, embarrassed—perhaps—by this coarseness. William took a deep breath.

"Priest says that the lad needs a place to live. Told
60 him, the boy could have a room at ours. He's paying, of course. He'll be good money for me and some company for you, when I am working."

The color in her cheeks retreated. "Are you sure? People might talk."

65 "Nonsense! You're the Miller's wife. They know your worth." He paused. "I know your worth. Like Caesar's wife, as they say, you are above suspicion."*

Abigail dropped her eyes. "As you say," she replied demurely.

70 So Absalom moved into the loft at the mill. At first, Abigail was unnerved by this nearness, but it was not long before she found that it was a boon to have Absalom about the grounds when William was not there. He claimed that he was studying, at which
75 she laughed, for she saw no books. She soon got into the routine of preparing his favorite eggs and bits of pickled beef exactly on time for his morning descent from the loft, long after William's departure for work. Absalom had a healthy appetite. "William is a very
80 lucky man!" he would exclaim, and Abigail would blush and giggle and give him a clip on the ear, just as she had once done with her younger brother.

Then, one warm morning—it was a Monday, she remembered later—Absalom seized her hand and
85 kissed it. She felt the warmth of his lips upon her skin.

She looked into those deep blue eyes. There was a stillness that seemed tangible.

She withdrew her hand. "No."

The world came rushing back. He looked at her,
90 astonished and wounded. She stepped back behind the table. She could hear the chickens clucking in the yard outside. She looked around and saw the sack of corn that was their feed.

"Take this and feed them, will you?" she said, and
95 gave him a maternal smile. "Caesar's wife," she added, by way of explanation. "We all have a choice to make in life. And when we do, then we keep to it or leave it."

Absalom nodded slowly and solemnly, and went to feed the chickens.

---

* "Caesar's wife must be above suspicion," Roman proverb

GO ON TO THE NEXT PAGE

7. The second paragraph of the passage (lines 8-22) suggests that Abigail is attracted to William because of his

   (A) jovial disregard of social norms
   (B) high social status and apparent affluence
   (C) popularity as a leader of the community
   (D) spirit of generosity and wealth of experience
   (E) unique perspective on issues of morality

8. Which of the following is one of the major "reservations" (line 16) about Abigail's marriage to William?

   (A) William is twenty years older than Abigail.
   (B) William is easily the richest man in the village.
   (C) William is a disingenuous businessman.
   (D) William cannot comprehend Abigail's emotions.
   (E) William sought approval from Abigail's parents.

9. After Abigail's marriage to William, "the other village women deferred to her" (lines 21-22) most likely because

   (A) Abigail's incongruous marriage inspires confusion
   (B) Abigail has grown sly and vindictive under William's influence
   (C) the women admire her pragmatism and frugality
   (D) Abigail's status in the community has improved significantly
   (E) the women are resentful of her newfound popularity

10. As described in the third paragraph, which of Absalom's features make a strong impression on Abigail?

    (A) his indigence and his indifference to religious matters
    (B) his laconic way of speaking and his spiritual purity
    (C) his refined gestures and his beautiful voice
    (D) his austere style of dress and his avoidance of social interaction
    (E) his tattered clothes and his captivating eyes

11. In lines 31-39 ("Waiting by . . . even"), Absalom's energetic appearance is contrasted with

    (A) William's clear signs of aging
    (B) Abigail's anxiety about her marriage
    (C) William's solemn approach to work
    (D) William's petty conversation with the priest
    (E) Abigail's superficial responses to wealth

12. In context, the "golden bangle" on Abigail's wrist (line 41) is best understood as

    (A) a sign of William's love of ornate objects
    (B) a subtle symbol of Absalom's ambition
    (C) a reminder of William's munificence
    (D) an object that does not deserve to be envied
    (E) an example of Abigail's rebellious spirit

13. William's comments in lines 53-55 ("You must . . . toothless") indicate that

    (A) older women are ill advised to admire much younger men
    (B) the community is often uniform in its social judgments
    (C) William enjoys ridiculing the foibles of his acquaintances
    (D) Abigail is unaware of her admiration of Absalom
    (E) the women in the church were intrigued by the sight of Absalom

14. In lines 59-62 ("Priest says . . . working"), it can be inferred that William wants Absalom as his boarder primarily because

    (A) Abigail has alerted William to her feelings of isolation
    (B) William shares the general admiration for Absalom
    (C) William will make money from providing the young man with lodgings
    (D) William has an established reputation for offering hospitality
    (E) William and the priest are close friends

15. In line 63, the word "retreated" most nearly means

    (A) surrendered
    (B) disappeared
    (C) retired
    (D) relaxed
    (E) accommodated

GO ON TO THE NEXT PAGE

Practice Test 2

Practice Test 2

16. It can be inferred from the statement in lines 74-75 ("He claimed . . . books") that Absalom's course of study is

(A) socially subversive
(B) carefully structured
(C) remarkably idiosyncratic
(D) spiritually rewarding
(E) possibly spurious

17. In lines 95-97 ("Caesar's wife . . . leave it"), Abigail responds to Absalom's advances by

(A) engaging Absalom in an intentionally inconclusive dialogue
(B) greeting Absalom's duplicitous nature with apparent outrage
(C) baffling Absalom with a set of arcane references
(D) explaining her state of mind with phrases used by her husband
(E) emphasizing her dislike of Absalom's lowly station in society

18. Absalom's actions in lines 98-99 ("Absalom nodded . . . chickens") emphasize his

(A) bitter resentment of Abigail's rebuke
(B) willingness to comply with Abigail's wishes
(C) inability to alter his modest lifestyle
(D) obliviousness to the demands of society
(E) admirable and well-developed work ethic

19. The passage as a whole can best be described as

(A) a narrative that details the outcomes of a woman's personal decisions
(B) an overt condemnation of cynicism and adultery
(C) a foreshadowing of social influences that would bring greater autonomy to women
(D) a bleak episode that features sequences of gratuitous humor
(E) a reflection on the precarious nature of marriages based on material gain

STOP

If you finish before time is called, you may check your work on this section only.
Do not turn to any other section in the test.

POST TEST ANALYSIS

This post test analysis is important if you want to see an improvement on your next test. Each section has a set of possible reasons for errors. Place check marks next to the ones that pertain to you, and write your own on the blank lines provided. Use this form to better analyze your performance. **If you don't understand why you made errors, there is no way you can correct them!**

1. **SENTENCE COMPLETION:**

   Problems with the sentence:
   - ❏ Wasn't familiar with phrases, idioms, or words in the sentence
   - ❏ Missed the clues or tones
   - ❏ Put your OWN word in the blank rather than one from the sentence
   - ❏ Completely avoided marking
   - ❏ Other: _____

   _____

   Problems with the answers:
   - ❏ Did not use process of elimination
   - ❏ Did not ignore unknown words
   - ❏ Did not use prefix/root/suffix knowledge to figure out the meaning of the unknown words
   - ❏ Did not match the clues and tones of the answer with those of the sentence
   - ❏ Did not recognize vocabulary words
   - ❏ Did not check answer to see if it fit
   - ❏ Other: _____

   _____

   Leaving questions unanswered:
   - ❏ Did not try
   - ❏ Did not fill in the blank(s) with words
   - ❏ Ran out of time
   - ❏ Other: _____

   _____

2. **SHORT READING COMPREHENSION:**

   - ❏ Did not read entire paragraph
   - ❏ Did not see more than one point
   - ❏ Missed contrast clues
   - ❏ Did not pinpoint thesis
   - ❏ Did not identify similarities and differences in Double Short Reading Comp
   - ❏ Other: _____

   _____

3. **LONG READING COMPREHENSION:**

   - ❏ Did not understand the question, line reference, or answers
   - ❏ Spent too much time reading the passages
   - ❏ Did not underline the line reference
   - ❏ Read too much or too little
   - ❏ Did not answer the specific question; instead analyzed its main idea
   - ❏ Did not do process of elimination based on facts in the passage
   - ❏ Couldn't find the false words
   - ❏ Couldn't choose between two possible answers
   - ❏ Did not use tone to help eliminate answers
   - ❏ When stuck at 2 guessed instead of pulling additional fact
   - ❏ Couldn't finish in time
   - ❏ Other: _____

   _____

ANSWER KEY

TEST 2

SECTION 1

#	Answer	LEVEL
1	B	(1)
2	B	(2)
3	A	(3)
4	B	(4)
5	E	(5)
6	C	(3)
7	D	(4)
8	B	(2)
9	C	(3)
10	C	(2)
11	E	(3)
12	C	(3)
13	D	(2)
14	D	(4)
15	D	(5)
16	D	(3)
17	C	(3)
18	C	(4)
19	A	(5)
20	A	(3)
21	A	(2)
22	D	(1)
23	A	(3)
24	E	(4)

SECTION 2

#	Answer	LEVEL
1	B	(1)
2	C	(3)
3	E	(2)
4	B	(3)
5	A	(3)
6	C	(4)
7	A	(4)
8	E	(5)
9	D	(3)
10	D	(4)
11	A	(3)
12	B	(5)
13	C	(3)
14	C	(2)
15	E	(2)
16	A	(2)
17	C	(3)
18	E	(4)
19	A	(3)
20	D	(2)
21	D	(3)
22	A	(4)
23	B	(4)
24	E	(3)

SECTION 3

#	Answer	LEVEL
1	C	(1)
2	C	(2)
3	D	(2)
4	A	(3)
5	B	(4)
6	C	(5)
7	B	(3)
8	A	(2)
9	D	(2)
10	E	(3)
11	A	(3)
12	C	(4)
13	E	(3)
14	C	(2)
15	B	(2)
16	E	(4)
17	D	(4)
18	B	(2)
19	A	(2)

Difficulty levels range from 1 - 5 with 1 being the easiest and 5 being the hardest.
For answer explanations please visit www.ies2400.com/criticalreading

PRACTICE TEST 3

SECTION 1

Time–25 minutes
25 Questions

> **Directions:** For each question in this section, select the best answer from among the choices given and fill in the corresponding circle on the answer sheet.

Each sentence below has one or two blanks, each blank indicating that something has been omitted. Beneath the sentence are five words or sets of words labeled A through E. Choose the word or set of words that, when inserted in the sentence, <u>best</u> fits the meaning of the sentence as a whole.

Example:

Jimmy opened his gas station in the ------- because he wanted to be in the middle of a metropolis.

(A) country
(B) suburbs
(C) periphery
(D) environment
(E) city

1. Since George can successfully guarantee the performance of all his high-tech products, his customers view him as an indisputably ------- and reliable salesman.

   (A) conspicuous   (B) reputable
      (C) prosperous   (D) fraudulent
        (E) opportunistic

2. A ------- work of literature, Aleksandr Solzhenitsyn's 1962 novel *One Day in the Life of Ivan Denisovich* was the first account of Stalinist repression ever to be published.

   (A) justified   (B) complicated   (C) pioneering
      (D) seditious   (E) fateful

3. As one would expect, ------- promotes cultural exchange, since people who inhabit large cities replete with diversity are more likely to be influenced by those ethnically different from themselves.

   (A) reorganization   (B) heterogeneity
      (C) permanency   (D) uniformity
        (E) worshiping

4. Capable of swimming 100 miles a day without needing to stop for rest or food, the blue whale is notable among marine mammals for its ------- nature.

   (A) precipitous   (B) voracious   (C) restless
      (D) indefatigable   (E) insatiable

5. Julie is ------- to a fault, so willing to please others that she is sometimes forced to ------- her own happiness.

   (A) complaisant . . forgo
   (B) belligerent . . evaluate
   (C) critical . . secure
   (D) dogged . . promote
   (E) tactful . . transform

6. Although the government granted free reign to ------- members of the business community, ordinary citizens still had only a hint of ------- in the conduct of their day-to-day business dealings.

   (A) common . . rebellion
   (B) dissident . . freedom
   (C) elite . . latitude
   (D) aristocratic . . diversity
   (E) permanent . . autonomy

7. When considering one's own feelings, it is best to be ------- about every detail of an interaction; failing to cover all ground can lead, unfortunately, to the ------- of one's psyche.

   (A) meticulous . . mollification
   (B) heedless . . destruction
   (C) myopic . . appeasement
   (D) subjective . . eradication
   (E) fastidious . . devastation

8. Known for its -------, the Gila monster is one of the stealthiest species of lizard on Earth.

   (A) exquisiteness   (E) sinuousness
      (C) alacrity   (D) refractoriness
        (E) furtiveness

1   1   1   Unauthorized copying or
reuse of any part of this
page is illegal.   1   1   1

The passages below are followed by questions based on their content; questions following a pair of related passages may also be based on the relationship between the paired passages. Answer the questions on the basis of what is <u>stated</u> or <u>implied</u> in the passages and in any introductory material that may be provided.

Questions 9-12 are based on the following passages.

Passage 1

Is it wise to perpetuate competition through body type? In the early 1900s, the profile of the ideal Olympic athlete was based on classical human
Line proportions. Imagine the range of human bodies
5   as a bell curve, with extreme body types at the far ends. The exemplary athletes of this time would occupy the middle of this curve. Consequently, athletes who would be considered average by today's standards were ideal for the Olympics in past eras.
10   Now, however, athletes are lauded for unique but preordained physical traits that set them apart from "average" sportsmen. To uphold the integrity of sportsmanship, we should commend excellence in training instead of applauding a lucky roll of the
15   genetic dice.

Passage 2

Olympic figure skating is a sport unlike any other, a sport in which months of training all boil down to a single performance. In these few minutes, the athlete must prove himself through strength, control, grace,
20   and finesse. Overall, figure skating rewards those with a balance of these aspects as opposed to those with the most power. Since the inception of the Olympics in 1924, the average figure skater has decreased in height by five inches; smaller, lighter bodies are optimal for
25   the jumping, spinning, and landing required by the sport. Does this mean that all figure skaters must be small? Of course not. Despite body types, athleticism will always be defined as personal perseverance and triumph over obstacles both mental and physical.

9.   The authors of both passages discuss which of the following?

(A) Changes in body type standards that have occurred over the course of the twentieth century
(B) Specific Olympic sports that have been transformed by the prioritization of new body types
(C) Athletic developments that are likely to prove detrimental if they persist into the future
(D) Specific courses of action that could counteract the current emphasis on extreme body types in athletics
(E) Events that were crucial to the evolution of the Olympics over the course of the twentieth century

10. It can be inferred that the author of Passage 1 most likely views the emphasis on "preordained physical traits" (line 11) as

(A) a phenomenon dependent on new research on the human body
(B) a source of controversy among sporting commentators
(C) a guaranteed means of success in contemporary competitions
(D) a factor that has transformed professional sporting regulations
(E) a generally deleterious factor in modern sportsmanship

11. Lines 26-29 of Passage 2 ("Does this . . . physical") involve a shift from

(A) an evenhanded consideration of sporting standards to a proposal for specific improvements
(B) an analysis of harmful new developments to an endorsement of traditional values
(C) a consideration of a single sport to a broad assertion concerning positive athletic traits
(D) a historical survey of figure skating to a prognosis concerning the future reception of this sport
(E) a survey of much-debated developments to a synopsis of desirable mentalities for athletes

12. The author of Passage 1 would most likely regard the statement in lines 22-26 of Passage 2 ("Since the . . . sport") as

(A) evidence that modern sports prioritize exaggerated physical traits
(B) a concession to new standards that are widely regarded as lamentable
(C) a development that should only alarm individuals involved in figure skating
(D) a creative method for gaining an unfair advantage in competition
(E) an indication that extreme body types can diminish a sport's popular appeal

GO ON TO THE NEXT PAGE

Questions 13-25 are based on the following passage.

In this passage, the author describes an international day of commemoration and explains how this event relates to the history of his own family.

This past weekend was the Weekend of Remembrance in Europe, America, and beyond. Commemorating the eleventh hour of the eleventh
Line day of the eleventh month—the moment when the
5 First World War ended—this anniversary symbolizes all the grief of family loss in a century more ravaged by warfare than any other. Here in Domfront, a small town in Lower Normandy, the mayor laid a wreath on the steps of our little war memorial. I sat in my
10 little house near the medieval ramparts that were built to protect the town centuries ago and over which the allied forces dropped their bombs in 1944, and thought of my Uncle Robert. I never met him, for he died two years before I was born, yet I know that he was
15 the central figure in a moment when my family was forever changed.

My maternal grandparents had four children: three boys—Peter, Robert, and Godfrey—and one daughter, my mother Joan. She was born after Robert and before
20 Godfrey, much to the delight of Granny, who always said that having a girl evened life out a bit. The boys were boisterous and mischievous, which pleased Grandpa, who had been a bit of a rabble-rousing character himself until he met Granny and started a
25 family and calmed down, to a degree. My mother took after him in some respects, and she could be fiery. She always said that, with three brothers around, she had to learn quite quickly how to give as good as she got. Laughing, she would relate the tale of the day when
30 her brothers chased her around the big field behind the house until she climbed a tree and pelted them with apples, and did so with devastating accuracy. The boys got spankings from Grandpa for harassing their sister: Joan got a lecture from Granny about how a lady
35 should behave. However, she said that a lecture from Granny was far worse than anything Grandpa could do. Granny had a way of making you feel very small.

It was not that Granny did not love my mother: she loved all her children. But Robert, my mother
40 said, was always Granny's favorite. Perhaps that was because he was the only child whose birth had been difficult. For a while he had been seriously unwell, and later he had had asthma attacks. Nonetheless, he grew up to be the best-looking of all the boys. My
45 mother said that all the girls in her class wanted to be her friends so that they would have better chances of getting near Robert. He was courteous and kind, but he also wanted to travel and see the world. He seemed to think that life was a great adventure that was meant
50 to be embraced. That is why he joined the Royal Air Force, because it gave him a chance to fly. Grandpa encouraged him; Granny kept her fears to herself and let him go.

And then came the telegram that broke the family:
55 "Missing, presumed dead." Robert's plane had been shot down over the Mediterranean; the sea was his grave. Granny became withdrawn. Every year that followed, on the eve of Robert's birthday, she would go into the front room of the house, take down from
60 the mantelpiece the silver frame that contained the last photo taken of Robert, and sit in the armchair there, holding the photo tightly. One year, when I was about five years old, I went quietly into the front room and clambered onto a chair beside her. I saw a tear on her
65 face, and I felt a great stillness.

Granny became aware of me. "This is your Uncle Robert," she said and offered me the photo, although she kept one hand on it, in case I should let it fall. He looked so young. He lounged nonchalantly against a
70 stone wall, beyond which was a calm sea. One of his hands held a cigarette, the other was shoved into his trouser pocket. His RAF cap was pushed back rakishly. His jacket was slung over the wall behind him. You could tell it was hot, because his sleeves were rolled
75 up. He was laughing along with someone who was outside the camera shot. He seemed so happy and so carefree, like a younger Grandpa.

"Nothing lasts forever," Granny said quietly, and she caressed my hair so gently. "But we must
80 remember the joy he gave."

All that was a long time ago. The family went its separate ways, and now I am the last of them all, an old man with memories that are perhaps more important than the swirling, perpetual changes of
85 everyday life, changes that seem so demanding, at least when they are right before us. Remembrance Day, with its two minutes of silence, gives us a chance to think about what we have become and what we have lost.

13. This passage is best described as

(A) an account of the circumstances surrounding the death of a family member
(B) an essay that promotes peaceful means of resolving international conflicts
(C) an enumeration of the devastating effects of modern warfare
(D) a description of the changing reputation of a single family
(E) a biography of one of the narrator's apparent role models

GO ON TO THE NEXT PAGE

14. Lines 1-7 ("This past . . . other") primarily serve to

(A) explain the causes of a transformative historical event
(B) detail the destructive consequences of modern warfare
(C) provide essential information about an annual occurrence
(D) show how families reacted to the First World War
(E) describe a notable Weekend of Remembrance ceremony

15. In context, "fiery" (line 26) most nearly means

(A) destructive
(B) crass
(C) oversensitive
(D) vivid
(E) feisty

16. The author refers to his mother's childhood "tale" (line 29) to demonstrate that his mother exhibited

(A) personality traits that would make her renowned later in life
(B) idiosyncrasies that permanently alienated her from other children
(C) dissatisfaction with traditional roles for women
(D) the ability to successfully defend herself from her brothers
(E) an astonishingly high degree of physical resilience

17. In context, "relate" (line 29) most nearly means

(A) tell
(B) understand
(C) foreshadow
(D) connect
(E) memorize

18. What does the description in lines 35-37 ("However, she . . . small") suggest about the author's grandmother?

(A) Her dour attitude made her children resentful.
(B) Her disciplinary methods irked the author's grandfather.
(C) Her personal eloquence intimidated her children.
(D) Her moments of affection were signs of hypocrisy.
(E) Her verbal discipline was extremely effective.

19. According to the third paragraph, Robert was motivated to join the Royal Air force primarily by

(A) a need to flee from his stern upbringing
(B) a sense of patriotic duty and obligation
(C) a desire to explore what the world has to offer
(D) an urge to compensate for earlier infirmity
(E) a preoccupation with aeronautic technology

20. Lines 62-65 ("One year . . . stillness") establish a mood of

(A) calm indifference
(B) silent mourning
(C) inappropriate levity
(D) fearful hopelessness
(E) embattled perseverance

21. The description of the photograph in lines 68-77 conveys what impression of Uncle Robert?

(A) He was impetuous and uncompromising.
(B) He was indifferent to public perceptions.
(C) He was determined to achieve fame.
(D) He was untroubled and cheerful.
(E) He was motivated by patriotic zeal.

22. It can be inferred from the description of the photograph in lines 68-77 ("He looked . . . Grandpa") that the author of the passage

(A) was insecure about his own place in life
(B) experienced feelings of comfort and solace
(C) felt an overpowering sense of personal loss
(D) was afraid of dropping the framed photograph
(E) was intrigued by Uncle Robert's appearance

23. The final paragraph indicates that the author

(A) finds value in reminiscing about the past
(B) has lived a life that he finds unsatisfying
(C) wishes that he had emulated his Uncle Robert
(D) cannot relate to his chosen community
(E) sees little use for modern innovations

GO ON TO THE NEXT PAGE

24. For the author, "Remembrance Day" (line 86) serves as a reminder of

(A) the dissolution of his family and the misfortunes that befell most of his relatives
(B) the unpleasantness of solitude and the joy of solidarity
(C) both specific war casualties and general social changes
(D) the confusion and arbitrariness of life during a time of war
(E) an era of heroism that has been replaced by today's cynicism

25. The tone of the overall passage can best be described as

(A) pessimistic
(B) garrulous
(C) wistful
(D) tremulous
(E) clairvoyant

STOP

If you finish before time is called, you may check your work on this section only.
Do not turn to any other section in the test.

SECTION 2
Time–25 minutes
24 Questions

Directions: For each question in this section, select the best answer from among the choices given and fill in the corresponding circle on the answer sheet.

Each sentence below has one or two blanks, each blank indicating that something has been omitted. Beneath the sentence are five words or sets of words labeled A through E. Choose the word or set of words that, when inserted in the sentence, <u>best</u> fits the meaning of the sentence as a whole.

Example:

Jimmy opened his gas station in the ------- because he wanted to be in the middle of a metropolis.

(A) country
(B) suburbs
(C) periphery
(D) environment
(E) city

1. The works of mathematical prodigies Ramanujan and Galois, both of whom died young, continue to be ------- generations later as the basis for advanced theories.

    (A) ridiculed   (B) duplicated   (C) countered
       (D) utilized   (E) debated

2. Trying not to upset his boss, who prized ------- business conduct, Christopher attempted not to ------- convention when communicating with his colleagues.

    (A) orthodox . . deviate from
    (B) liberal . . stray from
    (C) adventurous . . protest against
    (D) traditional . . adapt to
    (E) timid . . comply with

3. Joanna's essay on her final exam was -------, pedestrian at best.

    (A) revealing   (B) inspired   (C) mediocre
       (D) noteworthy   (E) plagiarized

4. Peter admitted that the story his son told him was -------, though at first it had seemed to be an impossible tale.

    (A) confusing   (B) fabricated   (C) alluring
       (D) spurious   (E) plausible

5. People who are generally abstemious tend to allow themselves certain liberties during the holidays, occasions for ------- rather than -------.

    (A) freedom . . sovereignty
    (B) improvisation . . discipline
    (C) indulgence . . self-denial
    (D) jocularity . . hubris
    (E) self-control . . moderation

GO ON TO THE NEXT PAGE

2   2   2   Unauthorized copying or
reuse of any part of this
page is illegal.   2   2   2

Each passage below is followed by questions based on its content. Answer the questions on the basis of what is <u>stated</u> or <u>implied</u> in each passage and in any introductory material that may be provided.

Questions 6-7 are based on the following passage.

In June of 1967, Air Force pilot Robert Henry Lawrence became the first African-American astronaut. Sadly, he would never see a full space
Line mission. Lawrence's career was cut short in December
5 of the same year, when he lost his life in a jet crash at Edwards Air Force Base in California. Americans would have to wait another 15 years before an African American was actually launched into space (an honor that went to Guion "Guy" Bluford, Jr.,
10 a participant in the 1983 Challenger space shuttle explorations). Since then, America has been graced with African-American astrophysicists, African-American NASA administrators, and an African-American director of the Hayden Planetarium.
15 Such diversity came gradually; let us hope that it remains in place permanently.

6. The primary purpose of the passage is to

(A) discuss how astrophysics diversified African-American careers
(B) explain the social challenges that African Americans had to overcome
(C) highlight the achievements of African Americans in a specific professional field
(D) support the notion that astronauts can come from any background
(E) offer accounts of scientific discoveries by African Americans

7. The author's attitude in the final sentence is best described as

(A) qualified optimism
(B) tempered ambivalence
(C) dolorous resignation
(D) veiled enthusiasm
(E) abject disillusionment

Questions 8-9 are based on the following passage.

For want of a better phrase or an appropriate euphemism, I must openly state that "I hate musicals." In what universe does someone start
Line singing mid-sentence or even mid-rant? I don't like
5 reality television either; in essence, reality television shows are just musicals without the singing. Both are melodramatic, cloying, irritating forms of entertainment. Yet where pop culture is concerned, I'll always take a gratuitous car chase over a high-pitched
10 melody of regret or greeting. I will choose a low-key drama or a romantic comedy if pushed to decide. I don't mind a good cry or hysterical laugh, so long as the dialogue is delivered in an honest cadence and without a burst of trumpets and violins that serves no
15 other purpose than to manipulate my emotions.

8. The first sentence of the passage ("For want . . . musicals") primarily serves to

(A) account for a common objection
(B) question the reader's assumptions
(C) introduce a much-debated issue
(D) allude to a single experience
(E) state the author's overall position

9. In the last sentence, the reference to "a burst of violins and trumpets" serves as an example of

(A) a form of expression that is acceptable only outside of musical theatre
(B) a descriptive image that clarifies an otherwise abstract argument
(C) an overwrought tactic which musicals use to elicit audience responses
(D) a moment of humor in an otherwise serious analytical discussion
(E) a sign of how stage musicals have influenced other forms of entertainment

GO ON TO THE NEXT PAGE

2 2 2 2 2

Unauthorized copying or reuse of any part of this page is illegal.

Practice Test 3

Questions 10-16 are based on the following passage.

This selection, excerpted from an early twentieth-century work of nature writing, discusses the environment at and above tree-line in the Rocky Mountains of Colorado and in the Sierra of California.

The higher mountain-ranges rise far above the zone of life and have summits that are deeply overladen with ancient snow and ice. Yet the upper slopes and summits of the Rocky Mountains of Colorado and of the Sierra of California are not barren and lifeless, even though these highest reaches stand far above the timber-line. There are no other mountain-ranges on the earth that I know of that can show such varied and vigorous arrays of life above the tree-line as do these two ranges. How different are the climatic conditions in the Rocky Mountains and in the Sierra, where timber-line is at approximately eleven thousand, five hundred feet, or a vertical mile higher than it is in the Alps.

The tree-line appears to be both as old and as unchanging as the hills; however, like every frontier, that of the forest is aggressive, is ever struggling to advance. Here is the line of battle between the woods and the weather. The elements are insistent with "thus far and no farther," but the trees do not heed, and the relentless elements batter and defy them in a never-ending battle along the timber-line. Few trees in this forest-front rise to a greater height than twelve feet. The average height is about eight feet, but the length of some of the prostrate trees is not far from the normal height. Heavy wind and other taxing conditions give a few trees the uncouth shapes of prehistoric animals. One can even discern a vine-made ichthyosaurus crawling along, flat upon the earth.

The range is distinguished by a spate of lakes. Glaciers the world over have been the chief makers of lake-basins, large and small. These basins were formed in darkness, and hundreds and even thousands of years may have been required for the glaciers to carve and set the gems-like ponds whose presence now adds so much to the light and beauty of the rugged mountain-ranges. In descending from the mountain-summits, ponderous glaciers and ice rivers came down steep slopes and precipitous walls with such momentum that their great weight bore irresistibly against the earth. Among the lakes and tarns now lie fields of grass and meadows of luminous flowers.

These idyllic pastures are the home of many mountain sheep. Large numbers of these animals like to rest comfortably within the shattered shoulder of granite between Long's Peak and Mt. Meeker. Imagine the patriarchal ram, heavy and proud, looking down upon the world, but also scouting for enemies. The ram brays, disturbing a mountain lion,

who bounds among the scattered wreckage of granite and vanishes. Here is big game and its well-fed pursuer, in the mountain heights, above the limits of tree growth and almost three miles above the surface of the sea. Many flocks reside at an altitude of twelve thousand feet. Here the lambs are born, and from this place the herd makes spring foraging excursions far down the slopes into warmer zones, seeking out greenstuffs not yet in season on the heights. Warm coverings of soft hair protect these sheep from the coldest blasts. Winter quarters appear to be mostly in localities from which winds regularly sweep the snow. This sweeping prevents the snow from burying food beyond reach, and lessens the danger that these short-legged mountaineers will become snowbound. They commonly endure wind-storms by crowding closely against the lee side of a ledge. Now and then the sheep are so deeply drifted over with snow that many of the weaker ones perish, unable to wallow out. The snow-slide, the white terror of the heights, occasionally carries off an entire flock of these bold, vigilant animals.

10. The primary purpose of this passage is to

(A) marvel at the natural landscape of the Rocky Mountains
(B) explain the origins of a breed of Rocky Mountain sheep
(C) contest a claim about the danger of the Rocky Mountains
(D) detail the evolutionary history of the Rocky Mountains
(E) describe the author's excursions in the Rocky Mountains

11. In the first paragraph, the author mentions the "Alps" (line 14) in order to

(A) argue that the Rocky Mountains rise much higher than most other American ranges
(B) question the accuracy of a widespread claim about mountain life
(C) indicate an important feature of the topography of an American mountain range
(D) deny the supposition that the Alps and the Rocky Mountains are intrinsically different
(E) compare the predominant species of animal life in two distant mountain ranges

GO ON TO THE NEXT PAGE

© Integrated Educational Services, 2014 :: www.ies2400.com

12. The author claims that the forest is "aggressive" (line 17) most likely because

    (A) humans should take caution when encountering the animals within
    (B) trees in the forest date back to prehistoric times
    (C) the level of the tree-line has not changed for many years
    (D) the tree-line is relentless in its expansion up the mountain
    (E) the weather at this level of the mountain forbids exploration

13. In context, the "ichthyosaurus" described in line 29 is most likely

    (A) a denizen of the woods
    (B) a wind-battered tree
    (C) a collection of fossils
    (D) a ruin of an old structure
    (E) an intricate pattern in rock

14. The word "ponderous" (line 39) most likely means

    (A) profound
    (B) clumsy
    (C) foundational
    (D) formidable
    (E) grueling

15. According to the author, the "big game and its well-fed pursuer" (lines 52-53) are significant because they

    (A) have evolved over hundreds of years as hunter and prey
    (B) manage their lives thousands of feet above sea level
    (C) represent the battle of the tree-line against the elements
    (D) explore a habitat that will never be able to support life
    (E) have escaped the attention of the vast majority of naturalists

16. Based on the information in the last paragraph, which of the following poses the greatest threat to the mountain sheep?

    (A) Human encroachment
    (B) Thin ice
    (C) Mountain lions
    (D) Wind storms
    (E) Avalanches

GO ON TO THE NEXT PAGE

Practice Test 3

Questions 17-24 are based on the following passage.

This passage looks into the reasoning behind a relatively modern philosophical movement.

Where did our obsession with and absolute insistence on having every individual liberty we can possibly imagine come from? What is at the root of
Line our preoccupation with gadgets that magnify and
5 emphasize our own self-importance? How did we justify, and pass off as a need, our desire to follow our every whim and to have the freedom to ignore any data that shows the pitfalls of choosing such radical autonomy? It all began with Ralph Waldo
10 Emerson's "Self-Reliance". This ever-popular and widely-taught essay can be at least partly credited with inflating our perceptions of self worth, for better or for worse.

Let's rewind. I remember my English teacher
15 in high school starting the class with, "Nothing is at last sacred but the integrity of your own mind." Upon hearing this, I was intrigued. In my sixteen years, nobody had ever given me the complete freedom to own my own thoughts; furthermore,
20 nobody had told me that this ownership was a good thing. Emerson writes about conformity and why it is essentially evil incarnate. Simply, conformity is not only wrong because of what one may conform to, but also wrong for its own sake. We are not
25 merely at risk of being misguided by false ideas: any inclination towards following any idea that is not our own is misguidance itself.

What, then, should we do if we do not conform? "Self-Reliance" gives people the freedom to decide
30 for themselves what is wrong and what is right, and moreover depicts this self-determination as more sacred than the dictates of any social law. After reading that part of his essay, I at sixteen felt empowered. Was I really ordained with the power
35 to choose, without limit? This idea constitutes heaven for almost any teenager. I could decide what was acceptable and what wasn't based on my own reasons. I could write my own testament and carve it in stone.
40 The problem with this is that what we construe as wrong or right, good or bad, varies on a daily basis. This variance may guide us to wrong decisions, dangerous choices that are not beneficial for us in the long run. So what then? Emerson says that this
45 is okay; we should not let our fickle natures stop us from being true to ourselves. We should speak what we think and, if what we say today contradicts what we say tomorrow, then that's part of the process we must go through to learn who we are. And if these
50 many changes of mind cause us to be misunderstood, that's fine too. In fact, it's better than fine, because as Emerson declares in his remarks on history's greatest figures, "to be great is to be misunderstood."

Now let's fast-forward to the present day. I am
55 no longer in high school and I can take a step back and see the damage "Self Reliance" has actually done in giving generation after generation belief in such unbridled freedoms. This essay has prompted our society to adopt a very egotistical world view,
60 one that puts us at the center of the universe. "Self-Reliance" is essentially an endorsement of a self-satisfying, self-affirming, self-centered mentality. In the United States, this stubborn adherence to the self is to blame for decades of political gridlock. There is
65 little agreement because there is little compromise. Emerson's words have become gospel: "A man is to carry himself in the presence of all opposition as if everything were titular and ephemeral but he."

Maybe it's not such a bad thing to have our own
70 views and thoughts, and to adhere to them most of the time. But maybe listening to others' views and thoughts, and being affected by them, doesn't equal conformity. After all, humility is a virtue that doesn't have to contradict self-reliance.

17. The primary purpose of the passage is to

(A) recount a personal journey through high school
(B) deliver a critique of Ralph Waldo Emerson's writing
(C) discover the contradictions in a well-known philosophy
(D) articulate one person's quest for ideological freedom
(E) warn against the dangers of egotistical politics

18. The first paragraph primarily serves to

(A) argue that a single ideology is the root of all problems in contemporary society
(B) explain the historical reception of a classic and widely taught-text
(C) present "Self-Reliance" as the cause of our growing egos
(D) ask questions that use data to argue against pursuing personal freedom
(E) warn the reader about specific pitfalls that threaten misguided youth

19. On the basis of the quotation in lines 15-16 ("Nothing is . . . mind"), Emerson would most likely agree with which of the following?

(A) Conformity is essential for a social harmony.
(B) Outside influences are inherently misguiding.
(C) Ethical integrity is the most important trait.
(D) Reasoning is learned, not innate.
(E) Freedom gives you power over others.

GO ON TO THE NEXT PAGE

20. The author views the contradictions described in lines 45-49 ("We should . . . are") as

(A) empowering
(B) paralyzing
(C) unpopular
(D) problematic
(E) acceptable

21. In context, the "political gridlock" (line 64) is primarily caused by

(A) inability to commit
(B) unbiased voting
(C) too little patriotism
(D) lack of cooperation
(E) utopian schemes

22. In line 66, the word "gospel" most nearly means

(A) widely sanctioned
(B) deeply religious
(C) profoundly beautiful
(D) historically evanescent
(E) morally compromised

23. In context of the passage, the author would define "humility" (line 73) as

(A) being modest about your achievements
(B) believing in commonplace political ideas
(C) respecting the viewpoints of others
(D) finding the humor in everyday situations
(E) feeling embarrassment about philosophical uncertainty

24. The author uses the last paragraph primarily in order to

(A) challenge the reader's assumptions
(B) contradict Emerson's teachings
(C) reiterate a point made earlier in the essay
(D) question the usefulness of an essay
(E) reword the thesis of Emerson's work

STOP

If you finish before time is called, you may check your work on this section only.
Do not turn to any other section in the test.

SECTION 3
Time–20 minutes
18 Questions

Directions: For each question in this section, select the best answer from among the choices given and fill in the corresponding circle on the answer sheet.

Each sentence below has one or two blanks, each blank indicating that something has been omitted. Beneath the sentence are five words or sets of words labeled A through E. Choose the word or set of words that, when inserted in the sentence, <u>best</u> fits the meaning of the sentence as a whole.

Example:

Jimmy opened his gas station in the ------- because he wanted to be in the middle of a metropolis.

(A) country
(B) suburbs
(C) periphery
(D) environment
(E) city

---

1. Significantly taller than most other animals of the same type, the Lord Derby Eland stands as high as eight feet, making it the ------- of all antelope species.

   (A) rarest   (B) haughtiest   (C) sleekest
      (D) loftiest   (E) stoutest

2. I always ------- the better of my -------, and therefore make my accomplishments seem much bigger than my failings.

   (A) emphasize . . defeats
   (B) undermine . . exploits
   (C) recollect . . deeds
   (D) downplay . . attainments
   (E) highlight . . judgments

3. Insisting that artists should ------- the public about rising trends in experimental art, sculptor Georg Makarov has implored the art world to exchange its ------- leanings for ones he considers more avant-garde.

   (A) apprise . . imperative
   (B) edify . . conventional
   (C) educate . . innovative
   (D) encourage . . sophisticated
   (E) warn . . conservative

4. Once hired, a new employee would do well to master the tasks assigned by the management as soon as possible: promotions are given only to the most -------.

   (A) convivial   (B) fortuitous   (C) radiant
      (D) adept   (E) pretentious

5. He was respected more for his ------- than for anything else; his ability to find the nuances in a work and pinpoint the failures of any piece of writing was among the traits that made him -------.

   (A) fastidiousness . . contemptuous
   (B) indulgence . . famous
   (C) acumen . . effective
   (D) complaisance . . glamorized
   (E) judgment . . prodigious

6. Although the company director receives frequent reports of worker disgruntlement, the accounts are rarely -------, since hard evidence of the various grievances is difficult to obtain.

   (A) anecdotal   (B) circumstantial
      (C) concomitant   (D) duplicitous
         (E) substantiated

GO ON TO THE NEXT PAGE

Practice Test 3

The two passages below are followed by questions based on their content and on the relationship between the two passages. Answer the questions on the basis of what is <u>stated</u> or <u>implied</u> in the passages and in any introductory material that may be provided.

Questions 7-18 are based on the following passages.

The following two passages are adapted from articles that discuss the status of acting as a form of art.

Passage 1

Acting is not an art, but it is a craft. In one of the most famous scenes in *Hamlet*—an instructive address to a group of traveling players—William Shakespeare
Line made it quite clear what he required of the actors in
5 his plays. He wanted performers "to hold a mirror to nature." He wished them to avoid grand gestures and to refrain from "tearing a passion to tatters," aware that actors often over-play their parts to grab an audience's attention. An actor does not create a character; the
10 playwright does. The actor should never forget that he is not the center of the audience's interest. The audience believes in the *character*, not in the actor.

Despite these realities, actors often sound quite self-important when talking about what they call
15 their "art." They talk about artistic self-analysis and reflection, about the use of affective memory, about drawing on sense impressions and deepest emotions. They explain how they "experience different roles, manifesting emotions and feelings through visual and
20 vocal means," as one veteran actor put it. But these are defensive mechanisms, of course. It is difficult for professionals to come to terms with the fact that acting, particularly onstage, is both ephemeral and unpredictable. In performing a role, an actor may run
25 through exactly the same movements and gestures, deliver the same vocal tricks and intonations every night, but that does not mean that his acting will resonate in exactly the same way each time he plays the role. Lawrence Olivier, regarded by many of his
30 peers as the greatest actor of the twentieth century, was found in his private dressing room after a particularly moving performance of *Othello*, weeping streams of tears. His visitors were perplexed: "What is wrong? You were simply brilliant tonight! You were great!"
35 Lawrence managed to sob out: "I know it was great, but I don't know how I did it, so how can I be sure I can do it again?"

The truth is that actors are not artists in their own right. They are tools used by the dramatist; their job
40 is to present the characters the dramatist has created in order to tell his story as clearly as possible. To this end, actors need to present their assigned characters as truly as possible. This does not mean that they have to become the people they are playing. (If that were so,
45 then Shakespeare's Othello would really strangle his wife to death at every performance, leading to rather obvious problems.) However, each actor does have to present his or her character as a person with whom the audience can identify, or at least as somebody the
50 audience can recognize. Noel Coward, another man of the theatre, stated the case bluntly for his actors: "It's not difficult: enter, hit your mark, speak the words clearly, and then get off the stage."

Passage 2

Acting is more than mere craft. To categorize
55 acting as a craft is to liken actors to plumbers: they are certainly adept in what they do, but there is no genuine production of art. In this view, the actor is the mere transposition of the playwright's words from page to presence, from vision to visage, from ideas to
60 identity. Yet the actor is not a dumb instrument used to implement the playwright's work, but rather an artist who adds universal depth to a specific character. Whether dramatists want to accept this reality or not, an actor is the bridge into the dramatist's world, and
65 part of that connection lies within a basic human need to relate to something concrete: the actor is the touchstone. An actor's physical attributes, his deliberate vocal inflections, and even his smallest gesture fuse into someone that the audience can
70 identify and place in a specific context. And the viewers, despite the dramatist's abstract intentions, also supply an exceedingly indispensable characteristic of the Theatre: interpretation.

Without actors, a playwright would never
75 be able to effectively communicate his or her intentions to the audience. It is indeed possible to read a playwright's script, but part of full theatrical experience is witnessing the physical manifestation of the playwright's characters through the actors who
80 bring in their own experiences, skills, and training to fully embody unique stage personalities. Although performed many times, the character of Troy Maxson in August Wilson's *Fences* will always be inextricably tied to any given actor's portrayal, each performer
85 providing a new vantage from which to view and interpret Wilson's character.

As with any mode of art, it is difficult to perceive and judge what *is* truly defined as art, but defining what *isn't* may be even more important. The truth is
90 that acting, like all art, is an intangible concept because its merit is governed by a system that is primarily subjective—meaning that there is no standardized and indisputable method for distinguishing an outstanding performance from an inept one. Rather, a meaningful
95 critique of acting depends on considerations of

GO ON TO THE NEXT PAGE

delivery and execution in a given moment. To put it plainly, acting is like figure skating. The actor can be trained and versed in his craft, but at the end of it all, the performance itself is the art, not the actor. Should
100 this mean that acting is definitely an art form? The concept of "art" is perhaps too convoluted to provide any clear answer. But it is unmistakable that acting, at the very least, goes beyond the realm of craft. Acting is a mode of expression that transcends simple
105 showmanship and performance by linking an audience directly to a playwright's profound, universal truths.

7.   The authors of both passages would most likely agree that acting requires

(A) removal of personal life and experiences from an actor's mind during a performance
(B) relentless rehearsal to ensure that stage performances are consistent
(C) artistic flair and deep emotional introspection during a performance
(D) recognition that actors are fundamentally inferior to directors and dramatists
(E) performances that represent a dramatist's intentions in a compelling manner

8.   The author of Passage 1 discusses Shakespeare in the first paragraph in order to

(A) indicate that the passage's assertions about actors and dramatists are consistent with the ideas of a legendary playwright
(B) substantiate the claim that all playwrights aim to create passionate and redemptive theatre spectacles
(C) imply that Shakespeare's success as a playwright depended on his ability to communicate with his actors
(D) anticipate later claims about the various misinterpretations that surrounded Olivier's performance of Shakespeare's *Othello*
(E) demonstrate that many of Shakespeare's plays poke fun at the foibles and pretensions of actors and actresses

9.   In Passage 1, the phrase "these realities" in line 13 refers to

(A) the fact that many modern actors use self-analysis to craft emotionally striking performances
(B) the idea that the audience is not focused on the individual actor, but on the performance delivered
(C) the demanding hours and grueling professional duties that many actors face
(D) the realization that no actor is capable of doing justice to the works of an ingenious playwright such as Shakespeare
(E) the significant part that an actor plays in translating a given character from script to performance

10. The author of Passage 1 characterizes actors who discuss their work (lines 15-21) as

(A) adept at connecting with an audience by evoking familiar memories and emotions
(B) capable of counteracting the inherent uncertainty of live performance
(C) compensating for an ultimate lack of control over the quality of their performance
(D) relying too much on vocal inflection and dramatic gesture to captivate an audience
(E) needlessly concerned with the challenge of reflecting reality in their performances

11. The tone of the parenthetical statement in Passage 1, lines 44-47, is

(A) somber
(B) cautionary
(C) humorous
(D) salacious
(E) derisive

12. The author of Passage 1 would most likely view the role of the actor described in lines 57-60 ("In this . . . identity") of Passage 2 with

(A) justified skepticism
(B) qualified approval
(C) respectful dissent
(D) complete agreement
(E) open indignation

GO ON TO THE NEXT PAGE

Practice Test 3

13. In context, "depth" (line 62) most nearly means

    (A) distance
    (B) melancholy
    (C) meaning
    (D) remoteness
    (E) judgment

14. The author of Passage 2 mentions the "viewers" in line 71 primarily in order to

    (A) emphasize that the production and experience of theatrical art involves more than just the intentions of the dramatist
    (B) mock the willful ignorance of theater-goers who view acting as little more than a craft
    (C) discourage attendance at plays that feature simplistic and unambiguous roles
    (D) demonstrate that the historical context of a script will always overshadow the playwright's expressed intentions
    (E) claim that the interpretation of a performance is more important than the actual execution of a play

15. The author of Passage 2 uses the phrase in lines 76-77 ("It is . . . script") most likely in order to

    (A) explain how actors prepare for their roles
    (B) call attention to an overlooked reality
    (C) acknowledge a potential counter-argument
    (D) summarize a central principle of the passage
    (E) imply skepticism about a common practice

16. Which of the following does the author of Passage 2 indicate about "art" (line 87)?

    (A) It cannot be possessed by any single consumer, and consequently can never be destroyed.
    (B) It is a subjective construct that resists most forms of critical analysis.
    (C) It will always be incompatible with popular types of showmanship.
    (D) It cannot be evaluated systematically and is therefore open to interpretation.
    (E) It relies on firm and unwavering standards that art critics have yet to discover.

17. Noel Coward, mentioned in lines 50-53 of Passage 1, would be criticized by the author of Passage 2 for

    (A) failing to acknowledge the role that enunciation plays in an effective performance
    (B) departing radically from Shakespeare's ideas of proper acting
    (C) displaying no interest in theater's ability to convey psychological insights
    (D) communicating his ideas about acting in an uncouth fashion
    (E) understating the true responsibilities of the actor on stage

18. Which contrast best describes how the author of each passage views the position of the actor?

    (A) As mercenary and opportunistic in Passage 1; as idealistic and self-denying in Passage 2
    (B) As useful but limited in Passage 1; as invaluable and transformative in Passage 2
    (C) As changing heedlessly in response to popular taste in Passage 1; as guided by a unique set of virtues in Passage 2
    (D) As altering radically from one era to the next in Passage 1; as stable throughout history in Passage 2
    (E) As a source of justified satire in Passage 1; as deserving absolute respect in Passage 2

STOP

If you finish before time is called, you may check your work on this section only.
Do not turn to any other section in the test.

POST TEST ANALYSIS

This post test analysis is important if you want to see an improvement on your next test. Each section has a set of possible reasons for errors. Place check marks next to the ones that pertain to you, and write your own on the blank lines provided. Use this form to better analyze your performance. **If you don't understand why you made errors, there is no way you can correct them!**

1. **SENTENCE COMPLETION:**

   Problems with the sentence:
   - ❑ Wasn't familiar with phrases, idioms, or words in the sentence
   - ❑ Missed the clues or tones
   - ❑ Put your OWN word in the blank rather than one from the sentence
   - ❑ Completely avoided marking
   - ❑ Other: _____

   _____

   Problems with the answers:
   - ❑ Did not use process of elimination
   - ❑ Did not ignore unknown words
   - ❑ Did not use prefix/root/suffix knowledge to figure out the meaning of the unknown words
   - ❑ Did not match the clues and tones of the answer with those of the sentence
   - ❑ Did not recognize vocabulary words
   - ❑ Did not check answer to see if it fit
   - ❑ Other: _____

   _____

   Leaving questions unanswered:
   - ❑ Did not try
   - ❑ Did not fill in the blank(s) with words
   - ❑ Ran out of time
   - ❑ Other: _____

   _____

2. **SHORT READING COMPREHENSION:**
   - ❑ Did not read entire paragraph
   - ❑ Did not see more than one point
   - ❑ Missed contrast clues
   - ❑ Did not pinpoint thesis
   - ❑ Did not identify similarities and differences in Double Short Reading Comp
   - ❑ Other: _____

   _____

3. **LONG READING COMPREHENSION:**
   - ❑ Did not understand the question, line reference, or answers
   - ❑ Spent too much time reading the passages
   - ❑ Did not underline the line reference
   - ❑ Read too much or too little
   - ❑ Did not answer the specific question; instead analyzed its main idea
   - ❑ Did not do process of elimination based on facts in the passage
   - ❑ Couldn't find the false words
   - ❑ Couldn't choose between two possible answers
   - ❑ Did not use tone to help eliminate answers
   - ❑ When stuck at 2 guessed instead of pulling additional fact
   - ❑ Couldn't finish in time
   - ❑ Other: _____

   _____

ANSWER KEY

TEST 3

SECTION 1

#	Answer	Level	#	Answer	Level	#	Answer	Level	#	Answer	Level
1	B	(1)	7	E	(4)	13	A	(1)	19	C	(2)
2	C	(2)	8	D	(5)	14	C	(3)	20	B	(2)
3	B	(3)	9	A	(4)	15	E	(4)	21	D	(3)
4	D	(3)	10	E	(3)	16	D	(3)	22	E	(4)
5	A	(3)	11	C	(2)	17	A	(2)	23	A	(4)
6	C	(4)	12	A	(4)	18	E	(1)	24	C	(4)
									25	C	(3)

SECTION 2

#	Answer	Level	#	Answer	Level	#	Answer	Level	#	Answer	Level
1	D	(1)	7	A	(3)	13	B	(2)	19	B	(4)
2	A	(2)	8	E	(3)	14	D	(4)	20	D	(2)
3	C	(3)	9	C	(4)	15	B	(2)	21	D	(3)
4	E	(4)	10	A	(3)	16	E	(3)	22	A	(3)
5	C	(5)	11	C	(3)	17	B	(3)	23	C	(3)
6	C	(4)	12	D	(3)	18	C	(4)	24	B	(5)

SECTION 3

#	Answer	Level	#	Answer	Level	#	Answer	Level	#	Answer	Level
1	D	(2)	6	E	(5)	11	C	(3)	16	D	(5)
2	C	(1)	7	E	(3)	12	D	(3)	17	E	(3)
3	B	(3)	8	A	(4)	13	C	(2)	18	B	(4)
4	D	(3)	9	B	(3)	14	A	(4)			
5	C	(4)	10	C	(4)	15	C	(4)			

Difficulty levels range from 1 - 5 with 1 being the easiest and 5 being the hardest.
For answer explanations please visit www.ies2400.com/criticalreading

PRACTICE TEST 4

SECTION 1
Time–25 minutes
24 Questions

Directions: For each question in this section, select the best answer from among the choices given and fill in the corresponding circle on the answer sheet.

Each sentence below has one or two blanks, each blank indicating that something has been omitted. Beneath the sentence are five words or sets of words labeled A through E. Choose the word or set of words that, when inserted in the sentence, <u>best</u> fits the meaning of the sentence as a whole.

Example:

Jimmy opened his gas station in the ------- because he wanted to be in the middle of a metropolis.

(A) country
(B) suburbs
(C) periphery
(D) environment
(E) city

1. Some students complained that the teacher, rather than treating them as his -------, befriended them and expected them to -------.

    (A) equals . . surrender
    (B) peers . . learn
    (C) underlings . . resist
    (D) pupils . . reciprocate
    (E) protégés . . falter

2. Surpassing all expectations in his performance, George erased all memories of his earlier, slipshod work and received several -------.

    (A) accolades   (B) circumventions
        (C) considerations   (D) lectures
            (E) securities

3. Although he frequently describes ------- as the loftiest quality, philosopher George Pendal is best known for the ------- nature of his writing.

    (A) emotion . . instinctive
    (B) innuendo . . speculative
    (C) acumen . . sardonic
    (D) logic . . intellectual
    (E) reason . . visceral

4. Every spring, animal shelters are ------- cats and dogs, since these animals experience a ------- in population during the warmer months.

    (A) inundated with . . surge
    (B) besieged by . . dearth
    (C) devoid of . . upturn
    (D) lacking in . . growth
    (E) disrupted by . . shortage

5. In the 1960s, sending a man to the moon seemed like the most exciting adventure of the time; however, this feat has been replicated so often that some people now find televised space launches -------.

    (A) exhilarating   (B) wasteful   (C) droll
        (D) exorbitant   (E) tedious

GO ON TO THE NEXT PAGE

1   1   1   Unauthorized copying or
reuse of any part of this
page is illegal.   1   1   1

Practice Test 4

Each passage below is followed by questions based on its content. Answer the questions on the basis of what is <u>stated</u> or <u>implied</u> in each passage and in any introductory material that may be provided.

Questions 6-7 are based on the following passage.

I stared deeply into his menacing eyes, taking
note of his sinister grin from the periphery of my
vision. What did he want from me? The cat tipped his
Line hat and adjusted his bowtie as he continued down the
5 cobblestone road. I couldn't help but feel a profound
mea culpa as the cat sauntered along, as if my presence
had ordained a sense of guilt that only the cat could
know and understand.
    I'll never know if I would have been truly sorry
10 for stealing the cabbage from the farmer. But what
does it mean to be sorry, when you have no choice? As
the cat vanished into the horizon, I wagged my bushy
tail and hopped back toward my hole under the hill.

* *mea culpa*: a Latin phrase meaning "guilt" or "my fault"

6. Which best characterizes the relationship between
    the first paragraph and the second paragraph?

    (A) The first paragraph uses a term
        unconventionally while the second
        paragraph offers a standard explanation.
    (B) The first paragraph explores a moment
        of high emotion that is elucidated in the
        second paragraph.
    (C) The paragraphs offer incompatible
        explanations of a single strange incident.
    (D) The second paragraph humorously digresses
        from the topic discussed in the first
        paragraph.
    (E) The first paragraph links a personal anecdote
        to the broader topic addressed in the second
        paragraph.

7. The literary device primarily used in this
    passage is

    (A) hyperbole
    (B) simile
    (C) allegory
    (D) personification
    (E) anachronism

Questions 8-9 are based on the following passage.

To excel in their military endeavors, the ancient
Romans did not rely on physical prowess alone,
important though this was. Roman warriors would
Line regularly perform training exercises with weapons
5 weighing twice as much as the swords and spears that
they carried into war. Yet should sheer strength and
agility fail these soldiers, siege engines and heavy
artillery could still turn the tide of battle. The "foot and
horse" warriors of the Roman legions were supported
10 by battering rams, stone-throwing catapults, and
devices known as scorpions, which launched blades
and javelins into enemy ranks. For the enemies of
Rome, the best battle strategy was often a quick and
unconditional surrender.

8. The primary purpose of the passage is to

    (A) explain the reasons for a civilization's
        ultimate downfall
    (B) highlight a little-known tactic in ancient
        warfare
    (C) discuss the difficulty of deploying artillery on
        the battlefield
    (D) provide an informative synopsis of a military
        strategy
    (E) detail the technological advances of a military
        culture

9. In context, the author regards the "training
    exercises" (line 4) as

    (A) essential to all military endeavors
    (B) ancillary to a well-supplied arsenal
    (C) obsolete in light of technical advances
    (D) insufficient to guarantee victory
    (E) critical in establishing superiority

GO ON TO THE NEXT PAGE

1   1   1   Unauthorized copying or
reuse of any part of this
page is illegal.   1   1   1

Questions 10-16 are based on the following passage.

The following passage is adapted from a 2012 essay written by an origami enthusiast.

If you fold a square of paper in half, then fold the sides to the middle and again once more, you will then hold in your hands a crude, but functional,
Line paper airplane. We all made toys like this when we
5 were young, whether they were paper airplanes, paper footballs, paper cranes, or paper boxes. It was easy: all you had to do was get a piece of paper, fold it around a few times until it formed the shape you wanted, and then you had a new toy, innocuous and amusing.
10   Simple? Today, mathematicians and scientists say otherwise. In recent years, origami, or the art of sculpturally folded paper, has become a crucial factor in many fields of mathematics and science, including research involving space equipment and medical
15 technology. For hundreds of years, origami was just an art form. For hundreds of years more, it was just a popular past-time. Now, with the astounding speed of technological breakthrough that marked the turn of the 21st century, origami has become an application
20 that may one day save lives.
    Robert J. Lang, a physicist and origami artist, tells us in his recent TED talk that origami has much more to do with mathematics than one would think. He explains that he can turn a single square sheet of
25 paper into virtually any shape. By simply partitioning the paper with multiple creases, one can create the foundation of a complex origami form. Lang has created a computer program that is able to turn a basic stick figure into a pattern of circle creases that
30 you can fold into a base for your origami figure. But the relation between origami and math doesn't stop at flaps and circles. What scientists have realized over the years is that origami can be used to reshape designs to fit size constraints.
35   When scientists at the Lawrence Livermore National Laboratory took on the project of sending a telescope with a lens of 100 meters in diameter into space, they were met with an obvious stumbling block: How on Earth (or in space) were they going to fit such
40 a large telescope into such a small rocket? Dividing the glass lens into separate parts that could fold and unfold was one possibility, but even after folding the circular lens numerous times, the scientists were left with a result that was not nearly small enough. The solution,
45 though, was anything but impossible for an origami artist. The National Laboratory engineers were able to collaborate with origami artists to come up with a pattern for folding the lens down until it was only five meters in diameter—still the largest lens in the world,
50 but much more manageable.
    As you can see, origami is much more than folding a piece of paper into a flower or a bird. What wasn't possible before due to size constraints can

now be achieved through the use of origami concepts.
55 Maybe the paper airplane you folded as a child will one day take the shape of a real airplane and carry technology to new, unseen heights.

10. The author states "We all . . . young" (lines 4-5) in order to

(A) encourage present-day children to try a new art form
(B) highlight the simplicity and universality of a craft
(C) refute misconceptions about activities that appeal to children
(D) create a connection between the reader and individuals described in biographical anecdotes
(E) portray a craft as unsophisticated and suitable only for immature persons

11. The author mentions "mathematicians and scientists" (line 10) in order to

(A) propose further statistical research on the use of origami in science
(B) introduce a stance on the perceived simplicity of an art form
(C) discredit scientists for relying on arts and crafts in solving complex problems
(D) contradict the view presented in the first paragraph about the childishness of origami
(E) lend credibility to a point made about the aesthetic applications of origami

12. The author includes a rough timeline for origami in lines 15-20 ("For hundreds . . . lives") primarily in order to

(A) question the usefulness of an art that has taken so long to become pragmatic
(B) substantiate the claim that origami has been medically useful for hundreds of years
(C) discuss the evolution of origami over a vast period of time
(D) establish the average amount of time before an art form assumes practical uses
(E) express skepticism about the assimilation of origami by different cultures

13. The overall tone of the third paragraph can best be described as

(A) emphatic
(B) sarcastic
(C) grave
(D) condescending
(E) incredulous

GO ON TO THE NEXT PAGE

14. The situation described in lines 44-50 ("The
solution . . . manageable") is most analogous
to which of the following?

(A) A writer works with multiple illustrators to
     publish his first children's book.
(B) An artist works with naturalists to create
     better camouflage for observation.
(C) A biologist submits a piece of science fiction
     to an anthology.
(D) A group of engineers works collaboratively
     to solve a difficult electrical problem.
(E) A man hires an on-demand service to clean
     his house because he doesn't have the time.

15. The author's attitude toward origami is one of

(A) justifiable appreciation
(B) confused awe
(C) artistic interest
(D) muted disdain
(E) marked indifference

16. The primary purpose of the passage is to

(A) instigate an interest in the art of origami
     among children
(B) reminisce about the earliest days in the
     development of origami
(C) evaluate the modern implications of an
     ancient cultural practice
(D) disparage the use of artistic forms in
     contemporary medicine
(E) introduce the art of origami to radically
     different cultures

Practice Test 4

GO ON TO THE NEXT PAGE

1   **1**   **1**   **1**   **1**   **1**

Unauthorized copying or
reuse of any part of this
page is illegal.

Practice Test 4

Questions 17-24 are based on the following passage.

This passage is adapted from a nonfiction essay describing the author's experiences as a teacher living in Malawi, a country in Africa. Here the author discusses an edifying meeting with an African child.

Twenty years ago, I was a teacher of English at Saint Andrew's School in Malawi, one of the smallest and poorest countries in Africa. The school occupied
Line a large estate set back from the road leading from the
5 city of Blantyre to Ndirande, a huddled township squeezed between the flanks of a mountain. The school was founded by Malawi's first president in order to educate the children of expatriates living and working in the country. The school buildings were
10 solid and modern, the sports facilities were spacious and featured a large swimming pool. The students were white. Malawian children were educated, if at all, in villages, in the shade of baobab trees.

I had been in the country just four weeks when I
15 was invited on a trip to the very southernmost tip of the country, to Sucoma. There was a small private reserve there which, occasionally, hosted selected visitors. We met in the late afternoon warmth: me, the headmaster and his wife, the geography teacher and
20 his wife, who was a native Malawian. Gripping her hand was a small girl gazing up in awe and silence at the white adults.

"This is Twambi, my niece." said the wife of the geography teacher.
25 "Here with you on a visit?" asked the headmaster's wife.

"No. My sister's husband died and she has three other children. So Twambi is with us. She only speaks Chichewa."
30 "Oh. *Bwanji**, Twambi." The headmaster took off his hat and bowed solemnly.

Twambi giggled and hid her face in her aunt's skirt. We piled into the jeep and set off on what turned out to be a three-hour, dusty, jolting drive along a
35 deserted road which, more often than not, showed traces of tarmac. We arrived at the edge of the reserve as dusk was falling. We were brought to the lodges where we would spend the night, given a simple meal, and then shown to bed, for we were to wake at half
40 past four in the morning in order to reach the hide beside the water hole before daybreak.

In the morning, the company's truck dropped us about half a mile from our destination and we made our way through the surprisingly chilly darkness and
45 silence until we arrived. The hide was built on stilts and an alarmingly rickety ladder allowed us access to it. We sat beneath the thatched roof on tall stools and leaned forward to rest our elbows on the wooden shelf that ran the length of the structure. We peered
50 through an opening, gazing at the clearing a few yards away. There lay the still water of the water

hole, behind which a slope led up to a ridge of trees. No animals had gathered yet; we just had to wait. Bushes trailed down on either side of the incline, but
55 there appeared to be trails leading off between the bushes. On the far edge of the pool was a sandy shore. Large trees framed the scene.

Stillness and silence. We held our breath intently. A rustle in the undergrowth and a
60 procession of small deer—nyala, perhaps—picked their way, delicately, to the water's edge and dipped their heads. Above them, an owl eased through the air and posed itself upon a heavy branch. The placid bird hooted softly. A heron, white and stately, as if
65 by magic (for we had not seen it enter the scene) stood as rigid as a sentinel, and a fish eagle floated through the lightening air. The nyala paused, raised their heads, then turned and moved away through the bushes. They were replaced by other deer. A
70 hammerkopf called from the bushes, and this call seemed to be a cue, for a single line of warthogs, each with its tail pointing directly to the sky, trotted, almost comically, to their drinking place.

I do not remember all the animals we saw,
75 although the Malawian guide with us whispered the name of each animal or bird that took its turn at the water's edge. The light strengthened. It was as if a climactic moment were approaching. A group of female kudu came down to the pool and drank. Then,
80 in unison, they raised their heads and moved aside. At the top of the slope, silhouetted against the dawn, stood an adult male kudu. His head, raised proudly, showed off his towering, twisted, powerful horns. He stared across the pool, directly at the hide. Then, like
85 royalty, he moved down to the pool, lowered his head, and drank. He raised it, stared across the pool at us again, then turned and exited. The stage was bare. The sun had risen. We left the hide in awed silence.

In the jeep, on the way back, we talked to each
90 other and discussed what we had seen. Twambi sat between her uncle and aunt. She was singing in Chichewa.

"Is that a Malawian song she is singing?" the headmaster's wife asked. "What does it mean in
95 English?"

"It isn't really a song," answered Twambi's aunt. "She is repeating all the names of the animals she saw this morning. She sings so that she can put them in her memory. That is how children learn in the
100 village, under the baobab tree."

*Bwanji means "Hello" in Chichewa, the native language of Malawi

GO ON TO THE NEXT PAGE

17. The word "huddled" in line 5 most nearly means

(A) suppressed
(B) secretive
(C) compact
(D) spread out
(E) set back

18. The contrast in lines 9-13 emphasizes a distinction between

(A) the need to impress others and the need to feel personally satisfied
(B) the importance of competition and the value of compassion
(C) the love of nature and the love of learning
(D) differing sets of cultural and family priorities
(E) the education practices applied to two groups of students

19. Lines 20-33 ("Gripping her . . . skirt") serve to

(A) provide character sketches of the participants in the excursion
(B) highlight subtle egocentrism on the part of the headmaster
(C) imply that Twambi is heartbroken to be without her family
(D) suggest that Twanbi is outside of her comfort zone
(E) show reverence for the geography teacher and his wife

20. The "hide" described in lines 45-57 is used for

(A) observing animals without being detected
(B) resting overnight before continuing on a journey
(C) achieving a respite from the heat and sun
(D) the formal schooling of native Malawian children
(E) gathering equipment for zoological experiments

21. Lines 42-57 are distinctive for their use of

(A) scientific detail
(B) auditory evocation
(C) visual description
(D) speculative argumentation
(E) mystical foreshadowing

22. The author uses which of the following rhetorical devices in the description of the water hole in lines 62-87 ("Above them . . . bare")?

(A) hypothetical musing
(B) extended analogy
(C) historical allusion
(D) breezy colloquialism
(E) dramatic irony

23. The author's statement "I do not . . . edge" (lines 74-77) primarily serves to

(A) indicate a major memory lapse on the narrator's part
(B) signify that there were too many species at the water hole for anyone to remember by name
(C) suggest that the memorization technique used by Malawian children is effective
(D) demonstrate that the narrator's ability to recall details was compromised by astounding events
(E) imply that animal names are easier to remember in the Malawian language than they are in English

24. The reader can assume that the author included the last quotation in lines 97-100 to

(A) make a point about the true effectiveness of seemingly improper education techniques
(B) vent his frustration at the headmaster for assuming the girl was merely making up a song
(C) prove that the school for expatriates should include similar memory lessons and songs for its students
(D) admit that he feels guilty to be working an elite school while Twambi studies elsewhere
(E) demonstrate his fascination with African animals and how they relate to the Malawian people

STOP
If you finish before time is called, you may check your work on this section only.
Do not turn to any other section in the test.

Practice Test 4

SECTION 2
Time–25 minutes
24 Questions

Directions: For each question in this section, select the best answer from among the choices given and fill in the corresponding circle on the answer sheet.

Each sentence below has one or two blanks, each blank indicating that something has been omitted. Beneath the sentence are five words or sets of words labeled A through E. Choose the word or set of words that, when inserted in the sentence, <u>best</u> fits the meaning of the sentence as a whole.

Example:

Jimmy opened his gas station in the ------- because he wanted to be in the middle of a metropolis.

(A) country
(B) suburbs
(C) periphery
(D) environment
(E) city

1. Switzerland is a linguistically ------- country: French, German, Italian, and Romanche are all spoken in different parts of the nation.

    (A) generous   (B) concentrated   (C) rich
        (D) astonishing   (E) conflicted

2. Considered ------- public morals when they first appeared in the seventeenth century, novels treating controversial themes eventually captivated the public to gain widespread -------.

    (A) consistent with . . acceptance
    (B) harmful to . . currency
    (C) oblivious to . . support
    (D) reminiscent of . . uncertainty
    (E) supportive of . . ridicule

3. The professor possessed an amazing ability to ------- his thoughts clearly, and thus to get his point across with perfect ------- whenever the need would arise.

    (A) articulate . . opacity
    (B) diverge . . frankness
    (C) remonstrate . . clarity
    (D) convey . . coherence
    (E) transmit . . diffidence

4. As a species, squirrels are known for their -------; they are very adept at activities involving balance and muscle coordination.

    (A) agility   (B) lassitude   (C) maladroitness
        (D) ambidextrousness   (E) intractability

5. While Eric Clapton and Carlos Santana are ------- as two of the world's greatest guitarists, there are in fact many practitioners of the instrument who, though lacking such popularity, have ------- technical skills.

    (A) celebrated . . standard
    (B) censured . . commensurate
    (C) estimated . . calculable
    (D) overrated . . alternate
    (E) venerated . . equivalent

6. British politician Winston Churchill regarded medical discoveries as the finest examples of scientific -------, arguing that the achievements of his time were so ------- that they deserved to be sainted.

    (A) procession . . important
    (B) development . . somber
    (C) pretentiousness . . intrepid
    (D) betterment . . significant
    (E) amelioration . . confounding

7. Trying to appear unaffected by her recent disappointment, Marcy assumed an air of ------- whenever her friends asked about her activities.

    (A) nonchalance   (B) recalcitrance
        (C) munificence   (D) wariness
            (E) ambivalence

8. As an active champion of -------, Henry Kissinger urges nations to resolve their disputes through peace talks rather than through acts of war.

    (A) autonomy   (B) retribution
        (C) appeasement   (D) diplomacy
            (E) conflict

GO ON TO THE NEXT PAGE

2   2   2   Unauthorized copying or
reuse of any part of this
page is illegal.   2   2   2

The passages below are followed by questions based on their content; questions following a pair of related passages may also be based on the relationship between the paired passages. Answer the questions on the basis of what is <u>stated</u> or <u>implied</u> in the passages and in any introductory material that may be provided.

Questions 9-12 are based on the following passages.

Passage 1

The TV channels are full of the death of Nelson Mandela. I so vividly remember watching him walk out of Robben Island (where he had been imprisoned
Line for a long stretch of his life). Soon, the spectacle of
5 his emancipation would be followed by the sight of queues of South Africans voting for the very first time. We do not always realize how lucky we are, for all the faults of our democracies. Mandela was much admired by the Angolan pupils I taught—second on their list of
10 great African leaders only to Agostinho Neto, who had been Angola's own version of Mandela. Some of the best essays my students wrote were about what these two men meant to the future of all of Africa.

Passage 2

Nelson Mandela, or the "Father of the Nation"
15 to many South Africans, left us with a cold reminder of the work that remains to be done in dismantling institutionalized racism. His critics often denounced him as a communist and a terrorist, mostly because he battled the inequality of certain economic and social
20 structures. But what is truly interesting about Mandela and others like him is the inevitable imprisonment they face because of their beliefs. What does it say about our democracies that the solution to opposing ideologies is a steel cell? Threaded into the fabric of
25 our psyches is the terrifying thought that any legitimate idea of change must be met with such unwarranted and unmitigated reactions.

9. In contrast to that of Passage 2, the tone of Passage 1 is more

   (A) ambivalent
   (B) condemnatory
   (C) agitated
   (D) pedantic
   (E) personal

10. Both passages mention Nelson Mandela as an example of

   (A) a proponent of social and economic inequality
   (B) an individual vilified by a national government
   (C) a leader who has inspired his fellow Africans
   (D) a role model for present-day schoolchildren
   (E) a universally successful social reformer

11. Unlike Passage 2, Passage 1 includes which of the following?

   (A) An analysis of modern democratic principles
   (B) A refutation of commonly accepted definitions
   (C) An expression of praise for Mandela's values and beliefs
   (D) A discussion of a specific incident in Mandela's life
   (E) An overview of two different traditions

12. The author of Passage 2 would most likely respond to lines 7-8 of Passage 1 ("We do . . . democracies") by asserting that

   (A) Mandela's personal struggle has overshadowed his political successes
   (B) Mandela's reforms have been largely ignored by the modern media
   (C) even democratic governments can be guilty of harsh repressions
   (D) future policies in South Africa will nullify Mandela's accomplishments
   (E) society will gradually become unwilling to stigmatize reformers

GO ON TO THE NEXT PAGE

Practice Test 4

Questions 13-24 are based on the following passage.

This passage is adapted from a 2013 short story about a Midwestern man named Jermaine Wright, who has left his small town in Wisconsin to move to Boston, Massachusetts.

This was a new coffee shop. It was actually an old coffee shop, one of the oldest in America, first opened in 1874. But to Jermaine, it was a new
Line coffee shop. Everything was new to Jermaine. The
5 Northeast ran at a different speed than Jermaine did, but he found himself able to catch up, to run past the lazy ambling of his native Wisconsin. This was a new coffee shop, and he was a new Jermaine.

He didn't even necessarily want to leave
10 Wisconsin, but his therapist thought it would be a good exercise in independence and confronting his fears to move somewhere new, somewhere farther along. Frankly, Jermaine thought his therapist wanted a break from their sessions, and had even heard the
15 therapist say something of the sort to his receptionist, but Jermaine told himself that his old paranoid fears of worthlessness were just dogging him. Regardless of the reason for his new shift in location, Jermaine still called his therapist weekly, sometimes biweekly,
20 to which his therapist would reply, "Hello Jermaine, what's the crisis this time?"

Jermaine sat down with his coffee, a large-sugar-no-Splenda-soy-milk-no-dairy-hazelnut-and-as-little-froth-as-possible-brew, and thought about his new
25 roommate. Jeff was an odd fellow, a little too happy and a little too friendly for Jermaine, but Jermaine supposed the situation could be worse. Jermaine Wright and Jeff Wozniak. "Double JW!" Jeff said. "JW squared!" Jeff laughed. Jeff seemed to fancy
30 himself a comedian, but Jermaine couldn't manage to find him funny. He simply smiled and waited for it all to be over.

What's worse were Jeff's cleaning habits. Jeff would leave his clothing strewn all about the
35 apartment. Jermaine was rather strict about tidiness, but only once had he found the courage to confront Jeff about it, a situation resulting in Jeff's comment, "Oh yeah, thank goodness we no longer live with our mothers!" Jermaine answered with a weak smile, and
40 then a sigh, and he didn't bring up the topic again. He did begin to clean the apartment, a development to which Jeff adjusted immediately.

One day last week, and it had only been day three of living together, Jeff came home in a mood.
45 "I only told one little joke," Jeff said, "and merely pointing out an inequality doesn't make me a bigot. I mean, who would get all riled up over that?" Who would be all riled up? Jermaine thought. The only people who would get riled up would be those who
50 listen intently to what is being said, realize its effect on the societal landscape, and then admit that jokes at the expense of others only promote the inequalities that they claim to be 'merely pointing out.'

But Jermaine sipped his coffee, and pulled his
55 laptop from his bag. He'd done enough thinking about Jeff for the day, he told himself. He pulled up the document he was working on; he was a freelancer, often picking up government projects, but he'd been having problems lately. The websites
60 and his friends had all said it was so easy to change your address, but Jermaine was having a hard time finding all the authorities he had to inform of the change. They even wanted to change the address on his driver's license; it seemed that, until Jermaine did
65 this, his government employers would have a hard time locating where he was now. An immeasurable amount of work, yet it was supposedly no work at all. He would eventually get to it, but who could stomach a day in line at the motor vehicle agency?

70 When all was said and done, Jermaine missed his native Wisconsin. When he remembered his time there, he remembered his old life with a tender pain, as he might remember an old friend who had moved away long ago. He thought of his coworkers—here
75 was the pain, with none of the tenderness—and he thought of his neighbors. He thought of his family— oh, his mother never quite let him be, maybe she was the one thing he was truly glad to be rid of. But he remembered fondly the way Ontario Drive swooped
80 around in curves and buckled under bridges. He missed the flat plains, and the way you could see a hundred trees stretched out over what felt like a hundred miles, and the way a snow drift could create a monument in just one night.

85 He couldn't say he hated the Northeast, though he could say that Boston was not nearly as comfortable as Wisconsin was. He couldn't say Boston was less enjoyable, but he could say that it was more stressful. This area of America was just
90 so different for Jermaine. He didn't feel as lost as he thought he would, though. He didn't feel as helpless as he thought he would. He had come here to get a break from the everyday particulars, and he was certainly finding that, but with an important caveat:
95 all days are the same in some sense.

GO ON TO THE NEXT PAGE

2   2   2   Unauthorized copying or   2   2   2
                                   reuse of any part of this
                                   page is illegal.

13. Taken as a whole, this passage is best understood as an account of

(A) a man's impulsive escape from his normal life
(B) a traveler's respite in a big city before moving on
(C) a cloistered man's experience of new surroundings
(D) a recent transplant's situation with a new roommate
(E) a foreigner's attempt to settle in a new country

14. The phrase "The Northeast ran at a different speed than Jermaine did" (lines 4-5) suggests that

(A) the traffic in the city of Boston was maddeningly chaotic
(B) Jermaine found it necessary to slow down his lifestyle in the Northeast
(C) the pace of life in Boston differed from what Jermaine had experienced in Wisconsin
(D) there were only novel experiences to be had in this part of the country
(E) Jermaine could not adapt to the speed of his new surroundings

15. According to the information in the second paragraph, the therapist's tone in lines 20-21 ("'Hello, Jermaine . . . time'") is most likely one of

(A) concern
(B) curiosity
(C) contentment
(D) irritation
(E) solemnity

16. The depiction of Jermaine's coffee in lines 22-24 ("a large . . . brew") suggests that Jermaine is

(A) pragmatic
(B) heedless
(C) fastidious
(D) accountable
(E) pretentious

17. Jermaine's answering "with a weak smile, and then a sigh" in lines 39-40 indicates a feeling of

(A) fearfulness
(B) despondency
(C) gratification
(D) resignation
(E) serenity

18. In lines 25-42, Jermaine's attitude toward Jeff can best be described as

(A) grudging tolerance
(B) unqualified appreciation
(C) spiteful disdain
(D) uninhibited disgust
(E) paranoid anxiety

19. What is the best interpretation of Jermaine's answer to the question Jeff poses in line 47?

(A) Those who are too sensitive
(B) Those who are unhappy in life
(C) No one in particular
(D) Only Jermaine himself
(E) Those who are cognizant of social problems

20. In context, the sentence "An immeasurable . . . all" (lines 66-67) implies that Jermaine's process of changing his address is

(A) such an enormous amount of work that it will never be finished
(B) more arduous than had been initially anticipated
(C) too extreme a task for Jermaine to complete without formal assistance
(D) the primary source of Jermaine's discomfort in his new surroundings
(E) less time-consuming than Jermaine had anticipated

21. Lines 71-74 ("When he . . . ago") indicate that Jermaine remembers Wisconsin with

(A) wistful longing
(B) abiding hope
(C) unrestrained euphoria
(D) biting cynicism
(E) unexpected flippancy

22. According to lines 76-84 ("He thought . . . night"), what Jermaine misses most about Wisconsin is

(A) his mother
(B) his neighbors
(C) the topography
(D) the architecture
(E) the agriculture

GO ON TO THE NEXT PAGE

Practice Test 4

23. Lines 85-89 ("He couldn't . . . stressful") are notable chiefly for their use of

(A) repetition
(B) humor
(C) metaphor
(D) sarcasm
(E) allegory

24. The passage is narrated from the point of view of

(A) Jeff
(B) Jermaine
(C) Jermaine's mother
(D) a detached narrator
(E) Jermaine's therapist

STOP

**If you finish before time is called, you may check your work on this section only.
Do not turn to any other section in the test.**

SECTION 3

Time–20 minutes
19 Questions

Directions: For each question in this section, select the best answer from among the choices given and fill in the corresponding circle on the answer sheet.

Each sentence below has one or two blanks, each blank indicating that something has been omitted. Beneath the sentence are five words or sets of words labeled A through E. Choose the word or set of words that, when inserted in the sentence, best fits the meaning of the sentence as a whole.

Example:

Jimmy opened his gas station in the ------- because he wanted to be in the middle of a metropolis.

(A) country
(B) suburbs
(C) periphery
(D) environment
(E) city

---

1. Although algae is a food source for a variety of small fish, when allowed to grow unchecked it can ------- a dissipation of the oxygen levels essential to the survival of all marine life.

    (A) detract from   (B) vitalize   (C) ward off
       (D) corrode   (E) contribute to

2. Many people tend to think of computer viruses as -------, but this is untrue: only the programmer who developed and disseminated the virus can be deemed malicious.

    (A) maladjusted   (B) synthetic   (C) responsive
       (D) malevolent   (E) delicate

3. Winnie Hauser's writing style is -------: her sentences are long, full of parenthetical remarks, and burdened by the excessive use of subordinate clauses.

    (A) concise   (B) jaded   (C) original
       (D) rambling   (E) somber

4. Critics of recent research policies that require scientists to test males and females in every experiment have ------- these -------, citing rising costs and partisan politics.

    (A) embraced . . experts
    (B) avoided . . hurdles
    (C) denigrated . . expenses
    (D) applauded . . regulations
    (E) decried . . directives

5. Beethoven's Moonlight Sonata inspires ------- in listeners who are susceptible to being moved profoundly.

    (A) appeasement   (B) levity   (C) pathos
       (D) voracity   (E) whimsicality

6. Helen is ------- and -------: she is able to discern her own errors and is quick to take corrective action before anyone else notices them.

    (A) self-critical . . expeditious
    (B) pessimistic . . anxious
    (C) arrogant . . prompt
    (D) perspicacious . . dilatory
    (E) negligent . . punitive

GO ON TO THE NEXT PAGE

Practice Test 4

Practice Test 4

> The two passages below are followed by questions based on their content and on the relationship between the two passages. Answer the questions on the basis of what is <u>stated</u> or <u>implied</u> in the passages and in any introductory material that may be provided.

Questions 7-19 are based on the following passages.

The two passages below discuss the benefits and drawbacks of treating movie-going as a social activity.

Passage 1

If you can watch a movie by yourself at home, you can watch a movie by yourself in a public theater. Yet a lot of us tend to refrain from venturing
Line into the unknown—that black abyss lit by a single
5 sun, the silver celluloid screen. What exactly is the fear? Well, one obvious hurdle may be the social stigma of being alone amidst the sea of barnacles, each one clasped to the red velvet rocks. You, too, are a barnacle now. Oddly enough, the other barnacles
10 look at you with judgment, as if to say "how sad it must be to not have any friends." Ironic that we live in a society that lauds individual endeavors—the whole "do it yourself" attitude—but that, with the same swipe, disapproves of solitude in such settings.
15 I've always rather liked going to the movies alone, since going with others tends to be problematic. Imagine, for once, a moment in which leaving things—or just leaving them—to the very last minute might actually pay off. Think about it. How
20 many times have you gone to the theater with a gaggle of friends, only to discover that there weren't enough seats? "We got here only five minutes before the movie started! How is this possible?" Sometime in that five minutes, a legion of barnacles appeared
25 out of thin air. Of course, we all procrastinate. However, by flying solo, you are guaranteed a seat with a great vantage point—all with the prolonged comfort of arriving there at your own speed. Sure, you might be sitting next to second-date kisses. But
30 that lip smacking certainly beats straining your neck to sit with your friends in the headache-inducing "no man's land" at the very front.
Trapped at a horrendous movie because your friends can't seem to get enough of it? Well, if you
35 had plunged into such inanity alone, you could have surfaced at any time. No need to wait for a search-and-rescue; just decide that you want out and kick your way to freedom! On the flip side, you'll never be abducted by your tribe of friends and be forced to
40 watch a film that doesn't interest you in the least. You are free to venture in solitude and discover the world of film without encumbrance. Yet there is one downside to solitary viewing, and here I will actually make a concession. If you want to have a fruitful
45 discussion about a film with your friends, you will often face the irritating prospect that they have not

watched it yet. You're forced to keep your critiques secret, to clench down on your insights, until that moment of release. But . . . there's always an online forum.

Passage 2

50 As a film critic, I attend special screenings of the latest Academy Award contenders (although some are clearly everything but award-worthy). It's primarily a solitary experience, one that I have become accustomed to, even though there is something
55 fantastic about watching a movie with strangers in the dark. Whether you are witnessing a laugh-out-loud comedy or a weighty drama, you share raw emotional reactions, completely and utterly visceral, with persons you may never see again. It is a fleeting
60 affair, with the highs and lows of a tryst that could never possibly endure. There is some solace in this notion of sharing profound moments without the emotional burden of having to call the other person back.
65 Yet it is clear that movies are designed to be a collective experience. Have we forgotten the fun and joy of gathering together to watch a new release, then—right after—of having heated coffee-shop discussions about the director's intentions? Or even
70 just sharing a laugh, remembering how the main character in a slapstick farce took an exaggerated tumble down the stairs? Now, it seems that we are relegated to keeping those moments to ourselves or, even worse, to sharing them during online debates.
75 As a result, we miss out on the connectivity behind a true film experience.
Even when a film is subpar, you can commiserate with your friends, who share your awareness of the movie's follies. In fact, critiquing a bad movie
80 together can lead to deeply intellectual discussions. But if you watch such a movie alone or leave it early, you will be limited by your own constricted views—never hearing another person's viewpoint and never growing in your own perspective. This downside is
85 not limited to poorly constructed films, either. I remember watching a reshowing of Billy Wilder's *Sunset Boulevard*, a black-and-white classic, at an independent film event in New York City. I was attending in order to gain some material for my blog;
90 to my surprise, many other people had arrived there for leisure but without a single companion. It was a film event after all, and it had seemed that the proper

GO ON TO THE NEXT PAGE

etiquette would be to bring friends. Yet that was not the case. Instead, we all sat there with the grayscale
95 of the screen flickering on our solitary faces, vacant seats between each of us. It was sad. To best capture the true allure of watching a film collectively, I leave you with the departing words of Norma Desmond, the main character in *Sunset Boulevard*: "It's just us.
100 And the cameras. And those wonderful people out there in the dark."

7. Which best describes how the author of each passage views the prospect of watching a movie alone?

(A) As difficult in Passage 1; as desirable in Passage 2
(B) As soothing in Passage 1; as agitating in Passage 2
(C) As rewarding in Passage 1; as limiting in Passage 2
(D) As unlikely in Passage 1; as inevitable in Passage 2
(E) As exhilarating in Passage 1; as unexciting in Passage 2

8. Unlike the author of Passage 1, the author of Passage 2

(A) employs rhetorical questions at key points in the passage's argument
(B) utilizes an extended metaphor to explain movie-going
(C) quotes a work of scholarship that discusses modern film
(D) expresses contempt for arguments against the passage's thesis
(E) provides concrete references to a specific film

9. The use of the word "barnacles" (line 7) is an example of what literary device?

(A) Contradiction
(B) Euphemism
(C) Parody
(D) Digression
(E) Metaphor

10. Which of the following statements best characterizes the relationship between the first and the second paragraphs of Passage 1?

(A) The first paragraph records a number of complaints that are downplayed in the second paragraph.
(B) The first paragraph concludes with a paradox that is illustrated with an unusual case study in the second paragraph.
(C) The first paragraph satirizes a social routine that is discussed much more ambivalently in the second paragraph.
(D) The first paragraph presents rhetorical questions that are only answered in the final sentences of the second paragraph.
(E) The first paragraph introduces a practice that is analyzed using hypothetical scenarios in the second paragraph.

11. The author uses the sentence in lines 23-25 ("Sometime in . . . air") to indicate

(A) the absence of considerate behavior among film viewers
(B) the lack of space and comfort in many contemporary cinemas
(C) the speed with which movie-goers can fill up vacant seats
(D) the impossibility of balancing movie-going with other obligations
(E) that capricious temperaments of frequent visitors to movie theaters

12. The author of Passage 1 would most likely consider "a collective experience" (line 66) to be

(A) vexing, because most movie-goers are misinformed about aesthetic standards
(B) peculiar, because film viewers generally prefer to visit movie theaters alone
(C) optimal, because collective viewing should fuel meaningful forum discussions
(D) unnecessary, because solitary viewing offers superior benefits
(E) problematic, because such experiences lead viewers to over-rate banal movies

GO ON TO THE NEXT PAGE

Practice Test 4

13. In line 82 of Passage 2, the word "constricted" most nearly means

(A) myopic
(B) tightened
(C) fallacious
(D) uncomfortable
(E) ungenerous

14. In lines 91-96 ("It was . . . us") the author of Passage 2 presents a contrast between

(A) ambition and failure
(B) optimism and cynicism
(C) community and misanthropy
(D) expectation and reality
(E) tradition and rebellion

15. The author of Passage 2 suggests that *Sunset Boulevard* (line 99) is

(A) an extremely serious drama
(B) a well-constructed work of cinema
(C) a depiction of the movie industry
(D) a favorite of film connoisseurs
(E) a film that cannot be appreciated without companions

16. In the final paragraph of Passage 2, the author suggests that

(A) solitary movie-going has decreased public appreciation for great cinema
(B) the organizers of public film events often eschew sub-par films
(C) the benefits of collective movie-going are not dependent on the quality of a given film
(D) people who live in big cities are most likely to watch movies alone
(E) film journalists tend to avoid traditional forms of social interaction

17. The author of Passage 2 would most likely regard a "fruitful discussion" (lines 44-45) as

(A) guided by the use of social networking and online media
(B) dominated by the opinions of professional film critics
(C) unrelated to the personal enjoyment of classic film
(D) essential to the collective spirit of movie-going
(E) compromised by the inconveniences that movie-goers frequently face

18. The author of Passage 1 would view the "online debates" mentioned in line 74 of Passage 2 as

(A) illogical, because they draw together incompatible cinematic and digital media
(B) shortsighted, because they encourage bland consensus rather than intelligent dissent
(C) valuable, because they make movie-goers more intolerant of low-quality films
(D) paradoxical, because they prioritize visceral reactions over rigorous reasoning
(E) advantageous, because they allow viewers to share opinions of a given film

19. The author of Passage 1 would most likely respond to the discussion of the "independent film event" (line 88) by stating that the author of Passage 2

(A) is unaware of the increasing preference for solitary film viewing
(B) is uninterested in the process of vigorously analyzing works of cinema
(C) has intentionally obscured the distinctions between film and other forms of entertainment
(D) has downplayed the discomforts of watching a movie as a member of a group
(E) has irresponsibly attempted to justify the social stigmatization that film audiences often experience

STOP

If you finish before time is called, you may check your work on this section only.
Do not turn to any other section in the test.

POST TEST ANALYSIS

This post test analysis is important if you want to see an improvement on your next test. Each section has a set of possible reasons for errors. Place check marks next to the ones that pertain to you, and write your own on the blank lines provided. Use this form to better analyze your performance. **If you don't understand why you made errors, there is no way you can correct them!**

1. **SENTENCE COMPLETION:**

   Problems with the sentence:
   - ❑ Wasn't familiar with phrases, idioms, or words in the sentence
   - ❑ Missed the clues or tones
   - ❑ Put your OWN word in the blank rather than one from the sentence
   - ❑ Completely avoided marking
   - ❑ Other: _____

   _____

   Problems with the answers:
   - ❑ Did not use process of elimination
   - ❑ Did not ignore unknown words
   - ❑ Did not use prefix/root/suffix knowledge to figure out the meaning of the unknown words
   - ❑ Did not match the clues and tones of the answer with those of the sentence
   - ❑ Did not recognize vocabulary words
   - ❑ Did not check answer to see if it fit
   - ❑ Other: _____

   _____

   Leaving questions unanswered:
   - ❑ Did not try
   - ❑ Did not fill in the blank(s) with words
   - ❑ Ran out of time
   - ❑ Other: _____

   _____

2. **SHORT READING COMPREHENSION:**
   - ❑ Did not read entire paragraph
   - ❑ Did not see more than one point
   - ❑ Missed contrast clues
   - ❑ Did not pinpoint thesis
   - ❑ Did not identify similarities and differences in Double Short Reading Comp
   - ❑ Other: _____

   _____

3. **LONG READING COMPREHENSION:**
   - ❑ Did not understand the question, line reference, or answers
   - ❑ Spent too much time reading the passages
   - ❑ Did not underline the line reference
   - ❑ Read too much or too little
   - ❑ Did not answer the specific question; instead analyzed its main idea
   - ❑ Did not do process of elimination based on facts in the passage
   - ❑ Couldn't find the false words
   - ❑ Couldn't choose between two possible answers
   - ❑ Did not use tone to help eliminate answers
   - ❑ When stuck at 2 guessed instead of pulling additional fact
   - ❑ Couldn't finish in time
   - ❑ Other: _____

   _____

ANSWER KEY

TEST 4

SECTION 1

#	Answer	LEVEL
1	D	(1)
2	A	(3)
3	E	(2)
4	A	(3)
5	D	(4)
6	B	(4)
7	D	(2)
8	D	(3)
9	B	(4)
10	B	(3)
11	B	(5)
12	C	(4)
13	A	(2)
14	B	(3)
15	A	(1)
16	C	(3)
17	C	(2)
18	E	(1)
19	D	(4)
20	A	(3)
21	C	(2)
22	B	(3)
23	C	(4)
24	A	(2)

SECTION 2

#	Answer	LEVEL
1	C	(1)
2	B	(2)
3	D	(3)
4	A	(3)
5	E	(4)
6	D	(3)
7	A	(4)
8	D	(4)
9	E	(3)
10	C	(3)
11	D	(4)
12	C	(3)
13	C	(3)
14	C	(3)
15	D	(4)
16	C	(3)
17	D	(4)
18	A	(4)
19	E	(3)
20	B	(2)
21	A	(4)
22	C	(3)
23	A	(3)
24	D	(2)

SECTION 3

#	Answer	LEVEL
1	E	(1)
2	D	(2)
3	D	(2)
4	E	(3)
5	C	(4)
6	A	(5)
7	C	(4)
8	E	(4)
9	E	(2)
10	E	(5)
11	C	(3)
12	D	(3)
13	A	(5)
14	D	(4)
15	B	(3)
16	C	(3)
17	D	(2)
18	E	(3)
19	D	(5)

Difficulty levels range from 1 - 5 with 1 being the easiest and 5 being the hardest.
For answer explanations please visit www.ies2400.com/criticalreading

PRACTICE TEST 5

Practice Test 5

SECTION 1
Time–25 minutes
24 Questions

Directions: For each question in this section, select the best answer from among the choices given and fill in the corresponding circle on the answer sheet.

Each sentence below has one or two blanks, each blank indicating that something has been omitted. Beneath the sentence are five words or sets of words labeled A through E. Choose the word or set of words that, when inserted in the sentence, <u>best</u> fits the meaning of the sentence as a whole.

Example:

Jimmy opened his gas station in the ------- because he wanted to be in the middle of a metropolis.

(A) country
(B) suburbs
(C) periphery
(D) environment
(E) city

---

1. In the heat of the summer months, bees ------- far from their hives in search of pollen, though they tend to remain ------- their home colonies when both the pollen counts and the air temperature decrease in the fall.

   (A) waddle . . dormant in
   (B) fly . . away from
   (C) stay . . active in
   (D) venture . . close to
   (E) wander . . aggressive in

2. Now that he has assumed the role of bandleader, Veer has put on a needlessly ------- attitude and treats his friends with a haughtiness that he never displayed in the past.

   (A) dignified   (B) fraudulent   (C) self-effacing
   (D) euphoric   (E) supercilious

3. In Jim Munroe's travel-oriented novel *An Opening Act of Unspeakable Evil*, a group of ------- musicians wanders across America, playing the opening acts for more famous bands.

   (A) blithe   (B) transitory   (C) itinerant
   (D) talented   (E) hapless

4. While harmless to humans, Theobromine, an ingredient of the cocoa bean, is ------- to dogs and cats.

   (A) disgusting   (B) essential   (C) nutritious
   (D) deleterious   (E) recriminatory

5. The businessman was a very ------- negotiator whose bargaining skills allowed him to deal shrewdly with even the most affluent -------.

   (A) astute . . entrepreneurs
   (B) deceitful . . executives
   (C) favored . . arbiters
   (D) honest . . tycoons
   (E) feckless . . opponents

6. Coconut crabs are known to steal items from humans, opting to ------- materials from people's homes instead of ------- them from natural sources.

   (A) pilfer . . extracting
   (B) borrow . . garnering
   (C) harvest . . retracting
   (D) supplant . . absorbing
   (E) snatch . . delivering

7. There are many valid arguments in favor of capital punishment, but the idea that it is the only effective way to punish criminals is -------.

   (A) justified   (B) myopic   (C) pugnacious
   (D) gruesome   (E) punitive

8. The doctor prognosticated that, since the patient refused to ------- his diet by eliminating fats and sugars, weight loss surgery would be -------.

   (A) annihilate . . imperative
   (B) corroborate . . foolhardy
   (C) curtail . . prohibitive
   (D) exasperate . . beneficial
   (E) mitigate . . futile

GO ON TO THE NEXT PAGE

Unauthorized copying or
reuse of any part of this
page is illegal.

> The passages below are followed by questions based on their content; questions following a pair of related passages may also be based on the relationship between the paired passages. Answer the questions on the basis of what is stated or implied in the passages and in any introductory material that may be provided.

Questions 9-10 are based on the following passage.

Immigration has been and will always be a point of contention in American society. During the California Gold Rush of 1848 to 1855, Chinese
Line men, seeking work in the gold mines, immigrated to
5 America. But as the initial fervor dwindled and gold extraction became highly competitive, animosity toward Chinese laborers rose dramatically. Most were banished from mine work and forced to settle in enclaves on the outskirts of major cities such as San
10 Francisco. Without any other employment prospects, these immigrants often found low-end positions in restaurants and laundry facilities, and unknowingly gave rise to the unjust theory that Chinese immigration depressed wage levels.

9. In context, the author refers to the "California Gold Rush" in line 3 in order to indicate

    (A) a historical moment when immigration was a divisive issue
    (B) an event that initiated mass immigration to America
    (C) a time when accumulation of wealth was a pervasive social value
    (D) a period of American history that has been unjustly glorified
    (E) an instance when venture capitalism compromised local communities

10. The author would most likely DISAGREE with which of the following statements about immigration?

    (A) It has enabled individuals of Asian descent to find employment.
    (B) It has been actively regulated throughout American history.
    (C) It is currently an issue that stirs disagreement among Americans.
    (D) It has only been of relevance in the past few decades.
    (E) It had not been the true cause of salary problems in menial labor.

Questions 11-12 are based on the following passage.

Although the Humboldt squid isn't nearly as giant as the giant squid, it still grows to the length of an adult human; instead of legs, though, this reclusive
Line animal has tentacles with razor-sharp teeth on its
5 suckers, which can flay flesh from bone in seconds. The Humboldt squid, which normally lives deep in the ocean off the western coasts of Central and South America, has recently been seen close to the shore as far north as Canada. Some people blame the
10 overfishing of the squid's natural predators, while others blame climate change for this unusual spread; either way, this ruthless killer is getting farther from its own habitat—and closer to ours.

11. The tone of the first sentence is best characterized as

    (A) informative
    (B) cautionary
    (C) facetious
    (D) celebratory
    (E) understated

12. Based on the information in the passage, the author would most likely agree that

    (A) the Humboldt squid is the deadliest of all marine animals
    (B) due to its size, the giant squid is considered a more ferocious predator than the Humboldt squid
    (C) overfishing of the Humboldt squid is responsible for the recent explosion of its population
    (D) global warming is pushing the Humboldt squid into warmer waters
    (E) regardless of the cause, the dangers presented by the Humboldt squid cannot be ignored

GO ON TO THE NEXT PAGE

Practice Test 5

Questions 13-24 are based on the following passages.

The following two passages discuss the implications of quantum theory. Passage 1 is adapted from an editorial written in the 1950s. Passage 2 is taken from an essay written in 1969 entitled, "The Philosophy of Physics".

Passage 1

Perhaps more than in any other scientific field, quantum physics presents us with a bewildering array of paradoxes. For example, from a quantum
Line perspective, light can act as both a particle and a wave,
5 while a cat inside a box can be both alive and dead. Of course, these situations may strike us as absurd; a cat is either alive or dead, but never both at the same time. How can it be otherwise?

The answer, according to the scientists, has to
10 do with the idea of probability. Before the advent of quantum physics, it was assumed that the smallest units of matter, such as atoms and electrons, behaved like tiny billiard balls. As such, their motions were entirely predictable. According to quantum physics,
15 however, we live in a probabilistic universe, in which the smallest units of matter do not behave according to definite patterns. Instead, subatomic particles such as electrons are governed by probability functions— equations that indicate the likelihood that a given
20 particle will behave in a given fashion. Thus, in the revolution that was quantum physics, absolute certainty was trumped by relative *uncertainty*.

We still have not fully come to terms with the implications of this discovery—which, if accepted
25 fully, might prove truly disheartening. After all, are not our bodies made up of nothing more than subatomic particles? By extension, are not the discoveries of quantum physics also discoveries about our very selves? The prospect of a "quantum self" turns out to
30 be nothing short of depressing. If I accept the quantum theory, then I must admit that I am little more than a probability function, and that my behavior, like that of the electron, is unpredictable and random. As such, I cannot be accountable for my failures, nor can I take
35 credit for any of my successes.

It was this very prospect—that quantum physics seemed to nullify any responsibility that we might have for our actions—that infuriated even Einstein himself. After much wrestling with these startling
40 new perspectives, the exasperated Einstein famously shouted, "God does not play dice!" Like Einstein, I too cannot accept the fact that I am little more than a random number generator. I can only hope that, like the host of scientific theories that have come before it,
45 the quantum theory will one day be disproven.

Passage 2

Even among physicists themselves, the complexities of quantum theory can prove mystifying. After all, concepts such as simultaneity—that is, that an object can exist in two different places at the very
50 same time—are inherently befuddling. As a result of all this confusion, various misinterpretations of quantum theory have taken root outside, and even within, the scientific community. Perhaps the greatest misunderstanding of all has arisen over the postulation
55 that the universe is probabilistic in nature. In order to clarify the confusion, we must ask ourselves: What does it mean for something to be probabilistic?

Consider the simple example of a coin toss, a very familiar case of probability: there is a 50%
60 possibility that the coin will come up heads, and a 50% possibility that it will come up tails. Quantum probability is based on similar laws of chance, but involves more complex alternatives. One of the central tenets of quantum theory is that subatomic particles
65 are governed by probability functions—mathematical equations that describe the relative likelihoods of different particle behaviors. And because our bodies happen to be made up of subatomic particles, some have extrapolated from this fact to conclude that we
70 ourselves are little more than "walking slot machines," governed by nothing more than random chance. As such, our behavior is not our own, and our "choices," seemingly made of our own volition, are far more akin to the erratic spins of a roulette wheel. However, such
75 interpretations of quantum theory are the product of a gross misunderstanding—namely, that if the outcome of something is probabilistic or uncertain, then it is necessarily unpredictable. But nothing could be farther from the truth.

80 Consider once again the toss of a coin. While the outcome of a single coin toss is uncertain, over the long term—say, if I were to toss the coin 1,000 times in a row—the behavior of the coin begins to fit a predictable pattern. And while human beings are
85 certainly more complex than coins, we are still largely creatures of habit. Observe us for a while, and our own patterns and predilections begin to emerge.

For instance, if I am feeling tired, there is a probability that I will take a nap. There is also the
90 probability, however, that I will make myself an espresso and continue writing these words. If my deadline is in two hours, I might be more inclined to make the espresso and keep working. In contrast to the 50/50 probability of any coin flip, the
95 probability for my behavior can change according to my circumstances: I am still left with an enormous measure of freedom. As it stands, the implications of quantum theory are far more liberating than its detractors seem to realize.

GO ON TO THE NEXT PAGE

1   1   1   1   1   1

Unauthorized copying or
reuse of any part of this
page is illegal.

13. Which of the following best describes the relationship between the passages?

(A) Passage 1 introduces a scientific problem which is solved in Passage 2.
(B) Passage 1 chronicles the evolution of a scientific theory for which Passage 2 describes the modern applications.
(C) Passage 1 analyzes the repercussions of a discovery that does not alarm the author of Passage 2.
(D) Passage 1 presents recent findings by the scientific community which are corroborated by a personal account in Passage 2.
(E) Passage 1 presents a balanced overview of a scientific debate in which Passage 2 takes a clear position.

14. In context of the second paragraph, the statement "absolute certainty . . . *uncertainty*" (lines 21-22) refers to

(A) a constantly changing universe
(B) the behavior of subatomic particles
(C) an evolution in scientific thought
(D) a need for greater personal accountability
(E) the randomness of individual behavior

15. Passage 1 suggests that the "implications of this discovery" (line 24) are depressing because

(A) they cause us to behave in random and unpredictable ways
(B) they lead us to believe that we have no control over our destinies
(C) they reduce human experience to the level of inconsequence
(D) they remind us that we have no more substance than do subatomic particles
(E) they suggest that lack of certainty makes life no longer worth living

16. The question in lines 27-29 ("By extension . . . selves?") serves to

(A) question the applicability of a scientific theory in describing human existence
(B) suggest that quantum physics is too depressing to accept as fact
(C) introduce an innovative approach to analyzing human behavior
(D) emphasize a similarity in the composition of structures of different sizes
(E) examine how quantum physics may contribute to personal insights

17. "Einstein" in the final paragraph of Passage 1 is characterized as

(A) irresponsible and outrageous
(B) thoughtful and methodical
(C) religious and philosophical
(D) frustrated and emphatic
(E) insightful and innovative

18. The example of the coin toss in lines 58-61 of Passage 2 serves primarily to

(A) analyze the outcomes in an equal probability experiment
(B) compare the probabilities of two different theories
(C) draw parallels between a practical application and a theoretical model
(D) disprove quantum theory through scientific inquiry
(E) clarify the meaning of an idea central to the passage

19. In line 65, the word "functions" most nearly means

(A) actions
(B) formalities
(C) purposes
(D) usages
(E) models

20. The "scientists" (line 9) would most likely react to the description of human behavior in lines 67-74 ("And because . . . wheel") with

(A) agreement
(B) amusement
(C) indifference
(D) alarm
(E) hostility

GO ON TO THE NEXT PAGE

1   1   1   Unauthorized copying or
                        reuse of any part of this
                        page is illegal.   1   1   1

Practice Test 5

21. In context of the third paragraph of Passage 2, the author characterizes the "misunderstanding" (line 76) as the result of

(A) a narrow view that does not take into consideration the effects of repeated patterns of behavior
(B) an incorrect application of a simplistic theoretical model to a complex case
(C) an unfortunate miscalculation of outcomes in a probability experiment
(D) a correct interpretation of human behavior despite our idiosyncrasies
(E) a logical conclusion to a fully-substantiated theory

22. The perspective presented in the final paragraph of Passage 2 most directly contradicts which statement in Passage 1?

(A) "light can act as both a particle and a wave" (line 4)
(B) "their motions were entirely predictable" (lines 13-14)
(C) "As such, I cannot be accountable for my failures" (lines 33-34)
(D) "God does not play dice!" (line 41)
(E) "quantum theory will one day be disproven" (line 45)

23. The author of Passage 2 would most likely respond to the questions in lines 25-29 of Passage 1 ("After all . . . selves?") by

(A) affirming that the tenets of quantum theory reduce human behavior to a series of preordained choices
(B) emphasizing the differences in the compositions of subatomic particles and of complex organisms
(C) highlighting the relative unpredictability of natural occurrences by presenting a hypothetical scenario
(D) indicating that our choices are governed more by conscious responses to external factors than by random influences
(E) confirming that quantum physics can help us understand the thoroughly chaotic nature of human existence

24. The author of Passage 1 would most likely respond to the statement "I am . . . freedom" (lines 96-97) in Passage 2 with

(A) qualified appreciation
(B) unbridled optimism
(C) mild skepticism
(D) vigorous objection
(E) righteous indignation

STOP

If you finish before time is called, you may check your work on this section only.
Do not turn to any other section in the test.

SECTION 2
Time–25 minutes
24 Questions

Directions: For each question in this section, select the best answer from among the choices given and fill in the corresponding circle on the answer sheet.

Each sentence below has one or two blanks, each blank indicating that something has been omitted. Beneath the sentence are five words or sets of words labeled A through E. Choose the word or set of words that, when inserted in the sentence, best fits the meaning of the sentence as a whole.

Example:

Jimmy opened his gas station in the ------- because he wanted to be in the middle of a metropolis.

(A) country
(B) suburbs
(C) periphery
(D) environment
(E) city

1. A successful experiment in physics often has ------- applications; it will improve the entirety of the discipline, not simply enhance a single area of thought.

    (A) multitudinous   (B) unorthodox   (C) scant
    (D) precarious   (E) unprecedented

2. While the television show uses standard characterizations, fans argue that it is a representation of a ------- historical period, even if the people it depicts are -------.

    (A) atrocious . . quotidian
    (B) captivating . . commonplace
    (C) energizing . . debatable
    (D) clumsy . . complicated
    (E) cogent . . honest

3. Adverbs, when used descriptively, are certainly ------- element of writing; nonetheless, most expert writers agree that, when these words are overused, they ------- an article.

    (A) an evocative . . dilute
    (B) a banal . . permeate
    (C) a creative . . disseminate
    (D) an odd . . temper
    (E) a vivid . . improve

4. The controversial university policy incited a prolonged ------- by professors who could not be ------- by even the most conciliatory administrative gestures.

    (A) rebellion . . oppressed
    (B) revolution . . censored
    (C) suspension . . propitiated
    (D) insurrection . . placated
    (E) mutiny . . extolled

5. Pharmaceutical companies have strengthened the composition of the flu vaccine in order to better fight the ------- strain of the disease that is expected to break out this year.

    (A) formulated   (B) salubrious   (C) flaccid
    (D) robust   (E) innocuous

GO ON TO THE NEXT PAGE

Practice Test 5

Practice Test 5

The passages below are followed by questions based on their content; questions following a pair of related passages may also be based on the relationship between the paired passages. Answer the questions on the basis of what is <u>stated</u> or <u>implied</u> in the passages and in any introductory material that may be provided.

Questions 6-9 are based on the following passages.

Passage 1

As a professional psychiatrist, I have to make a conscious effort to remind myself that not everybody is my patient. This applies even to the characters
Line that I find on the page. Recently I have been reading
5 *Anna Karenina*, and I have been laboring mightily to figure out why exactly the title character acts the way she does. Does Anna suffer from a form of obsessive compulsive disorder? Does she languish under a repressed trauma? Does she have an Electra Complex?
10 Undiagnosed and untreated paranoid schizophrenia? Does any of this matter? Probably not as much as my basic enjoyment of the book matters, but enjoyment is difficult when all this professional apparatus gets in the way.

Passage 2

15 One of the principal characters in Henry James's novel *The Wings of the Dove* is young woman named Milly Theale, who suffers from a chronic disease that James, for whatever reason, decided to leave unnamed. Modern critics have labored to figure out what Milly's
20 malady is. They have devised possibilities as different as tuberculosis, leukemia, diabetes, and pancreatic cancer. My own possibility is that James didn't know or care what Milly's exact affliction was, and that neither should we. To eliminate ambiguity at every
25 turn is to turn a novel into a dead, gray thing, a tiny medical case study instead of a teeming imagined world.

6. Unlike Passage 2, Passage 1 is primarily concerned with

    (A) the intentions of a classic novel's author
    (B) the fulfillment gained from scholarly analysis
    (C) the factors that explain a character's behavior
    (D) the shortcomings of modern literary criticism
    (E) the plausibility of a female protagonist

7. The author of Passage 1 would most likely characterize the "ambiguity" mentioned in line 24 of Passage 2 as

    (A) antediluvian
    (B) rudimentary
    (C) vexing
    (D) comprehensive
    (E) unwarranted

8. Which of the following in Passage 2 best exemplifies the questions in lines 7-11 ("Does Anna . . . matter?") of Passage 1?

    (A) "leave unnamed" (line 18)
    (B) "Milly's malady" (lines 19-20)
    (C) "devised possibilities" (line 20)
    (D) "My own possibility" (line 22)
    (E) "didn't know or care" (lines 22-23)

9. Both authors make use of

    (A) extended analogy
    (B) historical allusion
    (C) direct citation
    (D) personal voice
    (E) statistical analysis

GO ON TO THE NEXT PAGE

2   2   2   Unauthorized copying or
reuse of any part of this
page is illegal.   2   2   2

Questions 10-15 are based on the following passage.

The following passage is adapted from an essay on ethical living. Here, the author describes the phenomenon of theft in everyday life.

Most of us have been the victim of theft at one
time or another. The act provokes multiple reactions
within us: shock, fear, insecurity, a sense of betrayal
Line and violation, anger and resentment are among the
5 first emotions that sweep through us when we realize
that something has not simply been mislaid but has
been deliberately taken from us. We are outraged that
someone could do anything like that. The irony is that
very few of us have not stolen something at least
10 once in our lives.

There is no use denying it, dear reader, however
desperately you try to do so. Can you honestly raise
your hand and plead "not guilty" to the charge? Can
you really claim that you never put your hand into the
15 cookie jar and swiped a cookie when your mother's
back was turned? Have you never filched a coin from
the jar where the family stores loose change? After
all, it was only a couple of cents and will never be
missed and anyway you will replace it later. Really?
20 You can be quite honest here, for you are not alone.
How many times are we ripped off in the supermarket
by believing that the label on the package is accurate,
or, indeed, that a hamburger contains 100% beef with
neither soy nor horse included? Ask an adult if he or
25 she has never (hand on heart) committed fraud by
writing a check for more money than was in his or
her account, in the hope that, with a bit of luck, that
sum might be there soon enough. I know people who
stay in the most expensive hotels in the world: some
30 of them never consider leaving without purloining an
ashtray, or a towel, despite (or perhaps because of)
the label on the item with the hotel's name and logo.

Well, of course, you can claim that none of the
above can *really* be counted as stealing. These acts
35 cannot *really* be counted as part of major crime,
right? Take shoplifting, for example. Of course, *I
know* that school children today are *far* better
behaved than they were when I was a kid; back in
those dark times, furtively purloining a chocolate bar
40 from the candy store near the school gates was a
pretty common occurrence. And while we're on the
subject of school, don't tell me that you have never
plagiarized, even just a little, in order to get an
assignment done on time, and hoped that the teacher
45 was only half reading what you handed in. And do
teenagers still purchase false ID cards, I wonder?
I once worked in a very famous boarding school and
had to sign my name to a release form that allowed
the kids to go home for the weekend; they then came
50 back with the forms countersigned by their parents or
guardians. Years later I discovered, from reading
through pages on Facebook, that quite a few of the

signatures—including some of mine, amazingly—
were false. In another school, a student once "found"
55 my checkbook and tried to use it in order to buy a
camera. Silly boy! He had no idea that I was already
guilty of stealing, for the reasons given above.

Why do we feel such turmoil of aggression when
someone cons us? I suspect that it is because, at the
60 bottom of our hearts, we feel rather guilty. The only
thing we can do to comfort ourselves is to claim
innocence. We are set such a bad example by
everyone around us. To quote an old piece of advice,
"Don't steal, don't lie, and don't cheat. The
65 government hates competition."

10. The "irony" mentioned in line 8 is most
analogous to which situation?

(A) A grocer increases the price of his produce,
then gripes about how few customers
continue to shop at his store.
(B) An employer is upset with his employee for
tardiness when the employer himself is
chronically late to his appointments.
(C) A student gets upset when a classmate
reveals sensitive information about her, and
in turn the student divulges all the
classmate's secrets.
(D) A politician disputes the validity of a law,
then is arrested for breaking that very same
law.
(E) An honest mechanic is left with the bill
when an unscrupulous customer leaves
without paying.

11. The author's rapid succession of rhetorical
questions in lines 12-19 ("Can you . . . Really?")
is most likely intended to

(A) encourage the reader to rebel against
common social norms
(B) mark a progression from descriptions of
misdemeanors to accounts of serious
crimes
(C) question the integrity of people working in
the food industry
(D) provoke a discussion about finance and
family values
(E) alert the reader to his or her own possible
culpability

GO ON TO THE NEXT PAGE

2   2   2   Unauthorized copying or   2   2   2
                                  reuse of any part of this
                                  page is illegal.

12. The purpose of line 20 ("You can . . . alone")
is to

   (A) raise doubt about the amount of truthfulness
       in American society
   (B) provide a commentary on the psychological
       effects of dishonesty
   (C) offer reassurance so that the reader can
       perform a truthful self-evaluation
   (D) suggest a correlation between moral
       rectitude and meaningful companionship
   (E) claim that honesty is a fundamental
       drawback in today's increasingly licentious
       world

13. According to the author, in lines 21-32 ("How
many . . . logo") theft is

   (A) ubiquitous
   (B) inexcusable
   (C) arduous
   (D) abnormal
   (E) greedy

14. In the third paragraph, lines 47-57 ("I once . . .
above") utilize which rhetorical device?

   (A) paradox
   (B) analogy
   (C) vivid imagery
   (D) anecdote
   (E) alliteration

15. What is the function of the "old piece of advice"
given in the final paragraph?

   (A) To offer a touch of humor that resonates
       with the author's themes
   (B) To exhort readers to resist dishonest
       governmental policies
   (C) To undermine earlier points about the
       inevitability of theft
   (D) To encourage further discussion about the
       social usefulness of deceit
   (E) To absolve readers of guilt with a moment of
       reassuring comedy

GO ON TO THE NEXT PAGE

Questions 16-24 are based on the following passage.

The following passage is adapted from an essay by a science journalist. The author here discusses the Human Genome Project, a much-publicized initiative in genetic biology.

Since its emergence, genomics (the science of determining what our genes are and how those genes function) has certainly made some strange
Line philosophical and political bedfellows. It is true that
5 genomics techniques are proving to be the most powerful tools in science since the advent of quantum mechanics. Yet, strangely, this entire field of inquiry also forces some rather pointed and profound questions about humanity as a species. How did we
10 get here? And why do groundbreaking techniques seem like easy routes to potentially destructive ends?

It all started quite innocently, and with the best of intentions: the 1990s were heralded as the Decade of the Genome. The Human Genome Project (HGP),
15 as it was called, emerged from the clamor of molecular biologists and biochemists from a range of backgrounds, and emerged for a good reason: decades after the discovery of DNA's double-helix geometry by Watson, Crick, and Franklin, we humans
20 still knew little about what makes up a gene, how many genes there are, or why so much apparently useless or "junk" DNA nevertheless remains so critical to normal human development.

Seemingly anxious to answer these questions as
25 quickly as possible, the organizers of the HGP followed an unconventional research format. Structuring the Project as a data-identification competition, the administrating National Institutes of Health (NIH) decided to "let the best person win."
30 Maverick biochemist J. Craig Venter ended up beating the competition using his unexpected "shotgun" technique: identify each base pair of genes and allow the computers and the other competitors to figure out where the delineations are and what they
35 mean.

As the Decade of the Genome came to a close, we had discovered that it only takes about 25,000 genes to make a human a human: this was a striking discovery, because prior estimates went as high as
40 100,000 genes. We also found out that we share a whopping 75% of our DNA with pumpkins and about 89% with deer. Perhaps most importantly, the Human Genome Project yielded the startling conclusion that junk DNA (base pairs with no function for humans)
45 isn't junk; in many cases, such DNA is nearly identical to the active DNA of other species. On a molecular level, this may be the best possible confirmation of modern evolutionary theory. Suddenly, humanity had an entire dictionary of
50 genetic information—a scientific vocabulary of revelatory lucidity—at its fingertips.

However, these amazing advances require us, as a species, to think seriously about the good and the bad potentialities presented by genomics research.
55 Science is, by definition, amoral. One of the first tenets of the Scientific Method is for the researcher to put personal biases aside and strive to remain an objective observer, a scrupulous recorder of universally-verifiable observations and conclusions.
60 In other words, keep the science scientific.

Yet the social, and properly subjective, application of genomic research would have a transformative impact. Genomic screening has the potential to eliminate every disease known to
65 man—every single one. Even aging, on a molecular level, is considered to be a form of pathological affliction. In fact, through the "magic" of genomics, you can not only screen out genetic anomalies but also enhance the very properties that are passed on to
70 the next generation. Instead of allowing evolution to run its course and humanity to gradually grow more robust, we could eliminate weakness, eradicate aging, and permanently warp human-influenced ecosystems all over the world.
75 As I write these words, the first introduction of a modified gene into human offspring has been reported by the American press. If the potential for good is so great, then why is the scientific community almost entirely polarized by this measure? On the one
80 hand, we may well have the power to cure everything, including aging and all its ravages. On the other hand, we are forced to admit that we are still very primitive creatures and that we do not understand the many implications that accompany the
85 modification of a single gene. After all, if the first 25 years of the nascent field of genomics have taught us anything, it is that the malfunction of one gene can have a host of consequences; genes work in concert with one another. The Human Genome Project
90 reminds us that every organism—from a person to a pumpkin—is a delicate construct. Are we willing to tamper with the very foundations of biology?

16. The primary purpose of this passage is to

(A) establish an unambiguous position in a growing ethical discussion
(B) relate a scientific breakthrough to a well-known historical scenario
(C) discuss an emerging branch of science and its cultural implications
(D) laud the major researchers in a new field of genetic biology
(E) show how genomics contradicts the standard scientific method

GO ON TO THE NEXT PAGE

2   2   2   Unauthorized copying or
                                  reuse of any part of this   2   2   2
                                  page is illegal.

Practice Test 5

17. The parenthetical statement in lines 1-3 primarily serves to

(A) outline a thesis
(B) allude to a debate
(C) provide a timeline
(D) define a term
(E) note an incongruity

18. The word "this" in line 38 most likely refers to

(A) an unexpected disclosure
(B) a sudden realization
(C) an antiquated ideal
(D) a recent issue
(E) a compelling revelation

19. As described in the fourth paragraph, the discoveries made about the genome were

(A) fortuitous
(B) arbitrary
(C) anachronistic
(D) remarkable
(E) intimidating

20. The statement in lines 52-54 ("However, these . . . research") marks a shift from

(A) a largely interrogative analysis to a series of vehement assertions
(B) a tone of apparent enthusiasm to an attitude of dispassionate dismissal
(C) a discussion of a research endeavor to a contemplation of its consequences
(D) a summary of historical events to an unlikely hypothesis about the future
(E) an explanation of an esoteric field to a listing of commonplace ideas

21. Lines 63-74 ("Genomic screening . . . world") suggest which of the following about genomics?

(A) It has been misunderstood on moral and ethical grounds.
(B) It has helped to promulgate a new theory of human aging.
(C) It has prompted modifications to the Scientific Method.
(D) It has intrigued both non-specialists and casual observers.
(E) It has the potential to drastically change human life.

22. In context, the reference to "primitive creatures" (line 83) serves to emphasize the idea that

(A) radical scientific advances are often detrimental to human society
(B) humans lack knowledge of the indirect effects of gene manipulation
(C) humans have learned relatively little from existing genomics research
(D) the utilization of modified genes is regarded as finally unnecessary
(E) diseases and aging will inevitably be eradicated as civilization advances

23. In line 91, "delicate" most nearly means

(A) complex
(B) precarious
(C) sensitive
(D) tenuous
(E) abstruse

24. The tone of the overall passage can best be described as

(A) wistful
(B) quixotic
(C) pugnacious
(D) thoughtful
(E) ingenuous

STOP

If you finish before time is called, you may check your work on this section only.
Do not turn to any other section in the test.

SECTION 3
Time–20 minutes
19 Questions

Directions: For each question in this section, select the best answer from among the choices given and fill in the corresponding circle on the answer sheet.

Each sentence below has one or two blanks, each blank indicating that something has been omitted. Beneath the sentence are five words or sets of words labeled A through E. Choose the word or set of words that, when inserted in the sentence, <u>best</u> fits the meaning of the sentence as a whole.

Example:

Jimmy opened his gas station in the ------- because he wanted to be in the middle of a metropolis.

(A) country
(B) suburbs
(C) periphery
(D) environment
(E) city

1. Ironically, the people ------- their totalitarian ruler only to replace him with an equally ------- regime.

   (A) elected . . draconian
   (B) overthrew . . despotic
   (C) usurped . . democratic
   (D) reinstated . . dictatorial
   (E) deposed . . magnanimous

2. Norman's impartiality and evenhandedness may impress Alexandra, yet she is unable to explain how such merits ------- with his ------- adherence to an overbearing style of management that detracts from his positive qualities.

   (A) appraise . . enigmatic
   (B) justify . . subtle
   (C) negate . . stubborn
   (D) coexist . . unwavering
   (E) reunite . . tenuous

3. The blogger wrote in a style that, while nuanced and full of wordplay, managed to remain -------: her work was undeniably straightforward.

   (A) revitalizing   (B) holistic   (C) unequivocal
      (D) officious   (E) byzantine

4. Employers have found that by ------- the cues that keep employees happy in the workplace, the conditions that lead to increased ------- can be successfully instituted.

   (A) analyzing . . indolence
   (B) hindering . . punctuality
   (C) ignoring . . objectivity
   (D) studying . . productivity
   (E) consulting . . laziness

5. The members of the committee soon learned that their new chairwoman was highly -------, tending to react unpredictably to new proposals and routine assignments alike.

   (A) critical   (B) dependable   (C) erratic
      (D) facetious   (E) meticulous

6. In the Middle Ages, a tradesman was seen as a ------- if he experienced an excessive amount of luck in practicing his craft; however, today we know that swindlers don't need ------- on their side to carry out their devious schemes.

   (A) charlatan . . adversity
   (B) dignitary . . fortune
   (C) deceiver . . compulsion
   (D) pickpocket . . serendipity
   (E) mountebank . . chance

GO ON TO THE NEXT PAGE

3   3   3   3   3   3

Unauthorized copying or reuse of any part of this page is illegal.

The passage below is followed by questions based on its content. Answer the questions on the basis of what is <u>stated</u> or <u>implied</u> in the passage and in any introductory material that may be provided.

Questions 7-19 are based on the following passage.

This passage explores the contributions to the world of literature by female authors, particularly those of the eighteenth and nineteenth centuries.

It is a truth universally acknowledged that, until the nineteenth century, women did not involve themselves in the writing of novels. However, like most universally acknowledged truths, this one is not
5 completely accurate. For instance, Aphra Behn was a popular playwright and did produce a few novels. Yet after her burial in Westminster Abbey in 1689, the popularity of both her novels and her plays declined very quickly. There has been no rediscovery of her
10 qualities as a writer by scholars of English literature. Perhaps the epitaph on her tomb inadvertently summed up the general opinion:

"Here is a Proof that Wit can never be Defense enough against Mortality."

15 In addition to Aphra Behn, there is the marginally better-known Fanny Burney, who wrote the novels *Camilla* and *Cecilia* at the end of the eighteenth century. Today, literary scholars have a tendency to neglect her novels, while the general public remains in
20 complete ignorance of these books. Indeed, if Burney is remembered at all, it is for her more famous Diary. This work caused King George III, one morning when he discovered Burney in the act of making an entry, to sneer at her and quickly remark, "Scribble, scribble,
25 scribble, Mrs. Burney?"
There are reasons for this dearth of female novelists before 1800, the first being that the novel was a relatively new genre of writing. The earliest recognized novelist in England is Samuel Richardson
30 who produced *Pamela, or Virtue Rewarded* in 1740. Richardson's success prompted Henry Fielding to write *Joseph Andrews* and *Tom Jones*, which in turn encouraged Smollett, Sterne, and Goldsmith to try their hands at the new literary genre. Based on the structure
35 followed by their narratives, these novels are classified as "picaresque"—a term indicating that the novel is really a series of unrelated actions, the only unifying factor being the presence of the central character or "picaro." The author is omnipresent, constantly
40 commenting on events, making moral judgments on characters and actions: telling the reader what to think, in effect. One may well understand why a demure lady of the eighteenth century might not be encouraged to participate in this imperious form of writing.
45 In the final years of the eighteenth century, a new sub-genre of the novel appeared. Gothic horror involved inexplicable happenings in creaking

mansions, skeletons, ghosts, darkness, sudden death, and the presence of the supernatural, all orchestrated
50 with flashes of lightning, gales of wind, and torrents of pouring rain. Horace Walpole started it all with *The Castle of Otranto* in 1764, but there were women writers who created important specimens of this kind of novel. For instance, Anne Radcliffe wrote *The*
55 *Mysteries of Udolfo*, a best-seller. It is not read today outside of college English courses. Nonetheless, the modern reader of horror novels still enjoys Mary Shelley's *Frankenstein*, which Shelley wrote during a very wet summer in Switzerland in 1818 as part of
60 a story-telling contest involving herself, her husband, and her friend Lord Byron. The others gave up on the challenge, but Ms. Shelley followed through with the task and crafted a literary classic.
When considering the rise of women novelists,
65 we have to pay attention to the arrival of the Gothic novel in general and to the fame of Anne Radcliffe in particular. Then, in the last year of the eighteenth century, a sharp witted young lady named Jane Austen passed her time and amused her family by
70 writing a small book that punctured the posturing absurdity of the Gothic genre with a hard dose of common sense. Austen had not written anything before, and her book did not get published until 1817, after her death. However, *Northanger Abbey*
75 marked the moment when women began to write novels and show men how to do it. Jane Austen is the leader of the regiment of women writers who so often dominated the literature of the nineteenth century.
Indeed, for many devotees of fiction, Austen
80 remains the foremost English novelist. She never patronizes her reader and she never tells her reader what to think. The action is mostly domestic: events are related indirectly through the reactions of characters who only hear news of a public event after it has
85 happened. We see such events through the eyes of those who are not on the spot. Jane Austen is not concerned with action and history, but with reaction, a far more familiar experience in real life. Through her down-to-earth emphasis, laced with common sense and a distinct
90 awareness of irony, Jane Austen communicates and shares an understanding of what life is really like. To read *Sense and Sensibility*, or *Persuasion*, or any other of the six major novels she wrote, is to see precisely what life was really like for the majority of women who
95 lived in the late eighteenth century. She speaks for them all, quietly but clearly. She allowed a woman's point of view to be listened to and, eventually, considered.

GO ON TO THE NEXT PAGE

3   3   3   Unauthorized copying or
reuse of any part of this
page is illegal.   3   3   3

The nineteenth century is rightly deemed the period when the novel came to fruition. Who are the
100 authors who make us feel the real inequalities of that century, who present a woman's point of view with nuance, yet consistently present women as independent individuals? These authors are Mary Ann Evans ("George Eliot"), Elizabeth Gaskell, Charlotte Brontë,
105 Emily Brontë, Anne Brontë. And the first of them was Jane Austen. Their great-great-great grand-daughters should be proud.

7. The primary purpose of the passage is to

(A) compare the literary accomplishments of nineteenth-century men and women
(B) trace the role of female authors in the development of the novel
(C) discuss which writers were most popular in the Gothic horror genre
(D) designate Jane Austen as the single-most influential author in eighteenth-century fiction
(E) discredit the notion that few female authors wrote actively before the nineteenth century

8. In context of lines 1-5, the author considers the concept of a "truth universally acknowledged" to be

(A) relaxed
(B) absolute
(C) flawed
(D) dispensable
(E) mandatory

9. In lines 7-9 ("Yet after . . . quickly"), the author indicates that

(A) Behn's death also marked the end of her influence
(B) only after death did Behn become famous
(C) no truly great author achieves popularity while living
(D) writers should be judged based on their books alone, not based on their lifestyles
(E) a humorous epitaph can lead an otherwise obscure author to fame

10. The tone of George III's remark ("Scribble, scribble, scribble, Mrs. Burney?") in lines 24-25 can best be described as

(A) inquisitive
(B) buoyant
(C) encouraging
(D) sardonic
(E) contemplative

11. On the basis of the information found in lines 34-42, ("Based on . . . effect"), which of the following would MOST likely be associated with a picaresque novel?

(A) The author leaves the conclusion open to interpretation.
(B) A character persistently follows clues until he solves a mystery.
(C) A protagonist narrates related events from her past.
(D) The perspective jumps from one character to the next.
(E) A central character witnesses altercations that are only loosely linked.

12. The sentence in lines 42-44 ("One may . . . writing") can best be described as

(A) a possible explanation for the author's thesis
(B) the author's primary motivation for writing
(C) a counterargument that the author has anticipated
(D) a claim for which the author provides no evidence
(E) a researched conclusion that the author has worked towards

13. The passage indicates that Horace Walpole wrote novels that employed

(A) supernatural phenomena
(B) traditional history
(C) ancient folklore
(D) political tirades
(E) romantic undertones

14. The word "punctured" (line 70) most nearly means

(A) stabbed
(B) perforated
(C) deflated
(D) damaged
(E) infused

GO ON TO THE NEXT PAGE

15. The author suggests that Jane Austen's book "*Northanger Abbey*" (line 74) broke from the Gothic horror genre by

  (A) conforming to the practices of picaresque novels
  (B) opposing fantasy with everyday practicality
  (C) poking fun at conventions popularized exclusively by male writers
  (D) exerting a noticeable influence on eighteenth-century authors
  (E) offering farcical scenes that feature famous novelists from Austen's time

16. The significance of the statement "events are . . . happened" (lines 82-85) is that Jane Austen

  (A) "did not . . . death" (lines 73-74)
  (B) "is the . . . century" (lines 76-78)
  (C) "is not . . . life" (lines 86-88)
  (D) "speaks for . . . clearly" (lines 95-96)
  (E) "allowed a . . . considered" (lines 96-97)

17. From lines 80-82 ("she never . . . think"), it can be inferred that Austen improved the state of the novel by

  (A) allowing readers to draw their own conclusions
  (B) giving her stories clear historical timelines
  (C) employing omnipresent narration
  (D) creating works devoid of the supernatural
  (E) appropriating from male writers the format of the Gothic novel

18. The author's statement about *Sense and Sensibility* and *Persuasion* in lines 91-95 ("To read . . . century") assumes that

  (A) a prolific career is the mark of a great novelist
  (B) Jane Austen's sensitivities allowed her to understand the lives of ordinary women
  (C) Jane Austen's writings were widely read
  (D) male authors were incapable of portraying realistic female psychology
  (E) Jane Austen had never intended for her novels to be used for social inquiry

19. In context, why should the "great-great-great grand-daughters" (line 106) be "proud" (line 107) of their distant relatives?

  (A) These writers stood up to male bureaucracy and fought for women's dignity.
  (B) These writers shaped the course of the novel for decades to come.
  (C) These writers were best-selling authors of Gothic horror novels.
  (D) These writers guaranteed the popularity of the female picaresque novel.
  (E) These writers taught the men of their generation more polite writing techniques.

STOP

If you finish before time is called, you may check your work on this section only.
Do not turn to any other section in the test.

POST TEST ANALYSIS

This post test analysis is important if you want to see an improvement on your next test. Each section has a set of possible reasons for errors. Place check marks next to the ones that pertain to you, and write your own on the blank lines provided. Use this form to better analyze your performance. **If you don't understand why you made errors, there is no way you can correct them!**

1. **SENTENCE COMPLETION:**

   Problems with the sentence:
   - ❑ Wasn't familiar with phrases, idioms, or words in the sentence
   - ❑ Missed the clues or tones
   - ❑ Put your OWN word in the blank rather than one from the sentence
   - ❑ Completely avoided marking
   - ❑ Other: _____

   _____

   Problems with the answers:
   - ❑ Did not use process of elimination
   - ❑ Did not ignore unknown words
   - ❑ Did not use prefix/root/suffix knowledge to figure out the meaning of the unknown words
   - ❑ Did not match the clues and tones of the answer with those of the sentence
   - ❑ Did not recognize vocabulary words
   - ❑ Did not check answer to see if it fit
   - ❑ Other: _____

   _____

   Leaving questions unanswered:
   - ❑ Did not try
   - ❑ Did not fill in the blank(s) with words
   - ❑ Ran out of time
   - ❑ Other: _____

   _____

2. **SHORT READING COMPREHENSION:**

   - ❑ Did not read entire paragraph
   - ❑ Did not see more than one point
   - ❑ Missed contrast clues
   - ❑ Did not pinpoint thesis
   - ❑ Did not identify similarities and differences in Double Short Reading Comp
   - ❑ Other: _____

   _____

3. **LONG READING COMPREHENSION:**

   - ❑ Did not understand the question, line reference, or answers
   - ❑ Spent too much time reading the passages
   - ❑ Did not underline the line reference
   - ❑ Read too much or too little
   - ❑ Did not answer the specific question; instead analyzed its main idea
   - ❑ Did not do process of elimination based on facts in the passage
   - ❑ Couldn't find the false words
   - ❑ Couldn't choose between two possible answers
   - ❑ Did not use tone to help eliminate answers
   - ❑ When stuck at 2 guessed instead of pulling additional fact
   - ❑ Couldn't finish in time
   - ❑ Other: _____

   _____

ANSWER KEY

TEST 5

SECTION 1

#	Answer	LEVEL
1	A B C ● E	(1)
2	A B C D ●	(3)
3	A B ● D E	(3)
4	A B C ● E	(3)
5	● B C D E	(4)
6	● B C D E	(4)
7	A ● C D E	(5)
8	A B C D ●	(5)
9	● B C D E	(3)
10	A B C ● E	(3)
11	● B C D E	(3)
12	A B C D ●	(4)
13	A B ● D E	(3)
14	A B ● D E	(4)
15	A ● C D E	(3)
16	A B C D ●	(4)
17	A B C ● E	(2)
18	A B C D ●	(4)
19	A B C D ●	(3)
20	● B C D E	(4)
21	● B C D E	(4)
22	A B ● D E	(5)
23	A B C ● E	(4)
24	A B C ● E	(3)

SECTION 2

#	Answer	LEVEL
1	● B C D E	(2)
2	A ● C D E	(2)
3	● B C D E	(3)
4	A B C ● E	(4)
5	A B C ● E	(4)
6	A B ● D E	(4)
7	A B ● D E	(3)
8	A B ● D E	(4)
9	A B C ● E	(1)
10	A ● C D E	(4)
11	A B C D ●	(3)
12	A B ● D E	(3)
13	● B C D E	(3)
14	A B C ● E	(2)
15	● B C D E	(4)
16	A B ● D E	(3)
17	A B C ● E	(1)
18	A B C D ●	(3)
19	A B C ● E	(3)
20	A B ● D E	(3)
21	A B C D ●	(3)
22	A ● C D E	(3)
23	● B C D E	(4)
24	A B C ● E	(2)

SECTION 3

#	Answer	LEVEL
1	A ● C D E	(1)
2	A B C ● E	(2)
3	A B ● D E	(3)
4	A B C ● E	(3)
5	A B ● D E	(4)
6	A B C D ●	(5)
7	A ● C D E	(3)
8	A B ● D E	(3)
9	● B C D E	(2)
10	A B C ● E	(3)
11	A B C D ●	(3)
12	● B C D E	(3)
13	● B C D E	(4)
14	A B ● D E	(4)
15	A ● C D E	(3)
16	A B ● D E	(4)
17	● B C D E	(3)
18	A ● C D E	(2)
19	A ● C D E	(3)

Difficulty levels range from 1 - 5 with 1 being the easiest and 5 being the hardest.
For answer explanations please visit www.ies2400.com/criticalreading

PRACTICE TEST 6

1   1   1   Unauthorized copying or
reuse of any part of this
page is illegal.   1   1   1

SECTION 1
Time–25 minutes
24 Questions

Directions: For each question in this section, select the best answer from among the choices given and fill in the corresponding circle on the answer sheet.

Each sentence below has one or two blanks, each blank indicating that something has been omitted. Beneath the sentence are five words or sets of words labeled A through E. Choose the word or set of words that, when inserted in the sentence, best fits the meaning of the sentence as a whole.

Example:

Jimmy opened his gas station in the ------- because he wanted to be in the middle of a metropolis.

(A) country
(B) suburbs
(C) periphery
(D) environment
(E) city

1. The plant life of the Malaysian rainforest is -------: it includes wildflowers, deciduous trees, tropical shrubs, pines, and bamboo.

    (A) prominent   (B) diverse   (C) educational
        (D) healthy   (E) poisonous

2. The architectural designs were lauded as both ------- and -------: they were at once streamlined and original.

    (A) cheap . . revolutionary
    (B) opulent . . innovative
    (C) severe . . striking
    (D) sleek . . creative
    (E) worthwhile . . redundant

3. Using succinct updates, the magazine publishes the ------- of various experts as a means of ------- its main articles, thus giving readers a more complete understanding of a range of subjects.

    (A) adventures . . vindicating
    (B) findings . . undermining
    (C) opinions . . supplementing
    (D) proposals . . discharging
    (E) retractions . . underscoring

4. The use of camouflage can have dangerous repercussions: although animals cannot distinguish camouflage from the environment, allowing hunters to remain -------, other hunters cannot do so either, which can prove -------.

    (A) concealed . . prudent
    (B) conspicuous . . precarious
    (C) invisible . . alienating
    (D) perceptible . . unsafe
    (E) cloaked . . perilous

5. While he certainly made an interesting argument, his assertions turned out to be -------, based more on his own questionable interpretations than on verifiable fact.

    (A) transgressive   (B) fractious   (C) specious
        (D) convoluted   (E) objective

GO ON TO THE NEXT PAGE

Practice Test 6

The passages below are followed by questions based on their content; questions following a pair of related passages may also be based on the relationship between the paired passages. Answer the questions on the basis of what is <u>stated</u> or <u>implied</u> in the passages and in any introductory material that may be provided.

Questions 6-7 are based on the following passage.

The rule of the animal world, it seems, is to follow the herd, the flock, the school, or the swarm; greater numbers mean greater cooperation, and ensure
Line survival. Yet there are animals of all types that thrive
5 in solitude. Some of these are small and self-sufficient (the sturdy desert grasshopper, the aptly-named hermit crab), but others are huge in size (the rhinoceros) or high on the food chain (the jaguar). Family groups for such antisocial animals seldom grow beyond a
10 single mother and the most recent set of offspring; this is certainly the case with the giant anteater. A male anteater will wander alone, crushing ant colony after ant colony, while a female will carry a child or two on its back until these offspring, too, go their singular
15 ways.

6. The passage suggests that collective living in the animal world is

(A) the primary mode of survival for mammals
(B) not the only successful means of functioning
(C) dependent on the size of the animal in question
(D) an adaptation passed on from parent to offspring
(E) an effective survival tactic in extreme conditions

7. The author would most likely DISAGREE with which of the following statements about the "Family groups" formed by solitary animals (line 8)?

(A) Adults of some of these types can also function in absolute solitude.
(B) Their positions in the food chain vary from species to species.
(C) They will always consist of a mother and her progeny.
(D) They tend to be temporary in nature and can be dissolved once the offspring mature.
(E) The familial structure does not need to include multiple generations.

Questions 8-9 are based on the following passage.

In 1915, Marcel Duchamp bought a snow shovel, suspended it from the ceiling of his studio, and declared it a full-fledged work of art. He even
Line gave this work a title, *In Advance of the Broken Arm*.
5 Duchamp's creation of this and other "readymade" artworks has been rightly viewed by most critics as a subversive gesture; after all, if a snow shovel or a hat rack or a bicycle tire can be held up as "art," where does the realm of "art" begin and the realm of
10 "non-art" end? But I like to think that there was a second, more positive side of Duchamp's agenda: a desire to make us look more closely at everyday life and find moments of artistic beauty where we least expect them.

8. It can be assumed that the "subversive gesture" (line 7) most likely refers to

(A) challenging an accepted view of aesthetics
(B) undermining the techniques used to examine art
(C) parodying popular traditions in sculpture
(D) rejecting the tenets of arts organizations
(E) propagating respect for experimental art

9. The author's reference to the "positive side of Duchamp's agenda" (line 11) indicates the author's belief that

(A) Duchamp's work is valuable mainly because it rejects traditional standards
(B) Duchamp's creative inspirations were groundbreaking in their practicality
(C) Duchamp's mode of sculpture only employed seemingly trivial objects
(D) Duchamp's artworks reveal a subtle reverence for the inconspicuous
(E) Duchamp's works of art often elicit feelings of humility and awe

GO ON TO THE NEXT PAGE

Questions 10-16 are based on the following passage.

The following is an excerpt from a turn-of-the-century book of essays on lightning and its relationship to humans.

In 1897, at Linguy, a man and his wife were sleeping quietly, when suddenly a terrible crash made them jump out of bed. They thought that their last
Line hour had come. Their chimney, broken to pieces, had
5 fallen in and its wreckage had filled the room; the gable-end of their house was put out and the roof threatened to come down. The effects of the thunderbolt in the room itself were less alarming than its effects outside, but were still very curious. For
10 instance, bricks from one wall had been dashed horizontally against the wall opposite, with such extraordinary force that they were to be seen embedded above a dresser upon which pots and pans were ranged, while the windows of the room had
15 been smashed to bits; a looking-glass, detached from the wall, stood on end whole and entire upon the floor, delicately balanced. Very odd indeed. A chair near the bed, upon which articles of clothing had been placed, had been spirited away to a spot near the
20 door. A small lamp and a box of matches were to be found undamaged upon the floor. An old gun, suspended from a beam, had been violently shaken and had lost its ramrod.
    The thunderbolt had actually frolicked over the
25 bed, leaving its occupants more dead than alive from terror but quite unhurt. It passed within a few inches of their heads, then passed through a wall fissure and into an adjoining dairy, where it carried a whole row of milk-cans, full of milk, from one side of the room
30 to the other, breaking the lids but not upsetting a single can. It broke four plates out of a pile of a dozen, leaving the remaining eight intact. It carried away the tap of a small wine barrel, which emptied itself in consequence.
35 The thunderbolt then finished its excursion by passing through the window without further breakage.
    One of the strangest tricks to which lightning is accustomed is undressing its victims. It displays
40 much more skill and cleverness in removing garments and coverings than is to be found in animals or even in many human beings. Lightning also displays the oddest infatuation with thievery. Sometimes it will snatch things right out of your
45 hand and carry them off.
    There is an instance of a mug being thus spirited away from a man, who had just been drinking out of it, and deposited undamaged in a nearby courtyard— the man himself remaining completely uninjured. A
50 youth of eighteen, holding up a missal from which he is singing, has it torn out of his hands and destroyed. A whip is whisked out of a rider's grasp. Two ladies,

quietly knitting, have their knitting-needles stolen. A girl is sitting at her sewing-machine, a pair of scissors
55 in her hand; a flash of lightning, and her scissors are gone and she is sitting *on* the sewing-machine. A farm laborer is carrying a pitchfork on his shoulder; the lightning seizes the implement, carries it off fifty yards or so, and twists its two prongs into corkscrews.
60 These phenomena are for the most part cases of lightning's jovial, innocuous trickery.

10. The phrase "They thought that their last hour had come" (lines 3-4) most likely means that the couple

    (A) was about to miss an important deadline
    (B) had finally decided to stop vacillating
    (C) would not be able to sleep again that night
    (D) knew that they would soon be forced from their home
    (E) did not expect to survive what came next

11. The characterization of the thunderbolt in the second paragraph portrays the bolt as

    (A) life-threatening and malevolent
    (B) frightening and uncontrollable
    (C) destructive yet necessary
    (D) disturbing yet mostly harmless
    (E) intentional and mesmerizing

12. Which best characterizes the function of the sentence in lines 35-37 ("The thunderbolt . . . breakage")?

    (A) A shift in the author's attitude
    (B) A conclusion to a moralistic tale
    (C) A culminating description of strange events
    (D) A sentiment unnecessary to the story
    (E) A transition from narrative to scientific inquiry

13. In context, the word "spirited" in line 46 most nearly means

    (A) animated
    (B) borrowed
    (C) taken
    (D) enlivened
    (E) haunted

GO ON TO THE NEXT PAGE

Practice Test 6

14. The last sentence of the passage suggests that

   (A) though frightening, lightning is never harmful to people
   (B) lightning is at the heart of most inexplicable disappearances
   (C) no people were hurt in the strange cases described earlier
   (D) the reliability of the accounts just offered may be subject to doubt
   (E) lightning is taken too seriously as a subject of scientific investigation

15. All of the following rhetorical devices are used in the passage EXCEPT:

   (A) personification
   (B) visual description
   (C) quoted dialogue
   (D) figurative language
   (E) anecdote

16. Which of the following best describes the organization of the passage?

   (A) The author moves from an extended account to a series of vignettes.
   (B) The author begins with broad generalizations and moves to scientific inquiry.
   (C) The author shifts from humorous reflection to practical advice.
   (D) The author begins with an unconventional theory but supports it with empirical evidence.
   (E) The author ultimately accepts a conclusion that the passage initially casts in doubt.

Practice Test 6

GO ON TO THE NEXT PAGE

Questions 17-24 are based on the following passage.

The following passage is taken from an essay on John Chapman, the folk hero who would become known as Johnny Appleseed. Here the author discusses new theories on Chapman's life.

Here comes Johnny Appleseed, with a sack for a shirt and a pot on his head, throwing apple seeds to and fro from a burlap pouch slung over his shoulder.
Line *Walking quickly, stick in hand—and barefoot, to*
5 *boot—he travels town to town, singing hymns to the children and never staying in one place for more than a few days.*

This classic tale of an altruistic conservationist always pleases children in classrooms and is always
10 a delight to tell around a lively campfire. But there are many who now believe that this folk hero's intentions, though indeed noble, may be not as suitable for children as were once thought. It is true, yes, that the real-life Johnny Appleseed, named John
15 Chapman, traveled the early United States from about 1790 to 1830, planting apple orchards. Yet apples grown from seed, specifically those apples left untreated and allowed to grow on their own, are known to be hard and sour; in fact, these are the
20 crabapples that Chapman was likely to have sown. The fruits of his labors are now thought to have been nearly inedible.

So why was Chapman so popular as an orchardist, and what kept his legacy alive for over
25 two hundred years?

According to Michael Pollan, author of *The Botany of Desire: A Plant's-Eye View of the World*, John Chapman could have been bringing the frontiersman something more than charm and
30 generosity. "Really, what Johnny Appleseed was doing and the reason he was welcome in every cabin in Ohio and Indiana," Pollan writes, "was that he was bringing the gift of alcohol to the frontier. He was our American Dionysus."
35 Pollan's theory, which is gaining clout among historians, postulates that the tart apples Chapman planted across the region were being used to make cheap, dirty alcohols such as applejack and hard cider —two brews distilled by leaving apple juice
40 outside and untended over harsh winter nights. Applejack in particular was popular because of the low cost and low required maintenance. In contrast, brewing beer required a skill level most frontiersman hadn't the time or resources to master, and was
45 thus an expensive habit to maintain. Chapman's "philanthropy" has indeed begun to appear in a more negative light: alcoholism was a common malady in the decades after the American Revolution, wrecking both the physical and mental state of those caught in
50 its throes. A military report from 1812 even claims that roughly 2,000 men were released from the

Continental Army in one year as a result of excessive drinking and disorder.

But whatever the cultural problems of a
55 blossoming America or the repercussions of Chapman's rampant sowing, the fact remains that John Chapman was a gentle man and a profound teacher. A missionary for the Swedenborgian Church, he could often been seen in the early dawn, sitting
60 beside a brook, hands clasped in his lap, serene in prayer. Chapman often refused payment for his work, instead bartering apples for services that he could not perform himself, such as tailoring, preparing food, or providing lodgings. He let the children of the
65 towns he visited shadow him while he worked, both teaching them divine lessons and instructing them in the art of apple germination. A unique product of his era, Chapman was a true pioneer, never settling into any confining trade or lifestyle, often opting to sleep
70 alone in the woods and rarely claiming any town as his true home.

17. The primary purpose of the passage is to

(A) relate a new spin on a historical figure
(B) perpetuate the myths surrounding John Chapman
(C) account for a cultural change in early America
(D) discuss a long-standing controversy
(E) undermine the heroism of an individual

18. In line 8, the word "classic" most likely means

(A) ancient
(B) popular
(C) typical
(D) orthodox
(E) elegant

19. Michael Pollan (line 26) would most likely answer the author's question in lines 23-25 ("So why . . . years?") by stating that Chapman

(A) contributed expertise in building public institutions for the communities he visited
(B) facilitated the immediate accessibility of alcohol
(C) traveled between communities to spread his religious convictions
(D) taught frontiersmen how to conserve their resources
(E) perpetuated his own legacy with exaggerated stories

GO ON TO THE NEXT PAGE

Practice Test 6

1   1   1   1   1   1

Unauthorized copying or
reuse of any part of this
page is illegal.

20. In line 46, the author uses quotation marks primarily in order to

(A) call attention to the effects of alcohol
(B) highlight a specialized term
(C) mock Chapman's ideals
(D) question the validity of an interpretation
(E) suggest that Chapman was intentionally deceptive

21. The reference to the "military report" (line 50) primarily serves to

(A) divulge a failure of the Continental Army's regulations
(B) distract from the seriousness of the author's argument
(C) shift the focus of the passage to unconventional views of history
(D) suggest that Chapman was involved in military life
(E) corroborate a claim made by the author

22. Based on information provided in the fifth paragraph, the author implies that Chapman's intentions "may be not as suitable for children as were once thought" (lines 12-13) because

(A) Chapman's activities contributed to a widespread social problem
(B) Chapman sold inedible apples to gullible customers
(C) Chapman used his products to compete unfairly with beer manufacturers
(D) Chapman's abandonment of traditional social roles is a source of controversy
(E) Chapman was indifferent to military reports and other documents criticizing his work

23. The function of the last paragraph is to

(A) prove that Chapman's values were characteristic of his time
(B) suggest that Chapman was personally opposed to the consumption of alcohol
(C) provide information that mitigates the earlier depiction of Chapman's work
(D) explain why Chapman joined the Swedenborgian Church
(E) encourage contemporary Americans to emulate Chapman's creativity

24. The last sentence of the passage portrays John Chapman as

(A) a charlatan
(B) a sojourner
(C) a missionary
(D) a benefactor
(E) a misanthrope

STOP

If you finish before time is called, you may check your work on this section only.
Do not turn to any other section in the test.

SECTION 2
Time–25 minutes
25 Questions

Directions: For each question in this section, select the best answer from among the choices given and fill in the corresponding circle on the answer sheet.

Each sentence below has one or two blanks, each blank indicating that something has been omitted. Beneath the sentence are five words or sets of words labeled A through E. Choose the word or set of words that, when inserted in the sentence, best fits the meaning of the sentence as a whole.

Example:

Jimmy opened his gas station in the ------- because he wanted to be in the middle of a metropolis.

(A) country
(B) suburbs
(C) periphery
(D) environment
(E) city   Ⓐ Ⓑ Ⓒ Ⓓ ●

1. The composition was unquestionably -------: every sentence was a reworded duplication of a statement taken directly from the Internet.

    (A) confusing   (B) controversial
        (C) convincing   (D) imitative
            (E) straightforward

2. It is amazing that so many hundreds of thousands of species manage to ------- in the dense jungles of the Amazon, even though their habitat is now being ------- by loggers and house builders.

    (A) thrive . . eradicated
    (B) navigate . . collected
    (C) flourish . . enriched
    (D) wane . . destroyed
    (E) commune . . maligned

3. As the result of enduring centuries of war, European societies in the Middle Ages became -------, splitting into different political groups based on alliance and family origin.

    (A) bureaucratized   (B) democratized
        (C) oppressive   (D) fractured
            (E) standardized

4. Martha's ------- annoyed her friends, who tired of her unpredictable and sudden whims.

    (A) capriciousness   (B) complacency
        (C) bombast   (D) negligence
            (E) righteousness

5. The once-optimistic board members were compelled to reassess their corporate strategy after the initial ------- of the marketing campaign gave way to a ------- revision of the company's sales forecast.

    (A) despondency . . pessimistic
    (B) drive . . standard
    (C) focus . . bleak
    (D) vigor . . vindicating
    (E) vitality . . dreary

6. Horace Walpole was a veritable ------- of Gothic fiction: he pioneered the genre in the late eighteenth century.

    (A) arbiter   (B) confabulator   (C) critic
        (D) prognosticator   (E) progenitor

7. After a lifetime spent studying classical music, Alyssa considered herself a ------- of the subject.

    (A) tyro   (B) debunker   (C) patron
        (D) connoisseur   (E) protector

8. Leopold Senghor of Senegal, a revered poet and leader of the then newly-liberated former French colony in Africa, ------- French culture, deliberately ------- the anti-European sentiment that had become prevalent across the continent.

    (A) analyzed . . endorsing
    (B) championed . . advocating
    (C) chided . . rebuffing
    (D) embraced . . promoting
    (E) espoused . . rebuking

GO ON TO THE NEXT PAGE

Practice Test 6

The passages below are followed by questions based on their content; questions following a pair of related passages may also be based on the relationship between the paired passages. Answer the questions on the basis of what is <u>stated</u> or <u>implied</u> in the passages and in any introductory material that may be provided.

Questions 9-12 are based on the following passages.

Passage 1

     Many will contend that video games have replaced reading, particularly the reading of fiction. While video games may have dispensed with actual bound pages, video games carry within them the kind
Line
5 of stories and episodes that are present in all literature. In some cases, the video game hero is faced with a calling to embark on a journey that can change his world for the better. Then, he meets a mentor who guides him along the way. The climax occurs when
10 the hero faces his deepest fear, often embodied by a central antagonist. He conquers that fear and returns to his world with newfound knowledge. This is the basis of many traditional narratives, except that this time the storytelling is pixelated.

Passage 2

15   Video games are not books. There is a level of intimacy that can only be achieved by brushing your hand on paper, by hearing the subtle tear of a page that has been turned too quickly, by peering into the deepest nuances of an author's words. It seems that
20 today's trend is to forgo this romance. Instead, droves of young people are satisfied with the "interaction" provided by computer programs, never truly experiencing the ways in which physical proximity to the written word fosters a unique bond between the
25 reader and the book.

9. The author of Passage 1 would most likely respond to Passage 2 by stating that

  (A) video game stories and episodes are likely to draw in viewers who are indifferent to printed books
  (B) video games depart from traditional narrative conventions in ways that warrant extended study
  (C) most modern readers consider physical contact with a book an inessential part of the reading experience
  (D) video games speak to human emotions by adapting classic storytelling techniques to a new medium
  (E) young people lose touch with an important aesthetic experience by focusing exclusively on video games

10. Compared to that of Passage 1, the tone of Passage 2 is more

  (A) wistful
  (B) evenhanded
  (C) histrionic
  (D) cynical
  (E) euphemistic

11. In lines 6-11 ("In some . . . antagonist"), the narrator of Passage 1 describes

  (A) a structure that video games share with more traditional narratives
  (B) a tactic that video game makers have adopted to compete with print media
  (C) a type of episode that is noticeably enhanced by pixelated storytelling
  (D) a use of perspective preferred by video game enthusiasts
  (E) a justification for the widespread rejection of bound and printed books

12. The author of Passage 2 would most likely respond to the claim in lines 3-5 of Passage 1 ("While video . . . literature") by asserting that

  (A) video games are popular mostly among young people who will eventually embrace printed books
  (B) interaction with a physical book can enrich the experience of stories and episodes
  (C) few of the stories offered by video games match traditional print narratives in detail and complexity
  (D) only the most sophisticated video games are worthy of comparison with printed books
  (E) printed books foster reading and comprehension skills that videogames inculcate much less effectively

GO ON TO THE NEXT PAGE

Questions 13-25 are based on the following passage.

This passage is taken from a humorous short story written early in the twenty-first century.

It's another April day with intermittent heavy showers. "Good for the garden!" says my neighbor, and yes, I can see that the plants I carefully installed in
Line the front last week are making some effort to emerge.
5 The clematis in the pot by the front door has survived the winter and is growing rampantly, although the clematis against the wooden fence merely displays a few timid green shoots. The apple tree is beginning to show buds here and there, but it still looks hesitant,
10 and there is no sign that a single one of the bulbs I planted in autumn is making an effort to push through. I sigh. I am a terrible gardener, really: all enthusiasm and no patience. I wonder if whoever moves into this house after I leave will keep the garden going.
15 My reverie is interrupted by the arrival of a white van, which double-parks outside my gate. On the vehicle's side are painted the words: "Mr. Dutton, Removals and Storage." I look at my watch. Mr. Dutton has arrived only an hour late. Mr. Dutton gets
20 out of his van and walks up the path. He is a rather stocky man. His hair is cropped close to his skull and he sports a small earring in his left ear. His right ear supports a cigarette. He wears heavy boots, a sagging pair of jeans, and a heavy belt, which is partially
25 obscured by his overhanging belly. His T-shirt is emblazoned with a motorcycle logo and he also dons an open, ill-fitting jacket with leather shoulder pads. The fingers of his right hand vigorously work his mobile phone. In his left hand he holds a crisp business
30 folder. He pauses at the gate, pockets his phone, grins broadly at me, and approaches the door with the air of a busy executive. I invite him in and show him the items that I need to send into storage; we then sit down in the front room while Mr. Dutton works out
35 the estimated price for the job, all the while pursuing a monologue that requires few interventions on my behalf.

Mr. Dutton tells me that he understands that I am going to work in Sudan, which is funny because he
40 had an uncle who was Sudanese. This uncle returned to that country over twenty years ago: Mr. Dutton hasn't heard from him since. He advises me against taking any animals with me (actually, the thought hadn't crossed my mind). It's just not a good idea, poor
45 climate for dogs, and people there don't often share our affection for pets. Mr. Dutton then informs me that he is paying top taxes in this country and that by the end of 2012 there will be an economic black hole because everyone paying top taxes will have moved
50 elsewhere—as they are already doing. Do I realize that there are 69 million people here in the UK (I hadn't)—80 million if I include Ireland (I hastily add Ireland)—which is why houses cost so much? I try to

work this logic out, but by the time I have, Mr. Dutton
55 has moved on to his interest in pre-Roman history. Do I realize that every thousand years, the earth suffers a cataclysmic disaster, as in 535 C.E. when Krakatoa exploded? (The actual date had escaped me.) It caused darkness for twenty years, and crop growth
60 became minimal. And that affected societies all over the world: the Ming Dynasty in China collapsed, as did the Aztec Empire in Mexico. If that were to happen today, this country would be finished. (I nod in agreement.) We would turn to cannibalism, since we
65 import all our food. We would not know what to do, although, of course, the answer resides in one word: N.A.S.A. According to Mr. Dutton, the U.N. should force everyone in the world to give up 5% of what they earn in order to finance spaceships, which would
70 bring about the colonization of both Mars and the Moon. That, he says, is the future, and the quotation for storage for one year will be 1055 pounds sterling. Will I be paying in advance? I nod my head; in view of the cataclysmic future, safe storage seems like a good
75 investment.

With that, Mr. Dutton takes his leave, telling me just before he goes that MTV is a brilliant channel, since its costumes and music give young people the opportunity to learn about the world, and that it has
80 been a pleasure to meet me, for I am clearly someone with a view to the future. More people like us, he apparently feels, are needed if we are to survive the present difficulties. I see him to the front door, and watch him take out his mobile phone, enter his car, and
85 roar off, driving with one hand. I look once more at the garden, shrug my shoulders, and go back indoors.

13. The episode presented in the passage is best described as a

(A) dispute with an apparent nonconformist
(B) passionate debate about contemporary issues
(C) disappointing visit from a new friend
(D) collaborative effort to address a conundrum
(E) meeting with an eccentric individual

14. In context, "installed" (line 3) most nearly means

(A) positioned
(B) updated
(C) invested
(D) activated
(E) constructed

GO ON TO THE NEXT PAGE

15. In context, the words "timid" (line 8) and "hesitant" (line 9) emphasize the idea that

(A) successfully cultivating plant life is often an impossible task
(B) the narrator is committed to the long-term survival of his garden
(C) the narrator is trying to downplay his incompetence as a gardener
(D) the narrator's garden is evidently not thriving
(E) weather conditions are preventing the plants from reaching full bloom

16. Lines 20-27 ("He is . . . pads") are best described as a

(A) historical allusion
(B) visual description
(C) bizarre fantasy
(D) psychological analysis
(E) needless caricature

17. In context, the phrase "works out" (line 34) is best understood to mean

(A) calculates
(B) accomplishes
(C) practices
(D) resolves
(E) represents

18. The phrase in lines 35-37 ("all the . . . behalf") conveys what impression of Mr. Dutton?

(A) He is an engaging speaker.
(B) He is a shrewd businessman.
(C) He is extremely garrulous.
(D) He is adept at multi-tasking.
(E) He feels desperately lonely.

19. The parenthetical phrases in the third paragraph are presented as

(A) the most common objections to Mr. Dutton's arguments
(B) hypothetical questions that are meant to be humorous
(C) responses that are juxtaposed to highlight Mr. Dutton's absurdity
(D) quotations from authorities on social and historical topics
(E) obscure facts that substantiate Mr. Dutton's proposals

20. The phrase in lines 54-56 ("but by . . . history") serves to emphasize

(A) the narrator's general incompetence in conversation
(B) the narrator's inability to pay attention to Mr. Dutton
(C) the large number of inaccuracies in Mr. Dutton's explanations
(D) the haste with which Mr. Dutton proceeds to another topic
(E) the subtlety of Mr. Dutton's lines of reasoning

21. The sentence in lines 64-65 ("We would . . . food") is best described as

(A) an apology
(B) a concession
(C) a decision
(D) a dismissal
(E) a conjecture

22. In the sentence in lines 71-72 ("That, he . . . sterling"), Mr. Dutton transitions from

(A) condemning society at large to praising the narrator's perceptiveness
(B) postulating a grand solution to dealing with daily matters
(C) theorizing about large problems to proposing a specific solution
(D) criticizing economic structures to accepting unpleasant contingencies
(E) predicting a bleak future to endorsing the narrator's pragmatism

23. In context, the tone of the phrase ("in view . . . investment") in lines 73-75 is best described as

(A) wry
(B) belligerent
(C) resentful
(D) idealistic
(E) timorous

GO ON TO THE NEXT PAGE

24. As he is presented in the passage, Mr. Dutton can best be characterized as

(A) urbane
(B) maudlin
(C) idiosyncratic
(D) frugal
(E) mercenary

25. In context of the entire passage, the final sentence ("I look . . . indoors") suggests that the narrator

(A) no longer considers the burdens of keeping a garden to be relevant
(B) can find deep pleasure in incongruous and ugly surroundings
(C) will later scrutinize Mr. Dutton's ideas at much greater length
(D) is not seriously agitated by his dialogue with Mr. Dutton
(E) has reached a subtle understanding of Mr. Dutton's principles

STOP

If you finish before time is called, you may check your work on this section only.
Do not turn to any other section in the test.

SECTION 3

Time–20 minutes
18 Questions

Directions: For each question in this section, select the best answer from among the choices given and fill in the corresponding circle on the answer sheet.

Each sentence below has one or two blanks, each blank indicating that something has been omitted. Beneath the sentence are five words or sets of words labeled A through E. Choose the word or set of words that, when inserted in the sentence, <u>best</u> fits the meaning of the sentence as a whole.

Example:

Jimmy opened his gas station in the ------- because he wanted to be in the middle of a metropolis.

(A) country
(B) suburbs
(C) periphery
(D) environment
(E) city

---

1. Edward found that grading his student's essays had ------- effect on him when he was stressed: after he finished a few, he always felt better.

   (A) an unsettling   (B) a trivial
      (C) an exacerbating   (D) a soothing
         (E) an informative

2. By the time he reached his teenage years, Pablo Picasso was ------- as an artist of ------- talent, winning accolades from the most demanding Spanish critics.

   (A) acknowledged . . exceptional
   (B) exonerated . . professional
   (C) disparaged . . superior
   (D) inspected . . extraordinary
   (E) described . . negligible

3. While we may be tempted to view psychics as -------, we should resist this urge and realize that these individuals merely manipulate obvious visual clues.

   (A) satirical   (B) prescient   (C) pretentious
      (D) omnipresent   (E) ethereal

4. It is quite common for strangers to confuse Purva's ------- with enthusiasm: because she is so talkative, they assume that she is -------.

   (A) reserve . . passionate
   (B) garrulousness . . tepid
   (C) diffidence . . zealous
   (D) wordiness . . apathetic
   (E) verbosity . . ebullient

5. Because he alone knows every recipe by heart and can recall each ingredient by name and amount, Emmanuel is ------- among all the cooks at his restaurant.

   (A) industrious   (B) representative
      (C) munificent   (D) preeminent
         (E) susceptible

6. Although the United States has no set class system, there is a considerable difference between the powerful business ------- and the common individual where income levels are concerned.

   (A) socialite   (B) magnate   (C) aristocrat
      (D) aesthete   (E) intellectual

Practice Test 6

> The two passages below are followed by questions based on their content and on the relationship between the two passages. Answer the questions on the basis of what is <u>stated</u> or <u>implied</u> in the passages and in any introductory material that may be provided.

Questions 7-18 are based on the following passages.

The following passages discuss two authors' respective experiences of a classic American film from the 1940s.

Passage 1

Meet Me in St. Louis is a film that, for middle-class Americans, depicted the quintessential goals and pleasures of family life in the wake of the Second
Line World War. At the heart of this musical feature are the
5 dreams and unexpected realities of the Smith family, who live around the time of the 1904 St. Louis World's Fair. The Smiths' greatest crisis involves a life-altering decision: whether to leave comfortable, homely St. Louis for a new life of opportunity in
10 bustling, aggressive New York City. But as the film plays out, there is really no contest. Since this is a film made by M.G.M., it offers that studio's complaisant and complacent panacea for social problems: "East, West: Home is Best."
15 Almost eighty years after it first appeared, *Meet Me in St. Louis* is still popular, not only in the United States (where it unfailingly appears on television every Christmas) but also nearly everywhere else in the Western world. The modern-day critic—or
20 cynic—might sneer at the movie's sentimental popularity and point out everything that is missing from this depiction of everyday American life. In the early twentieth century, apparently, everyone in St. Louis was financially well-off. There were no
25 mortgages to worry about, no strikes, no protests, no pollution, no conflicts in schools, no acts of violence of any sort. The film, apparently, epitomizes the axiom that optimism knows no bounds; *Meet Me in St. Louis* even calls to mind a sentence from
30 Voltaire's satirical work, *Candide*: "All is for the best in the best of all possible worlds." Like critics of this film, the sarcastic Voltaire was wary of such optimism, implying that ill-advised and ill-fated beliefs lead to self-destructive impracticality.
35 It is probably true to say that a film like *Meet Me in St. Louis* could not succeed in today's jaded market. Too much has happened in the intervening years for us to embrace the film's sunny premise. However, it is wrong to ridicule and dismiss the film,
40 which is far more carefully crafted than its most vehement critics realize. *Meet Me in St. Louis* does not pretend to be a picture of 1940s life: it is set at the beginning of the 1900s, and thus places its characters in an era when America was still relatively hopeful
45 about its future, as becomes evident during the film's upbeat finale at the St. Louis World's Fair. And for all

his caveats about optimism and his endorsements of "pragmatism," even Voltaire ended *Candide* with a reassuring request: "Let us cultivate our garden." It is
50 up to the reader of *Candide* and the audience of *Meet Me in St. Louis* to decide whether an optimistic outlook is a viable response or a foolish reaction to the realities of the world.

Passage 2

Meet Me in St. Louis is a film like no other. It is a
55 piece of stringy bacon wrapped in a bow, with grease trickling down its velveteen ribbons. And that is putting it lightly. This musical—like most musicals—artfully dupes its viewers into running the emotional gamut; infected with newfound optimism about the
60 realities of life, the audience ends this seven-course meal of an entertainment satiated, but on the brink of a food coma. *Meet Me in St. Louis* is a "gentle" escape, pounded into the mind by the jackhammering of musical overtures, overdone lighting, and
65 cloyingly cheerful lyrics. And why? Well, who would conceivably pay for an overpriced ticket to watch a performance that has a tragic ending?
Theatre elitists claim that *Meet Me in St. Louis* originated in film and not onstage, and that film
70 viewership involves much more economical prices. Family fun on the cheap. It is true that "showtunes" have been sown into the fabric of American identity. But film musicals like this one are forcing that cloth to rip at the seams. Every Christmas, this film
75 musical airs on some family channel to extol idealistic middle class values. The overarching conflict is simple: do the characters decide to move to the fast-paced city, or should they remain happy and content in their Midwestern existence? The conflict is
80 really not a conflict at all, but a trivial struggle, based on humdrum geographical woes yet worked up into a profound existential crisis. The predominantly suburban audience for *Meet Me in St. Louis* explains a lot about the film's outcome: of course the family's
85 patriarch chooses to stay "at home" and forgo the attractions of the city. What better way to feel comfortable about our choices than to see them validated in Technicolor before us—complete with song and dance?
90 In no way should the sentimentality of *Meet Me in St. Louis* be questioned; sentimentality is the film's essence. Seriously debating the necessity of tear-jerking emotion here would be comparable to

GO ON TO THE NEXT PAGE

seriously pondering the existence of Santa Claus. Yet
95 we must question the integrity of the film's
sentiments. What good can arise from such saturated
optimism? It would behoove us to consider watching
films that reflect the modern realities of life, that
remind us that glimmers of hope are the greatest gifts
100 because they lie in the palms of our hands, in our
direct control. But in this film, nothing is left to
interpretation; all the choices of perspective are
already made for us. Either be content with what you
have or struggle toward the hollow idealism on the
105 screen. Perhaps the film's broadcast during Christmas
is most befitting. After all, the holiday season is an
escape, a time for forgetting, before the start of yet
another year.

7. The statement, "East, West: Home is Best"
(line 14) serves to

(A) illustrate a guiding principle that led to the
Smiths' ultimate decision
(B) juxtapose the beneficial aspects of two
radically different positions
(C) create levity in an otherwise dismal situation
(D) indicate the negative aspects of two
drastically different geographical locations
(E) cast doubt on the need for optimism while
moving from East to West

8. According to the author of Passage 1, over the
"eighty years" (line 15) since the movie was
released, its appearance on television has become

(A) an unpopular idea
(B) an unfortunate occurrence
(C) a ubiquitous phenomenon
(D) an unorthodox custom
(E) an esoteric practice

9. According to the author of Passage 1, a "modern-
day critic" (line 19) would "sneer" (line 20) at
Meet Me in St. Louis because the film fails to
take into account the

(A) audience's final emotional response
(B) cultural impact of the Second World War
(C) financial responsibilities of 1940s families
(D) harsh realities of American life
(E) optimism exhibited by Americans in the
1940s

10. The list in lines 24-27 of Passage 1 ("There
were . . . sort") serves to

(A) underscore various social problems
neglected by a popular work of
entertainment
(B) catalog aspects of twentieth-century life that
the makers of *Meet Me in St. Louis* openly
criticized
(C) show what New York City was like after the
Second World War
(D) contrast the expectations of Americans in the
1940s with those of people living today
(E) enumerate the woes felt by Americans who
had served in the military

11. According to lines 27-34 ("The film . . .
impracticality"), Voltaire would most likely view
the optimism found in *Meet Me in St. Louis* with

(A) irritation, because optimism always leads to
disappointment
(B) skepticism, because optimism is not a
pragmatic approach to life
(C) appreciation, because optimism creates an
environment of productivity
(D) indifference, because optimism does not
impact society in any meaningful way
(E) approval, because optimism is an
appropriate strategy for political reform

12. The author of Passage 2 would most likely
respond to the claim in Passage 1, lines 39-41
("However, it . . . realize") with

(A) outrage
(B) sympathy
(C) disagreement
(D) regret
(E) acceptance

13. The statement in lines 54-56 of Passage 2
("It is . . . ribbons") is an example of which
rhetorical device?

(A) Understatement
(B) Metaphor
(C) Foreshadowing
(D) Allusion
(E) Personification

GO ON TO THE NEXT PAGE

14. The quotation marks used in line 62 of Passage 2 serve to

(A) express skepticism about the aptness of a particular term
(B) highlight a use of specialized language
(C) indicate that film reviewers have applied a particular epithet to *Meet Me in St. Louis*
(D) mock the arbitrary standards of the film industry
(E) acknowledge respected authorities in an ongoing debate

15. The author's claim in lines 79-80 of Passage 2 ("The conflict . . . struggle") serves to

(A) show how *Meet Me in St. Louis* initiated a new preference for city living
(B) qualify the main idea of the passage by providing opposing opinions
(C) undermine the notion that one's location has no bearing on one's happiness
(D) introduce a sentiment that the author later contradicts
(E) propose that *Meet Me in St. Louis* exaggerates a rather everyday dilemma

16. According to the last paragraph of Passage 2, the author feels that we should watch films that

(A) present realistic visions of life but still cause us to value hope and independence
(B) promote the idea that if one has hope then one can overcome any obstacle
(C) parody escapist entertainments such as *Meet Me in St. Louis*
(D) are completely at odds with the commercial spirit of the Christmas season
(E) depict life as an perpetual struggle for comfort and prestige

17. Both authors agree that *Meet Me in St. Louis* ultimately

(A) creates controversy about American ideals
(B) supports the idealistic values of everyday Americans
(C) constitutes an accurate depiction of reality
(D) makes a statement about the importance of pragmatism
(E) lampoons life in 1940s middle-class America

18. Which contrast best describes how the authors of each passage view the film *Meet Me in St. Louis*?

(A) As imprecise but artistic in Passage 1; as touching and satisfying in Passage 2
(B) As valuable but obscure in Passage 1; as nostalgic and irresponsible in Passage 2
(C) As cheerful and complex in Passage 1; as meaningful but misunderstood in Passage 2
(D) As patriotic but outdated in Passage 1; as unique and truthful in Passage 2
(E) As inaccurate but popular in Passage 1; as mawkish and inauthentic in Passage 2

STOP

If you finish before time is called, you may check your work on this section only.
Do not turn to any other section in the test.

POST TEST ANALYSIS

This post test analysis is important if you want to see an improvement on your next test. Each section has a set of possible reasons for errors. Place check marks next to the ones that pertain to you, and write your own on the blank lines provided. Use this form to better analyze your performance. **If you don't understand why you made errors, there is no way you can correct them!**

1. **SENTENCE COMPLETION:**

Problems with the sentence:
- ❑ Wasn't familiar with phrases, idioms, or words in the sentence
- ❑ Missed the clues or tones
- ❑ Put your OWN word in the blank rather than one from the sentence
- ❑ Completely avoided marking
- ❑ Other: _____

_____

Problems with the answers:
- ❑ Did not use process of elimination
- ❑ Did not ignore unknown words
- ❑ Did not use prefix/root/suffix knowledge to figure out the meaning of the unknown words
- ❑ Did not match the clues and tones of the answer with those of the sentence
- ❑ Did not recognize vocabulary words
- ❑ Did not check answer to see if it fit
- ❑ Other: _____

_____

Leaving questions unanswered:
- ❑ Did not try
- ❑ Did not fill in the blank(s) with words
- ❑ Ran out of time
- ❑ Other: _____

_____

2. **SHORT READING COMPREHENSION:**
- ❑ Did not read entire paragraph
- ❑ Did not see more than one point
- ❑ Missed contrast clues
- ❑ Did not pinpoint thesis
- ❑ Did not identify similarities and differences in Double Short Reading Comp
- ❑ Other: _____

_____

3. **LONG READING COMPREHENSION:**
- ❑ Did not understand the question, line reference, or answers
- ❑ Spent too much time reading the passages
- ❑ Did not underline the line reference
- ❑ Read too much or too little
- ❑ Did not answer the specific question; instead analyzed its main idea
- ❑ Did not do process of elimination based on facts in the passage
- ❑ Couldn't find the false words
- ❑ Couldn't choose between two possible answers
- ❑ Did not use tone to help eliminate answers
- ❑ When stuck at 2 guessed instead of pulling additional fact
- ❑ Couldn't finish in time
- ❑ Other: _____

_____

ANSWER KEY

TEST 6

SECTION 1

#	Answer	LEVEL
1	B	(1)
2	D	(2)
3	C	(3)
4	E	(4)
5	C	(4)
6	B	(4)
7	C	(5)
8	A	(2)
9	D	(3)
10	E	(1)
11	D	(3)
12	C	(3)
13	C	(2)
14	C	(4)
15	C	(2)
16	A	(3)
17	A	(2)
18	B	(3)
19	B	(4)
20	D	(2)
21	E	(3)
22	A	(3)
23	C	(4)
24	B	(5)

SECTION 2

#	Answer	LEVEL
1	D	(1)
2	A	(1)
3	D	(2)
4	A	(3)
5	E	(3)
6	E	(4)
7	D	(4)
8	E	(5)
9	C	(4)
10	A	(2)
11	A	(3)
12	B	(4)
13	E	(3)
14	A	(1)
15	D	(3)
16	B	(3)
17	A	(2)
18	C	(3)
19	C	(4)
20	D	(2)
21	E	(4)
22	B	(3)
23	A	(3)
24	C	(4)
25	D	(4)

SECTION 3

#	Answer	LEVEL
1	D	(1)
2	A	(2)
3	B	(3)
4	E	(4)
5	D	(3)
6	B	(5)
7	A	(3)
8	C	(2)
9	D	(4)
10	A	(3)
11	B	(4)
12	C	(1)
13	B	(2)
14	A	(3)
15	E	(2)
16	A	(4)
17	B	(3)
18	E	(2)

Difficulty levels range from 1 - 5 with 1 being the easiest and 5 being the hardest.
For answer explanations please visit www.ies2400.com/criticalreading

PRACTICE TEST 7

1   1   1   Unauthorized copying or
reuse of any part of this
page is illegal.   1   1   1

SECTION 1
Time–25 minutes
24 Questions

Directions: For each question in this section, select the best answer from among the choices given and fill in the corresponding circle on the answer sheet.

Each sentence below has one or two blanks, each blank indicating that something has been omitted. Beneath the sentence are five words or sets of words labeled A through E. Choose the word or set of words that, when inserted in the sentence, <u>best</u> fits the meaning of the sentence as a whole.

Example:

Jimmy opened his gas station in the ------- because he wanted to be in the middle of a metropolis.

(A) country
(B) suburbs
(C) periphery
(D) environment
(E) city

1. Regina's innovative costume design earned her so many ------- that any misgivings about her past ------- were now forgotten.

    (A) accolades . . blunders
    (B) criticisms . . miscalculations
    (C) laurels . . praises
    (D) judgments . . mistakes
    (E) commendations . . achievements

2. Rufus possessed the ------- necessary to execute complex finger exercises on the guitar, but he lacked the passion and originality that mark a true musician.

    (A) excitement   (B) expediency   (C) freedom
        (D) dexterity   (E) arrogance

3. The dearth of documentary records remaining after the destruction of the palace forced investigators to ------- the quotidian activities of the king and his attendants from the ------- reports of the few surviving courtiers.

    (A) analyze . . abundant
    (B) mitigate . . secondary
    (C) speculate . . written
    (D) envision . . contradicting
    (E) reconstruct . . anecdotal

4. Humans are a ------- species: among us are geniuses and fools, altruists and misers, poets and boors.

    (A) dominant   (B) controversial
        (C) homogeneous   (D) competitive
            (E) paradoxical

5. Designed to provide free technical and scientific training to anyone attending a two-year community college, recent legislation in Wisconsin is intended to ------- a state workforce that is currently regarded as -------.

    (A) bolster . . vibrant
    (B) upgrade . . substandard
    (C) finance . . productive
    (D) subsidize . . intellectual
    (E) hobble . . mediocre

6. After the disappearance of her beloved pet, Mabel found herself emotionally and psychologically -------, sinking deeper and deeper into disoriented melancholy.

    (A) aghast   (B) resilient   (C) eclectic
        (D) unmoored   (E) vengeful

7. Proponents of artificial intelligence often ------- their arguments when prompted, listing individual and specific reasons why such technology will benefit humanity.

    (A) truncate   (B) enumerate   (C) rescind
        (D) proselytize   (E) descry

8. As ------- as the liberation of the oppressed nation must have seemed, this altruistic endeavor has nevertheless led to irreparable -------.

    (A) sanctimonious . . aftereffects
    (B) serendipitous . . deliverances
    (C) providential . . ramifications
    (D) regressive . . consequences
    (E) byzantine . . catastrophes

GO ON TO THE NEXT PAGE

Practice Test 7

> The passages below are followed by questions based on their content; questions following a pair of related passages may also be based on the relationship between the paired passages. Answer the questions on the basis of what is <u>stated</u> or <u>implied</u> in the passages and in any introductory material that may be provided.

Questions 9-10 are based on the following passage.

"Facebook is so yesterday," my niece said with a smirk that only a fifteen year-old could pull off: one part innocence and one part arrogance. And then, as if
Line to prove her point and her prowess, she continued to
5 list the social media sites that are "so not yesterday." Vine, with its repeating videos and spastic edits. Twitter, with its desperate 140-character bids for attention. Instagram, with its legions of narcissistic "selfies." I felt a longing for the time before smart
10 phones, when whether you had call-waiting or three-way calling determined your level of cool. I smiled at her diatribe, allowing her the hubris of knowledge that surrounds today's youth, then skulked away to check how many "likes" my newest Facebook post had
15 gotten.

9. The primary purpose of the passage is to

(A) cast aspersions on the ideas of a young person who lacks practical experience of society
(B) demonstrate that once-popular forms of social media inevitably lose popularity over time
(C) show how two individuals from different age groups respond to communication technologies
(D) explain why older trends in technology have given way to fast-paced yet undesirable media
(E) generate sympathy for individuals who are unable to adapt to new forms of communication

10. In the passage, the author's reference to her "newest Facebook post" is best understood as

(A) an effort to persuade the reader
(B) a reference to obsolete technology
(C) a dismissal of more recent innovations
(D) an instance of nuanced empathy
(E) a moment of self-deprecating irony

Questions 11-12 are based on the following passage.

The human ear is an amazing mechanism. The visible part of the ear, the auricle, acts as a conical amplifier, picking up sounds and funneling them into
Line the deeper reaches of the organ. In terms of structure,
5 the ear functions in much the same way that a seashell does. If a shell were to have an opening at its pinnacle, and if the pinnacle were to be placed gently into the ear, then such an arrangement would greatly amplify the surrounding sounds. But that's not all when it
10 comes to the workings of the ear. Hearing is actually the ear's ancillary purpose: keeping the body in equilibrium is this versatile organ's more difficult, but more essential, task.

11. The author's tone towards the human ear is one of

(A) utter resentment
(B) disoriented amazement
(C) general bemusement
(D) undeserved fascination
(E) unqualified appreciation

12. The author describes hearing as an "ancillary purpose" (line 11) most likely because

(A) hearing is the most important task of the ear
(B) keeping the body balanced is more significant
(C) the ear must both discern sound and stabilize
(D) using tools, such as a shell, enhances sound perception
(E) the ear is a relatively unimportant organ

GO ON TO THE NEXT PAGE

Questions 13-24 are based on the following passages.

The following two passages consider the theories developed by Charles Darwin (1809-1882) and their application to the social and natural sciences. The first passage is taken from an essay on the history of ideas, while the second is adapted from a recent article by a business journalist.

Passage 1

Throughout the history of science, the most monumental discoveries are often described as "groundbreaking." This description is particularly apt,
Line for like an earthquake itself, the most stunning scientific
5 insights have often proved jarring to our sensibilities. Such was the case when Charles Darwin first published his seminal work, *On the Origin of the Species*, in 1859. It was in this text that Darwin first elucidated his theory of "natural selection"—that is, the gradual biological
10 process by which the most successfully adapted members of a species pass along their genetic information through reproduction. Over time, the population of a species will change to show increased numbers of optimized traits. Responding to this
15 phenomenon, biologist Herbert Spencer coined the term "survival of the fittest" to describe Darwin's theory.

Only the most rare and brilliant scientists transcend their own narrow fields, and subsequently penetrate the psyche of a culture at large. Darwin was
20 such a scientist. The theory of survival of the fittest has influenced the thinking of experts in fields as diverse as finance and sociology. For instance, Darwin's theory provided physical, concrete evidence for the abstract theories proposed by economist Adam
25 Smith a century earlier. According to Smith, the ideal economic environment for a society is free-market capitalism, a structure in which open competition among producers yields the best products for consumers, manufactured and sold at the lowest
30 possible prices. Smith even described the marriage of supply and demand in the marketplace as something that occurred quite naturally and organically—as if the entire process were orchestrated by an "invisible hand." When Darwin came along, his theory of how
35 nature selects the fittest individuals, thereby yielding the strongest and most robust populations, proved to be a strong justification for Smith's economic teachings.

Of course, the corollary to "survival of the
40 fittest" is that the weaker populations in nature will not survive over the long term. "Natural Selection," wrote Darwin, "almost inevitably causes extinction of the less improved forms of life." Is it any surprise then, as we look around the world today, that
45 capitalism has flourished across the globe—even in countries that once had purely communist economies, such as Russia and China? Clearly, a century and a half after the *Origin of the Species*, Darwin's theory continues to justify Adam Smith's economic ideal.

Passage 2

50 Every now and then, I do a little digging online and try to find out what has happened to the people I knew in college. I'm mostly curious whether my prophecies for them—or rather, for their careers and successes—have in any way come true. I am often
55 stunned and sometimes amused to see how wrong my prognostications are. I recently looked up one of my highest-achieving classmates, who graduated with an honors degree in physics and mathematics, then went on to earn his doctorate in the second of these
60 disciplines. Now, he works as a teacher in a primary school just outside Seattle: a comfortable life, but not the future of earth-shattering discovery that I had so confidently predicted for him. I also recently looked up a few of my dorm-mates from freshman year,
65 particularly two carefree young men who enjoyed sneaking apples and oranges out of the cafeteria and using them to play baseball on a nearby athletic field. (Nobody ever hit more than a single: the fruit usually burst upon impact.) Today, one is a successful
70 corporate lawyer, while the other owns a popular chain of Italian restaurants. I wonder if either remembers those apples.

How strange this all seems, from the perspective of classic economic theory. In college, many of us are
75 taught that the modern world is dictated by "social Darwinism," "survival of the fittest," "the strong against the weak." These ideas aren't exactly clichés, but they aren't exactly applicable to the modern job market. If they were, I could have determined my
80 classmates' futures as easily as Darwin himself determined which birds and which reptiles were best suited to which environmental conditions. It just is not so; in truth, the preferences of employers, businessmen, and deal-makers can be absolutely
85 inscrutable. Traits that are typically marks of the "weak"—an easygoing temperament, a servile nature, an irresponsible sense of humor—can sometimes seal an interview, if not make a career.

The cases I have considered may seem small
90 and, frankly, weird. Still, what are we to make of the many international businesses that seem ready to self-destruct but somehow survive, and thrive, year after year? How do we explain corporate behemoths such as Amazon.com, a company that has never made
95 a steady profit but is still valued at over $150 billion? Again, "survival of the fittest" posits that the market is guided by an "invisible hand," which supposedly maintains a logical balance of power. The way I see it, the owner of that invisible hand must be blind, or
100 insane, or possessed of a devious sense of humor.

GO ON TO THE NEXT PAGE

13. Which of the following statements best describes the relationship between the two passages?

(A) Passage 1 argues for the broad applicability of theories that are subjected to critical skepticism in Passage 2.
(B) Passage 1 chronicles the development of a theory that Passage 2 corroborates by drawing on personal experience.
(C) Passage 1 draws a firm connection between two thinkers who are construed as antagonistic to each other in Passage 2.
(D) Passage 1 predicts the widespread acceptance of an ideology that is shown to be unpopular in Passage 2.
(E) Passage 1 morally endorses a school of thought that is depicted as fundamentally unethical in Passage 2.

14. In context of lines 1-5 ("Throughout the . . . sensibilities") "monumental discoveries" (line 2) are best understood to be

(A) insights into the workings of geologic forces that inspire awe and admiration
(B) innovative concepts that provoke human sensitivities
(C) preposterous claims that go against all that we have come to accept as fact
(D) self-evident, universal theories that require neither experimentation nor proof
(E) the findings of Charles Darwin as chronicled in his book

15. It can be inferred from the description in lines 9-14 ("the gradual . . . traits") that

(A) only the fittest members of a species engage in reproduction
(B) genetic information dictates the expression of physical characteristics
(C) the evolution of a species always progresses in a positive direction
(D) the successful traits of one member of a species can be learned by other members of the same species
(E) all members of a species will successfully adapt to a given environment over time

16. The author of Passage 1 mentions the idea of "survival of the fittest" (line 16) most likely in order to

(A) provide a corroboration of Darwin's theory
(B) illustrate the immediate popularity of Darwin's ideas
(C) define a complex theory in colloquial terms
(D) introduce a concept that is later applied to other fields of activity
(E) suggest that Darwin's theory may have had devastating social consequences

17. The word "open" in line 27 of Passage 1 most nearly means

(A) unrestrained
(B) candid
(C) disclosed
(D) active
(E) gaping

18. The phrase "invisible hand" (lines 33-34) is used to describe

(A) an economy based on furious competition and low-cost production
(B) an abstract idea that was disproven by the advent of communism
(C) a mechanism whereby the needs of consumers and producers are mutually met
(D) a scientific theory that pre-dates the concept of natural selection
(E) an economy in a state of robust growth and strategic expansion

19. In the opening paragraph, the author of Passage 2 makes the assumption that

(A) all science majors make effective and compassionate teachers
(B) the attitude of a college student can be correlated with the level of his academic achievement
(C) there is a scientific way to predict the career choices made by an individual
(D) a person's performance in school is indicative of his career potential
(E) mathematics majors are expected to perform meaningful research

GO ON TO THE NEXT PAGE

1   1   1   Unauthorized copying or
reuse of any part of this
page is illegal.   1   1   1

20. In Passage 2, the references to "social Darwinism" (lines 75-76) and "survival of the fittest" (line 76) primarily serve to

    (A) define technical terms
    (B) introduce new theories
    (C) undermine an established authority
    (D) prove the validity of a claim
    (E) set up a counter-argument

21. The statement in lines 78-79 of Passage 2 ("They aren't . . . market") most directly disproves which of the following claims made in Passage 1?

    (A) "scientific insights . . . sensibilities" (lines 4-5)
    (B) "the most . . . reproduction" (lines 10-12)
    (C) "Darwin's theory . . . earlier" (lines 23-25)
    (D) "the ideal . . . capitalism" (lines 25-27)
    (E) "the weaker . . . term" (lines 40-41)

22. The sentence "It just . . . inscrutable" (lines 82-85) implies that

    (A) businesses base employment decisions on potential rather than on achievement
    (B) employers generally feel threatened by candidates who project strength and aggression
    (C) employees should be selected based on characteristics that indicate a high probability of career success
    (D) the hiring practices of businessmen sometimes go against accepted social norms
    (E) the motives of employers remain completely mysterious even to the most educated commentators

23. The word "marks" (line 85) most nearly means

    (A) designs
    (B) gradations
    (C) features
    (D) motifs
    (E) symbols

24. The tones of Passage 1 and Passage 2, respectively, can best be described as

    (A) sentimental . . conversational
    (B) sanguine . . sardonic
    (C) grandiloquent . . apprehensive
    (D) informative . . colloquial
    (E) pompous . . flippant

STOP

If you finish before time is called, you may check your work on this section only.
Do not turn to any other section in the test.

SECTION 2
Time–25 minutes
25 Questions

Directions: For each question in this section, select the best answer from among the choices given and fill in the corresponding circle on the answer sheet.

Each sentence below has one or two blanks, each blank indicating that something has been omitted. Beneath the sentence are five words or sets of words labeled A through E. Choose the word or set of words that, when inserted in the sentence, <u>best</u> fits the meaning of the sentence as a whole.

Example:

Jimmy opened his gas station in the ------- because he wanted to be in the middle of a metropolis.

(A) country
(B) suburbs
(C) periphery
(D) environment
(E) city

1. Although even ------- accept the role of genetics in determining personality characteristics, the mechanism by which genes cause the occurrence of such phenomena as eye color remains ------- even to scientists.

    (A) behaviorists . . factual
    (B) laymen . . inscrutable
    (C) polemicists . . questionable
    (D) intellectuals . . enigmatic
    (E) researchers . . irrefutable

2. Departing sharply from her frenetic and wild behavior on the basketball court, Kayla was much more ------- in person than I had expected.

    (A) composed   (B) frenzied   (C) contrite
        (D) unpredictable   (E) respectful

3. By taking necessary risks, the producers created a truly ------- television show, rather than the cautious and ------- program that many viewers were expecting.

    (A) uninspired . . superlative
    (B) exceptional . . lackluster
    (C) precarious . . extemporaneous
    (D) prosaic . . featureless
    (E) popular . . ingenious

4. Jeff Koons is esteemed by some as a sculptor and painter of remarkable -------, but I value him primarily as a satirist who ------- stale artistic conventions.

    (A) cogency . . appreciates
    (B) ostentation . . lampoons
    (C) panache . . exults
    (D) finesse . . flouts
    (E) cynicism . . derides

5. Surprisingly, the musical overture from the amateur senior citizen chorus was so ------- that even a national newspaper provided coverage of the performance.

    (A) soporific   (B) cacophonous
        (C) syncopated   (D) impeccable
            (E) acquiescent

GO ON TO THE NEXT PAGE

2   2   2   Unauthorized copying or
reuse of any part of this
page is illegal.   2   2   2

The passages below are followed by questions based on their content; questions following a pair of related passages may also be based on the relationship between the paired passages. Answer the questions on the basis of what is <u>stated</u> or <u>implied</u> in the passages and in any introductory material that may be provided.

Questions 6-9 are based on the following passages.

Passage 1

The writing of art history and the writing of criticism melded as never before in the early years of the twentieth century. Before, it had been fashionable
Line for philosophers to dabble in art criticism, as Denis
5   Diderot did in the late eighteenth century; it had also been common for art critics to tinge their tracts and essays with philosophical theory, as nineteenth-century writers such as John Ruskin and Charles Baudelaire did. Yet it was a historian of the modernist
10 era, Clement Greenberg, who truly brought these two disciplines together. Greenberg and his followers applied the same deft precision to classic philosophical distinctions that they applied to the canvases of Picasso and Matisse. And in so doing, they forever changed the
15 way we think about art.

Passage 2

No educated reader will deny that Clement Greenberg was a critic of real talent. The same praises, however, cannot be applied to Greenberg's disciples. Take the strange, sad case of Michael
20 Fried, a prominent art historian and a thorough "Greenbergian." Every piece of writing Fried has produced, at least from the 1980s on, is a garish mixture of over-precise description and pseudo-philosophical abstraction. The truth is that Greenberg
25 was a one-man movement, an art historian so idiosyncratic that his followers were doomed to be little more than Greenberg parodies. As they say, vinegar is the son of wine.

6. The authors of both passages consider Clement Greenberg to be

    (A) responsible for present-day art criticism disputes
    (B) revolutionary in combining philosophy and art criticism
    (C) integral to shaping current views of art history
    (D) limited in his influence by the failures of his disciples
    (E) vindicated by those who subscribed to his methods

7. The author of Passage 1 would most likely respond to the idea that Greenberg was a "one-man movement" (line 25, Passage 2) with

    (A) dissent, since Greenberg's followers aptly promulgated his practices
    (B) contention, because those inspired by Greenberg improved art evaluation
    (C) agreement, since Greenberg was atypical of the traditional art critic
    (D) indifference, because Michael Fried is comparable to Clement Greenberg
    (E) ambivalence, since Greenberg and his followers were equally influential

8. Unlike the author of Passage 1, the author of Passage 2 makes use of

    (A) direct citation
    (B) a poverbial statement
    (C) personal voice
    (D) an abstract speculation
    (E) extended analogy

9. The author of Passage 2 would most likely regard the statement "Greenberg and . . . Matisse" (lines 11-14) as

    (A) factually indisputable
    (B) unusually myopic
    (C) woefully vacuous
    (D) greatly misinformed
    (E) unduly laudatory

GO ON TO THE NEXT PAGE

Questions 10-16 are based on the following passage.

What are the best conditions for a given animal, once it has been removed from its natural habitat? In the following passage, a professor of biology considers how animals react to the conditions they encounter in captivity.

It is an utterly complicated feat to replicate an animal's natural habitat, whether that of a domesticated pet in the home, an exotic animal in the pet store,
Line or a wild beast in the zoo. Beyond providing the
5 basic necessities of food and water, there are other factors that must be considered: preventing mineral deficiencies, housing animals in social settings appropriate to their natures, regulating and controlling psychological or physiological behaviors, and more. A
10 simple oversight in something that we humans would never commonly consider, an addition or change that would not affect us in the least, can drastically affect the quality of life for an animal.

In one instance involving a prairie dog at a
15 rehabilitation center, the mere presence of an extra fluorescent light bulb instigated considerable weight gain for the animal. The surplus heat emanating from the lighting fixture caused the rodent to become sluggish and inert, thus decreasing its physical activity.
20 A neighboring cage that housed another prairie dog only had one bulb, which was enough to provide light without drastically altering the immediate environment. This second animal did not suffer from heat exhaustion and therefore maintained a healthy
25 weight. Both rodents were provided with the same diet; the sole factor contributing to this anomaly was the disorientation and stress induced by the extra bulb.

To take another case, young piglets raised on concrete floors in hog farms develop iron deficiencies
30 and then anemia, primarily because these animals normally absorb minerals from soil. While farmers prefer the cement flooring because it facilitates cleanup and good sanitation, concrete-based housing blocks the animals from exposure to a necessary component
35 of their biological makeup. To compensate for this, swine managers will supplement pigs' diets with iron injections in successive treatments. Whether the cost of the injections offsets the potential health risks to the livestock is a cause of contention between swineherds
40 and veterinarians.

Similarly, at Kruger National Park in South Africa, a reserve spanning 19,633 square kilometers, a wide assortment of animals is kept in recreated biomes; however, the problem remains that not all species
45 require the same living conditions. The elephant and the lion will keep watchful eyes on each other without much interference. But a hyena population residing too close to a pride of lions may be thrown into a state of anxiety and fury. Caimans need hydration from bodies
50 of water, cheetahs hunt in the arid expanse of the

Savannah, and Cape Buffalo require lush vegetation to eat—all to mimic their natural habitats. Not only are such different habitats expensive to create, but such measures necessitate remarkable man-power, time, and
55 energy.

Controlled fires are periodic occurrences at the park and are meant to replicate the phenomenon of lightning striking the plain. The electrical energy found in lightning can separate out the nitrogen atoms
60 in the atmosphere, and these atoms will then fall to the earth and combine with nitrates in the soil. This organic fertilization process helps to rejuvenate the land, promoting succulent plant growth for herbivores and recreating processes that occur in the wild at the
65 park. Thus, the park rangers can maintain the innate equilibrium between plant and animal life.

10. The author of the passage assumes that a good environment for a captive animal must

(A) faithfully recreate the animal's indigenous habitat
(B) meet criteria established by trained veterinarians
(C) foster improved social habits in different species
(D) entail thorough planning and exorbitant expenses
(E) dramatically improve an animal's quality of life

11. The inclusion of the phrase "whether that . . . zoo" in lines 2-4 primarily serves to

(A) distinguish levels of difficulty in re-creating natural habitats
(B) introduce an extended comparison
(C) condemn modern forms of animal captivity
(D) highlight an issue that has not been resolved
(E) emphasize the broad applicability of a claim

12. The phrase in lines 15-17 ("the mere . . . animal") conveys the relationship between

(A) a human intervention and an animal's means of adaptation
(B) an altruistic intention and a detrimental consequence
(C) a well-advised adjustment and an unexpected deviation
(D) a use of technology and a pervasive biological problem
(E) a minor oversight and a conspicuous ramification

GO ON TO THE NEXT PAGE

Practice Test 7

13. "This anomaly" in line 26 refers to

    (A) inevitable disorientation
    (B) an extra light source
    (C) unexpected weight gain
    (D) the close placement of two animals
    (E) a lack of basic nutrients

14. The author presents "a prairie dog" (line 14) and "young piglets" (line 28) as animals that

    (A) would coexist poorly in the wild
    (B) are vulnerable to slight changes in their habitats
    (C) have been harmed by cost-efficient habitats
    (D) have widely misunderstood nutritional needs
    (E) have received special attention from habitat ecologists

15. The hyena population's "anxiety and fury" (line 49) would be most likely caused by

    (A) abnormal proximity to another species
    (B) psychological resistance to domestication
    (C) increased competition for resources
    (D) the unavailability of natural prey
    (E) the desire to confront a natural predator

16. The author's description of the Kruger National Park suggests that creating a healthy space for animals is

    (A) dangerous
    (B) rewarding
    (C) confusing
    (D) demanding
    (E) tentative

GO ON TO THE NEXT PAGE

2   2   2   Unauthorized copying or
reuse of any part of this
page is illegal.   2   2   2

Questions 17-25 are based on the following passage.

In this passage, adapted from an essay on international relations, the author discusses the Duke of Wellington and his unique approach to social, political, and military events.

When asked to reveal the details of the battle of Waterloo in 1815, the Duke of Wellington replied, "The history of a battle is not unlike the history of
Line a ball . . . no individual can recollect the order in
5 which [the individual events] occurred." No one perhaps could be more certain of the truth of that statement than the Duke himself. On the fifteenth evening of June 1815, the night before the Battle of Waterloo, he was the guest of honor at a ball given
10 by the Duchess of Richmond in Brussels, just a short distance from the fields that witnessed the final overthrow of Napoleon Bonaparte. The juxtaposition of that evening of revelry and the ensuing days of bloody maneuvers and relentless battle has fascinated
15 historians. No doubt, the Duchess of Richmond would have been flattered by the accounts of her opulence that appeared in the journals of the time. In addition, that social occasion soon became the subject of a poem by Lord Byron (albeit not a very
20 good one). Later, scenes of the ball were used in several historical novels, not the least of which were Tolstoy's *War and Peace* and Thackeray's *Vanity Fair*. The apparent sangfroid displayed by the Duke at the ball, a nonchalance that has been sharply
25 contrasted with the dogged intensity of Napoleon's advance against the Grand Alliance, is both thrilling history and the stuff of legend.

Actually, much of what the general public accepts as the truth about Waterloo is little more than
30 legend or hearsay. Napoleon's approach caught the Grand Alliance off guard, separating the Russian and Austrian forces. On receiving the dire news during the Duchess's ball, Wellington admitted, "Napoleon has humbugged me, by God. He has gained twenty
35 four hours' march on me." Or so it is alleged. Famously, the Duke scanned a map of the area and pointed at the small village of Quatre Bras, where he had intended to halt Napoleon's advance, remarking, "We shall not stop him here; and so, I must fight him
40 here," as his finger stabbed the name "Waterloo." However, after the battle, Wellington claimed that he had always intended to meet the French on the fields of Waterloo: he had supposedly made that decision two days before the ball.

45 Even the details of the ball have become romanticized over the years. Instead of an elegant affair in the spacious rooms of a splendid townhouse on one of those tree-lined avenues we associate with European cities, the event was actually held in a small
50 coach house behind the Duke of Richmond's rented mansion in Brussels, an outlying structure with a low-lying, insignificant entrance. This building with, one may assume, few windows, had been papered for the occasion with a pattern of roses climbing a
55 trellis. There was sufficient room for a supper table at which guests could be seated and for highland reels performed by the Gordon Highlanders—or so a letter from a young girl who attended informs us. Less cheerfully, this young woman also reported
60 that rumors ran rampant among the guests, as one might expect with so many urgent messages arriving in search of the Duke. Another guest's letter tells us that officers, in evening dress, were being dispatched immediately to their regiments. Some younger
65 attendees attempted to dance, but many of those invited hurried away to watch the troops marching through the streets, either to reach the front line or to hastily withdraw from Brussels.

Whatever the true details may be, the events
70 of the Duchess of Richmond's ball and the battle of Waterloo are inextricably linked in the public's conception of that turning point in European history. They define something essential in the attitudes assumed by the English and the French
75 at that historical juncture. On one side charged the impetuous, desperate, Romantic passion of French idealism, embodied in Napoleon himself; on the other side stood the equanimity of the English, self-assured and aloof, led by the seemingly unworried
80 Duke of Wellington, treating the battle as if it were merely another item on his social calendar. Only after Napoleon's defeat did he admit, "It has been the nearest run thing you ever saw in your life." The attitude of Wellington—and of the Duchess
85 of Richmond—defined a very English approach to serious events: it is not foolishness to dance in the face of death, but a defiance of death and an awareness of the joy of life.

17. The primary purpose of the passage is to

(A) shed light on pivotal events that shaped England and France in the early decades of the nineteenth century
(B) point out the similarities and discrepancies between French and English battle tactics
(C) ruminate on the atmosphere of the ball thrown by the Duchess of Richmond for the Duke of Wellington
(D) deprecate the tactical stratagems utilized by Napoleon Bonaparte in his attempts to succeed in battle
(E) create doubt in the minds of readers as to the validity of various accounts of a major military campaign

GO ON TO THE NEXT PAGE

Practice Test 7

18. The "juxtaposition" referred to in line 12 is that of

(A) the nonchalance of the English soldiers and the passion of the French people
(B) the somber attitude of the Duke of Wellington and the ebullience of the Duchess of Richmond
(C) the jubilance of a social gathering and the struggle involved in a historical event
(D) the unswerving tenacity of Napoleon Bonaparte and the cavalier disposition of the Duke of Wellington
(E) the evanescence of social diversions and the finality of war

19. It can be inferred from lines 15-17 ("No doubt . . . time") that the "reports in the journals" depicted the

(A) Duke of Wellington as aggressive and intrepid
(B) presence of Lord Byron at the Duchess's Ball
(C) English as overly sentimental and effusive
(D) Duchess's ball as an event that facilitated a new alliance among Napoleon's enemies
(E) Duchess of Richmond as a munificent host

20. In lines 22-23, the author mentions *War and Peace* and *Vanity Fair* primarily to illustrate the

(A) contrast between the life of Tolstoy and that of Thackeray
(B) interest surrounding the ball and how this event has reverberated throughout history
(C) propensity of nineteenth century authors to perform intensive historical research
(D) creative genius behind the literature of the nineteenth century
(E) ability of historical events to influence the values espoused by major authors

21. The words "Actually" (line 28) and "Famously" (line 36) are used to distinguish between

(A) Wellington's strategic prowess and Napoleon's tactical swiftness
(B) the public persona of a historical figure and and the virtues he exhibited in private
(C) the validated historical record and the alluring yet misleading accounts of a pivotal event
(D) a rash military decision and a well-considered battle plan
(E) the celebration of a national hero and the vilification of his nemesis

22. In context, the word "romanticized" (line 46) most nearly means

(A) enamored
(B) popularized
(C) exaggerated
(D) ornamented
(E) immortalized

23. The various accounts making up the description of the ball in the third paragraph were compiled from

(A) anecdotal musings recorded long after the ball itself
(B) letters recovered from the Duchess of Richmond's private collection
(C) news reports chronicling the activities of social luminaries
(D) literature generated by popular nineteenth-century essayists
(E) the correspondences of those who were present at the social event

24. In the last paragraph, the attitudes of the French and the English, respectively, can best be summarized as

(A) ardently pertinacious and confidently levelheaded
(B) subtly optimistic and dangerously zealous
(C) discerningly shrewd and understandably enervated
(D) understatedly gracious and unflappably stolid
(E) ostensibly creative and unthinkingly complacent

25. The passage as a whole suggests that the Duke of Wellington can best be described as

(A) sycophantic
(B) flustered
(C) refractory
(D) composed
(E) cynical

STOP

If you finish before time is called, you may check your work on this section only.
Do not turn to any other section in the test.

SECTION 3
Time–20 minutes
18 Questions

Directions: For each question in this section, select the best answer from among the choices given and fill in the corresponding circle on the answer sheet.

Each sentence below has one or two blanks, each blank indicating that something has been omitted. Beneath the sentence are five words or sets of words labeled A through E. Choose the word or set of words that, when inserted in the sentence, <u>best</u> fits the meaning of the sentence as a whole.

Example:

Jimmy opened his gas station in the ------- because he wanted to be in the middle of a metropolis.

(A) country
(B) suburbs
(C) periphery
(D) environment
(E) city

---

1. After an initially ------- start, the football team surprised its fans by winning a series of pivotal games.

   (A) inherent   (B) uncompromising
       (C) felicitous   (D) inauspicious
         (E) protracted

2. Sustainable architecture focuses on ------- approaches to environmental conservation in building design, ensuring that our actions today do not ------- the living conditions of future generations.

   (A) innovative . . bolster
   (B) haphazard . . limit
   (C) conscientious . . damage
   (D) expensive . . diminish
   (E) standard . . enhance

3. Raj never has been able to ------- playing board games with his family after dinner, but his wife Jemima always loves an opportunity to ------- her winning strategies.

   (A) resist . . utilize
   (B) endure . . conceal
   (C) tolerate . . display
   (D) decline . . demonstrate
   (E) surrender . . yield

4. Dominic's propensity to wear outrageous fashions, such as argyle socks in bright colors, was not ------- by the more conservatively-dressed employees.

   (A) endorsed   (B) confuted   (C) harangued
       (D) rejected   (E) misconstrued

5. Herbal tea can be an excellent ------- for a severe headache, even though this beverage may not ------- the pain entirely.

   (A) cure . . remove
   (B) antidote . . exacerbate
   (C) remedy . . prognosticate
   (D) complement . . lessen
   (E) palliative . . eliminate

6. It took a few minutes before she realized that the student's ostensibly cooperative and approving comments were actually ------- in intent.

   (A) dilatory   (B) inquisitive   (C) obscure
       (D) subversive   (E) praiseworthy

Practice Test 7

The passage below is followed by questions based on its content. Answer the questions on the basis of what is <u>stated</u> or <u>implied</u> in the passage and in any introductory material that may be provided.

Questions 7-18 are based on the following passage.

In this passage, the author recounts the changes that were occurring in 1960s Britain and relates his experiences during that tumultuous age.

Someone once said, "If you can remember the sixties, then you weren't there." This may be a flippant remark, of course, but it does help to
Line perpetuate the clichés of flower power, Beatle-mania,
5 and free love. For those people who regard the sixties as a piece of history, this quote conjures up a spurious picture of what it was really like to be young at the time. I was there, and I remember the period very differently.
10   In 1960, I had my twentieth birthday. Legally, I was still a child: in those days, one was not regarded as an adult by society until one reached twenty-one. In the UK, at eighteen I could buy cigarettes and I could join the army (compulsory conscription,
15 a legacy of the Second World War, had only been abolished that very year), yet I could not buy alcohol or vote for the government that would send me to war. I could go to the cinema and watch any kind of film, but education on intimate relationships was
20 regarded as one of the duties of a parent, not as something that I would be introduced to at school. And my parents, much like many other parents, omitted that part of their responsibility. My parents were also living apart: divorce was a much more
25 complicated and expensive process than it is today. My mother was a teacher; my father was working in a pharmacy. My father earned in a week what my mother earned in a month, since equal pay did not exist. Although my parents would have to pay my
30 university tuition and lodging expenses, I guess I was lucky to have the chance to obtain a university education: fewer than 2% of high school graduates went on to universities in those days.
       At the time, I did not feel particularly lucky
35 to have earned a place at Birmingham University in Central England. I traveled down there from the North of England for an interview and had been unnerved, not excited, by what I had glimpsed of Birmingham: the city's center was chaotic, for it was
40 being redesigned and rebuilt, finally, fifteen years after the war, and dust and scaffolding and cranes and Irish accents were everywhere. While I could take that much in, I had been surprised when I got on the bus that would take me to the university to find that
45 the conductor was an affable Jamaican woman: I had never encountered anyone who wasn't born and bred in Yorkshire before. I was even more unsettled when she opened her mouth and spoke to me in the distinct accent, not of Kingston, Jamaica, but of Acock's
50 Green, Birmingham. I really was not sure that I was ready to be launched into this new world that was so completely different from what I thought England was like.
       Certainly, in retrospect, the sixties do seem to
55 have been the time when everything we had been used to was galvanized into new ways of living. Equally certain is the idea that the changes people today make such a fuss about were not the changes that were actually influential. People today have no
60 concept of how isolated each part of the UK was before the sixties, before there were motorways, high-speed trains, and inexpensive air travel. In 1960, there were only two television channels in the country. Neither channel began broadcasting before
65 the afternoon, and both closed at midnight at the latest. Above all, the channels of communication— television, radio, and print—were satellites of the government.
       With the benefit of hindsight, we can see that
70 there had been rumbles of discontent before 1960, of course. The warfare in Europe was long over, and people noticed that things in the UK were not developing as they were in evolving countries such as Germany, for example. That did not seem
75 right. As a teenager, I had wondered why only American films were ever in Technicolor. That did not seem right. There was also a radio channel called Radio Luxembourg, which was not really allowed for broadcast in the UK, and the DJs on
80 there were playing some pretty exciting stuff called Rock 'n' Roll, which was not often heard on the government-run BBC. That did not seem right. Most representative of the times was a show that opened in London's West End in February 1960, a
85 show that had not been scripted and rehearsed in the usual manner: this production had been improvised through rehearsals by the actors and musicians. It was called *Fings Ain't Wot They Used To Be*, and it was a smash hit.
90   The old ways of doing things were being challenged one-by-one, and an era of novelty and excitement had arisen.

GO ON TO THE NEXT PAGE

7. The author's primary purpose in writing this passage is to

   (A) reminisce about his spiritual growth during the 1960s
   (B) explain how the changes of the 1960s were not as critical as many commentators believe
   (C) survey the political, economic, and social upheaval in 1960s Britain
   (D) compare the changes in 1960s Britain and the 1950s United States
   (E) present experiences of obscure social changes in 1960s Britain

8. The author criticizes the "flippant remark" (line 3) in the first paragraph for

   (A) propagating a superficial understanding of the social impact of an era
   (B) providing an improbable reason for individual amnesia
   (C) condemning a group of people who lack sufficient background knowledge
   (D) misrepresenting the political issues that re-shaped society from the periphery
   (E) offending the hardworking middle class that stabilized a chaotic time

9. The author's description in lines 10-21 ("In 1960 . . . school") serves to

   (A) prove that laws related to age were much too permissive
   (B) show the positive and negative realities of 1960s British society
   (C) highlight the opportunities and limitations faced by young people in the 1960s
   (D) imply that parents were unhappy with the moral education of their children
   (E) deride compulsory conscription and other legacies of the Second World War

10. According to the description of the city, the author felt "unnerved, not excited" (line 38) because

   (A) he had wanted to attend a university in northern England instead
   (B) he was scared of the construction machinery and other new technologies
   (C) he witnessed chaos and diversity of a type he had never seen before
   (D) he would owe his parents money for his college tuition
   (E) he was intimidated and upset by the interviewers at Birmingham University

11. The author's experience on the bus in lines 42-50 ("While I . . . Birmingham") suggests that the most surprising aspect of Birmingham was its

   (A) diversity
   (B) elitism
   (C) transportation
   (D) architecture
   (E) comfort

12. The statements in lines 54-59 ("Certainly, in . . . influential") suggest that the author most likely believes that people today

   (A) ignore the changes in the decades leading up to the 1960s
   (B) realize the social impact of the profound changes of the 1960s
   (C) forget the violence and political upheaval of the 1960s
   (D) focus too heavily on unimportant changes from the 1960s
   (E) romanticize the gritty reality of the chaotic 1960s

13. The author suggests that Britain became less "isolated" (line 60) in part because of

   (A) an increase in trade with other nations
   (B) the need to travel in order to relieve boredom
   (C) advances in transportation technology
   (D) a social uprising against segregation
   (E) the larger variety of consumer goods shown on television

14. The statement "Above all . . . government" (lines 66-68) implies that the government

   (A) maintained control of the media
   (B) aided a popular movement for change
   (C) protected the privacy of its officials
   (D) lauded the increasing influence of television
   (E) controlled international communication fiercely

GO ON TO THE NEXT PAGE

15. The statement in lines 69-71 ("With the . . . course") suggests which of the following about the people of 1960s Britain?

(A) They should have acknowledged the unhappiness of their fellow countrymen earlier.
(B) They were unhappy with the state of affairs before change was demanded.
(C) They were staunchly opposed to many of the changes that would take effect.
(D) After the war, they did not think change was happening as quickly as in the US.
(E) They shouldn't have allowed some of the changes to take hold permanently.

16. The author most likely repeats the statement "That did not seem right" in the fifth paragraph (lines 69-89) in order to

(A) emphasize the dissatisfactions that catalyzed social change
(B) contrast personal experiences with national policies
(C) compare contemporary trends in international cinema
(D) express disgust for the decade's political changes
(E) endorse an opinion that was once unpopular

17. In relation to the passage as a whole, the author most likely believes that the play mentioned in the fifth paragraph was a "smash hit" (line 89) because its actors and musicians

(A) mocked conservative media personalities to great effect
(B) used shocking costumes to draw attention to social injustices
(C) refused to remain bound by contemporary conventions
(D) presented a coherent argument for ending traditional media practices
(E) reflected personal hopes and dreams for the next several decades

18. In context of the passage as a whole, lines 90-92 ("The old . . . arisen") indicate the author's belief that

(A) a large number of individual changes in perspective can lead to political and social changes across a nation
(B) governments consistently push social reforms that the public is reluctant to accept due to isolation
(C) traditions are essential for maintaining a culture, but younger generations inevitably fight against their elders
(D) technological advances in transportation and communication amplify social unrest and the desire for change
(E) no one who was alive in the 1960s expected any changes to society based on the experience of earlier decades

STOP

If you finish before time is called, you may check your work on this section only.
Do not turn to any other section in the test.

POST TEST ANALYSIS

This post test analysis is important if you want to see an improvement on your next test. Each section has a set of possible reasons for errors. Place check marks next to the ones that pertain to you, and write your own on the blank lines provided. Use this form to better analyze your performance. **If you don't understand why you made errors, there is no way you can correct them!**

1. **SENTENCE COMPLETION:**

   Problems with the sentence:
   - ❑ Wasn't familiar with phrases, idioms, or words in the sentence
   - ❑ Missed the clues or tones
   - ❑ Put your OWN word in the blank rather than one from the sentence
   - ❑ Completely avoided marking
   - ❑ Other: _____

   _____

   Problems with the answers:
   - ❑ Did not use process of elimination
   - ❑ Did not ignore unknown words
   - ❑ Did not use prefix/root/suffix knowledge to figure out the meaning of the unknown words
   - ❑ Did not match the clues and tones of the answer with those of the sentence
   - ❑ Did not recognize vocabulary words
   - ❑ Did not check answer to see if it fit
   - ❑ Other: _____

   _____

   Leaving questions unanswered:
   - ❑ Did not try
   - ❑ Did not fill in the blank(s) with words
   - ❑ Ran out of time
   - ❑ Other: _____

   _____

2. **SHORT READING COMPREHENSION:**
   - ❑ Did not read entire paragraph
   - ❑ Did not see more than one point
   - ❑ Missed contrast clues
   - ❑ Did not pinpoint thesis
   - ❑ Did not identify similarities and differences in Double Short Reading Comp
   - ❑ Other: _____

   _____

3. **LONG READING COMPREHENSION:**
   - ❑ Did not understand the question, line reference, or answers
   - ❑ Spent too much time reading the passages
   - ❑ Did not underline the line reference
   - ❑ Read too much or too little
   - ❑ Did not answer the specific question; instead analyzed its main idea
   - ❑ Did not do process of elimination based on facts in the passage
   - ❑ Couldn't find the false words
   - ❑ Couldn't choose between two possible answers
   - ❑ Did not use tone to help eliminate answers
   - ❑ When stuck at 2 guessed instead of pulling additional fact
   - ❑ Couldn't finish in time
   - ❑ Other: _____

   _____

ANSWER KEY

TEST 7

SECTION 1

#	Answer	LEVEL
1	A	(1)
2	D	(2)
3	E	(3)
4	E	(3)
5	B	(3)
6	D	(4)
7	B	(5)
8	C	(5)
9	C	(2)
10	E	(3)
11	E	(2)
12	B	(2)
13	A	(3)
14	B	(3)
15	B	(1)
16	D	(3)
17	A	(3)
18	C	(5)
19	D	(5)
20	E	(3)
21	C	(3)
22	D	(5)
23	C	(3)
24	D	(3)

SECTION 2

#	Answer	LEVEL
1	B	(2)
2	A	(1)
3	B	(3)
4	D	(4)
5	D	(5)
6	C	(3)
7	A	(5)
8	B	(3)
9	E	(2)
10	A	(1)
11	E	(3)
12	E	(5)
13	C	(3)
14	B	(2)
15	A	(2)
16	C	(2)
17	A	(1)
18	C	(3)
19	E	(2)
20	B	(5)
21	C	(5)
22	C	(2)
23	E	(3)
24	A	(3)
25	D	(4)

SECTION 3

#	Answer	LEVEL
1	D	(3)
2	C	(2)
3	C	(1)
4	A	(3)
5	E	(4)
6	D	(5)
7	C	(2)
8	A	(2)
9	C	(2)
10	C	(1)
11	A	(2)
12	D	(3)
13	C	(3)
14	A	(4)
15	B	(4)
16	A	(3)
17	C	(4)
18	A	(5)

Difficulty levels range from 1 - 5 with 1 being the easiest and 5 being the hardest.
For answer explanations please visit www.ies2400.com/criticalreading

PRACTICE TEST 8

1   1   1   1   1   1
Unauthorized copying or
reuse of any part of this
page is illegal.

Practice Test 8

SECTION 1
Time–25 minutes
24 Questions

Directions: For each question in this section, select the best answer from among the choices given and fill in the corresponding circle on the answer sheet.

Each sentence below has one or two blanks, each blank indicating that something has been omitted. Beneath the sentence are five words or sets of words labeled A through E. Choose the word or set of words that, when inserted in the sentence, <u>best</u> fits the meaning of the sentence as a whole.

Example:

Jimmy opened his gas station in the ------- because he wanted to be in the middle of a metropolis.

(A) country
(B) suburbs
(C) periphery
(D) environment
(E) city

---

1. As a member of the judging panel, Lenny is hardly -------: one of the contestants is his very own daughter.

    (A) impartial   (B) biased   (C) problematic
        (D) unqualified   (E) subjective

2. Despite the ------- façade of the recently refurbished train station, the materials used for the interior are ------- the historic origin of the building.

    (A) tasteful . . reflective of
    (B) quaint . . consistent with
    (C) new . . at odds with
    (D) garish . . loyal to
    (E) modern . . faithful to

3. In class, James proved to be a truly ------- poet: other students attempted to replicate his superlative rhymes, but none succeeded.

    (A) controversial   (B) complacent   (C) prolific
        (D) consummate   (E) inept

4. The most recent BMW roadster is -------for its precisely engineered systems, a ------- that can be credited with this vehicle's wide commercial appeal.

    (A) acclaimed . . superfluity
    (B) derided . . feature
    (C) celebrated . . flaw
    (D) coveted . . trait
    (E) romanticized . . characteristic

5. In an environment harshly critical of high-profile egoism, author Claudine Campbel's decision to shun the public spotlight was dictated more by ------- than by -------.

    (A) humility . . vanity
    (B) conceit . . practicality
    (C) contempt . . sentimentality
    (D) apprehension . . confidence
    (E) pragmatism . . modesty

6. Using historical data, mathematical models allow companies to ------- future revenues with a certain amount of accuracy, yet these forecasting programs cannot effectively account for an unexpected yet desirable -------.

    (A) calculate . . hindrance
    (B) predict . . windfall
    (C) estimate . . anticipation
    (D) glean . . profit
    (E) thwart . . production

7. The World Health Organization warned of an impending calamity: the recent outbreak of malaria in West Africa ------- a worldwide epidemic.

    (A) stymies   (B) conceals   (C) heralds
        (D) circumvents   (E) simulates

8. Mary is considered a worker of great -------: even under pressure, she remains extremely detail-oriented while maintaining an air of ease.

    (A) aplomb   (B) austerity   (C) pretension
        (D) omniscience   (E) panache

GO ON TO THE NEXT PAGE

1   1   1   Unauthorized copying or   1   1   1
                         reuse of any part of this
                         page is illegal.

The passages below are followed by questions based on their content; questions following a pair of related passages may also be based on the relationship between the paired passages. Answer the questions on the basis of what is <u>stated</u> or <u>implied</u> in the passages and in any introductory material that may be provided.

Questions 9-12 are based on the following passages.

Passage 1

    "Theatre" often refers to the conventions of Western-culture performance, taking the techniques developed by the Greeks as points of origin.
Line Eventually, these techniques permeated other Western
5 cultures that developed their own types of theatre. The Italians had the Commedia Del'Arte and the British became famous for the Elizabethan tragedy and comedy exemplified by Shakespeare. Over time, the constructs of Western theatre would become the rubric
10 for contemporary performance both on stage and on screen. In fact, the premises for most film storylines start with Aristotle's *Poetics*, one of the earliest works on dramatic theory; whether they know it or not, popular filmmakers owe gigantic debts to this Greek
15 philosopher's ideas on character, pacing, and conflict.

Passage 2

    To most, familiarity with "theatre" means familiarity with playwrights such as Shakespeare, Arthur Miller, and maybe David Mamet or Harold Pinter. Most would not consider or think of Eastern
20 theatrical conventions such as kabuki, the Beijing Opera, or Sanskrit Drama when questioned about the proverbial stage. And why is this so? Western hegemony has pervaded most conventional understandings of art in general. Unfortunately, this
25 means that Eastern dramatic theories and practices are cast to the wayside—often belittled for departing from "standard" theatrical criteria and almost always relegated to the position of theatre that "celebrates culture," when in reality the theatre of the East has
30 often guided the theatre of the West.

9.   The author of Passage 2 would most likely describe Passage 1 as

    (A) subversive
    (B) reserved
    (C) provincial
    (D) condescending
    (E) divisive

10. In Passage 1, Aristotle's *Poetics* is mentioned as a work of writing that

    (A) is alluded to regularly by accomplished classical dramatists
    (B) was instrumental in defining Western theatrical conventions
    (C) helped Western theatre to overshadow other types of playwriting
    (D) was studied by both Italian and Elizabethan writers
    (E) was designed to exert an influence across different media

11. The author of Passage 2 uses quotation marks in order to

    (A) indicate that published commentary is being referenced
    (B) imply that traditional definitions are waning in popularity
    (C) emphasize ideas that readers have trouble comprehending
    (D) call into question the aptness of particular terms
    (E) identify theatrical jargon that relates to the passage's argument

12. Compared to that of Passage 1, the tone of Passage 2 is more

    (A) libelous
    (B) impartial
    (C) ambivalent
    (D) meticulous
    (E) critical

GO ON TO THE NEXT PAGE

1   1   1   Unauthorized copying or
reuse of any part of this
page is illegal.   1   1   1

Practice Test 8

Questions 13-24 are based on the following passage.

This passage is adapted from an essay written in 2013 about humans and the relationship they establish with nature through gardening.

"God Almighty first planted a garden, and, indeed, it is the greatest of human pleasures" wrote Francis Bacon in his *Essays*. Very few of us would
Line choose to disagree with him. Whether we live in
5 stately homes with landscaped views or in small cottages with tiny pockets of land before them or, indeed, in apartments where we have to make do with a couple of window boxes, it seems that it is endemic to human nature to attempt to create a patch
10 of nature which expresses our feelings towards the fertile earth. Real aficionados spend hours consulting gardening catalogs, planning layouts for what are referred to as "outside rooms," creating areas for "mass planting," considering the values of sheltered
15 arbors, establishing which areas are to be made into shaded walks and which left open to the sun, or pondering the necessity of a water fountain. Mention a particular plant to these connoisseurs and they will immediately refer to it by its Latin name, recount the
20 variations of the original plant now available, discuss its soil needs and positioning, explain what care and tending it requires, and determine when it needs to be pruned and tamed.

For me, the best thing about gardening is that
25 you really do not need to have any specialized knowledge or experience to do it—although, admittedly, if you do have either of these two qualities, you can cut down on the mistakes that come from old-fashioned trial and error. When I lived in
30 Africa, I had a small garden and a gardener named Kennedy. He never knew the name of any plant that he put into the ground. If I asked Kennedy what he was planting, he would reply with a shrug, "It is red (or yellow, or blue, as the case might be)." He was
35 always right. No doubt, more professional gardeners would be shocked by so nonchalant an approach to nomenclature, but I always thought that Kennedy had the correct view of what a garden was all about. Color and contrast, light and shade: these are the
40 things that pass though the eye of the beholder and bring quiet contentment to his soul.

Of course, gardens began with a much more practical intention. The original English Cottage garden, which we admire today for its charm, calm,
45 and cheerfulness, was actually more like a medieval pharmacy. The leaves and flowers of the various plants were used, as antidotes and antiseptics, to ease physical and mental pain. Herbs were grown in the garden to add flavor and taste to meals. Fruits
50 provided essential vitamins to the body—not only the blackberry, raspberry, and strawberry, but also fruits that are far less seen these days: gooseberries, black,

red, and white currants, and mulberries. A small tree—apple, pear, or hazelnut—was often included.
55 These trees provided the vitamins necessary to keep people energetic and healthy through the winter months. Vegetables too provided natural Vitamin C and antioxidants, both necessary to the body.

Sadly, the vegetable garden nowadays has
60 been superseded by the supermarket: you no longer see the poles of peas that used to flourish in every garden. Freshly plucked peas are a thing of the past, which is a pity. When was the last time you ate a pea that had not been frozen? When I was a child,
65 I sat by my mother on the back doorstep, and she taught me how to pop a pea pod and push the lovely fat, deep-green peas into the colander, so they could be gently cooked. Believe it or not, there was a time when peas had a definite taste.
70 However, the desire to plant a seed and watch it grow and develop leaves and flowers and, perhaps, fruit has not yet disappeared. There is still something magical in the way that what in the winter months was seemingly barren, frozen mud gradually changes
75 into a green haze which grows in strength until, as the spring moves into summer, the ground becomes ablaze with color and scent and populated with insects and bees droning through the long sun-spread afternoons. With the insects come the birds, and
80 the garden's creation reaches completion before the beginning of that slow ripening of fruit and eventual decay that is autumn. Then all recedes into a winter stillness. The sequence is something we recognize and feel in the deepest parts of our souls, for it is a
85 metaphor for human life and a recognition that there is some powerful force with which we have yet to come to grips.

Thus, we rival that creation of the first garden by putting order into our small section of Nature.
90 The big stuff like forests and jungles and mountains and crevasses and rivers and lakes we can leave to Mother Nature. She clearly had a plan for the world. We can only imitate her on a smaller scale, and enjoy that small plot that we can shape.

GO ON TO THE NEXT PAGE

1   1   1   Unauthorized copying or
reuse of any part of this
page is illegal.   1   1   1

13. The primary purpose of this passage is to

(A) contemplate the true value of gardening and
reflect on what gardening means in a broad,
cultural context
(B) explain the natural human affinity for
gardening as a desperate response to the
forces of life and death that are found in
nature
(C) suggest that humans are powerless against
the advance of nature and that gardening is
a way to establish a feeling of security
(D) discuss the idea of the garden as it has
changed from its humble, practical
beginnings into the ostentatious act it is
today
(E) delve into the nostalgic feelings that a
freshly-planted garden can conjure

14. According to the first paragraph, the "real
aficionados" possess a mastery of all of the
following EXCEPT:

(A) soil care
(B) botanical Latin
(C) landscape design
(D) crop rotation
(E) plant strains

15. According to the passage, the "real aficionados"
(line 11) would mostly view "Kennedy"
(line 31) as

(A) pompous
(B) uncultured
(C) academic
(D) well-meaning
(E) illiterate

16. The contrast between the narrator's garden in the
second paragraph and the English Cottage
gardens of the third paragraph, respectively,
is one of

(A) aesthetics vs. pragmatism
(B) education vs. ignorance
(C) interest vs. boredom
(D) beauty vs. erudition
(E) uselessness vs. functionality

17. In line 60, the word "superseded" is closest in
meaning to

(A) collected
(B) passed
(C) replaced
(D) destroyed
(E) transcended

18. The sentence in lines 63-64 ("When was . . .
frozen?") primarily serves to

(A) contradict an earlier assertion
(B) question the reader
(C) highlight an irony
(D) discuss a failure
(E) emphasize a point

19. The sentence in lines 64-68 ("When I . . .
cooked") is notable for its use of

(A) artistic pretense
(B) whimsical reference
(C) cause and effect
(D) hyperbolic language
(E) personal anecdote

20. The word "definite" in line 69 most nearly means

(A) fixed
(B) plain
(C) decided
(D) distinct
(E) established

21. Which statement best summarizes the meaning
of the "metaphor" (line 85) the author presents in
the fifth paragraph?

(A) All things in nature will grow again in the
spring.
(B) All living things experience the cycle of life.
(C) All life comes to an end during winter.
(D) Humans must fight to escape the cold winter.
(E) Humans control the cycle of life.

22. The phrase "powerful force" in line 86 primarily
serves to

(A) exemplify a connection between humans
and nature
(B) suggest that humans are weak and powerless
(C) provide context for the following paragraph
(D) highlight nature's destructive powers
(E) recall an example that was previously
introduced

GO ON TO THE NEXT PAGE

Practice Test 8

23. In line 88, the word "rival" is closest in meaning to

(A) emulate
(B) scorn
(C) evaluate
(D) revere
(E) oppose

24. It can be inferred from the final paragraph that

(A) the creations of humans parallel those of the natural world
(B) humans have been designing natural landscapes for a long time
(C) humanity will always strive to overpower Mother Nature
(D) Mother Nature assiduously plans out each garden
(E) human action cannot ultimately affect forests and mountains

STOP

If you finish before time is called, you may check your work on this section only.
Do not turn to any other section in the test.

SECTION 2
Time–25 minutes
25 Questions

Directions: For each question in this section, select the best answer from among the choices given and fill in the corresponding circle on the answer sheet.

Each sentence below has one or two blanks, each blank indicating that something has been omitted. Beneath the sentence are five words or sets of words labeled A through E. Choose the word or set of words that, when inserted in the sentence, <u>best</u> fits the meaning of the sentence as a whole.

Example:

Jimmy opened his gas station in the ------- because he wanted to be in the middle of a metropolis.

(A) country
(B) suburbs
(C) periphery
(D) environment
(E) city

1. Most writing teachers do not want their students to expound at length about minor points; on the contrary, such instructors prefer essays that are ------- and direct.

    (A) provocative   (B) convoluted
      (C) discursive   (D) comprehensive
        (E) concise

2. Both ------- and -------, the dolphin displays a rare intelligence and a mild temperament that make it perfectly suited for training.

    (A) bright . . elucidating
    (B) clever . . docile
    (C) perspicacious . . contentious
    (D) obtuse . . gentle
    (E) preternatural . . lenient

3. Anastasia felt sure that her speech would be received positively, and indeed, her performance was met with -------.

    (A) insouciance   (B) covetousness
      (C) salutation   (D) abhorrence
        (E) accolades

4. Recent changes have ------- the process of pet licensing: what was once an onerous chore has now become less -------.

    (A) forestalled . . difficult
    (B) eliminated . . streamlined
    (C) improved . . expedient
    (D) facilitated . . arduous
    (E) promulgated . . burdensome

5. Physicists hoping to prove their theories by conducting experiments at the Supercollider Institute were ------- by protracted delays, many of them due to mechanical problems at the ------- facility.

    (A) frustrated . . exemplary
    (B) galvanized . . stressed
    (C) vexed . . beleaguered
    (D) gratified . . standard
    (E) exasperated . . bureaucratic

GO ON TO THE NEXT PAGE

The passages below are followed by questions based on their content. Answer the questions on the basis of what is <u>stated</u> or <u>implied</u> in the passages and in any introductory material that may be provided.

Questions 6-7 are based on the following passage.

Like any normal person, I could not wait to travel to Europe, the faraway land of magic and mystical fables, castles, and languages of love. My itinerary
Line read like the route of a modern-day gypsy—Paris,
5 Venice, Florence and Prague. Unfortunately, all of my expectations were delusions. As I entered each country, I could not help but notice how alike everything looked. Yes, old buildings and castles have different façades, but the differences no longer stand out when
10 the people surrounding these structures are dressed in similar clothing and clutch identical phones. Famed edifices are no longer breathtaking when each one has the kind of gift shop you are likely to find in the United States, or Canada, or probably everywhere in the
15 world.

6. The passage suggests that the author's travels were disappointing because

(A) she was upset by a series of deceptive stereotypes
(B) she could not relate to the other sightseers in Europe
(C) she was unable to differentiate between major tourist sites
(D) she encountered homogeneity in commerce and culture
(E) she was disoriented by the excessive merchandising

7. The author mentions the United States and Canada in order to

(A) imply that cultural exchange has accelerated considerably in the recent past
(B) suggest that specific features in different countries are nearly interchangeable
(C) emphasize the inability of tourists to appreciate diverse cultures
(D) indicate that differences in global architecture are mostly insignificant
(E) hint at future and potentially more desirable travel destinations

Questions 8-9 are based on the following passage.

Anthropologists have long noted that all human cultures possess some level of superstition or magical thinking. Recently, a new theory has attempted to
Line explain the benefits that such seemingly irrational
5 beliefs can yield. Since our brains are finite organs, a bit of magic keeps our attention spans from spreading too thin; a supernatural explanation can provide focus, and comfort. If we were to worry all day about the why and the how of the past and the future, we could
10 never prioritize the present for long enough to survive. Furthermore, now that survival isn't as difficult for all of us, we can seek new explanations of matters that extend beyond the present moment.

8. The primary purpose of the passage is to

(A) advocate the formulation of a new branch of anthropological study
(B) dismiss a method of reasoning that has inspired extended debate
(C) explain a survival mechanism that will soon become outmoded
(D) consider a phenomenon that has been subjected to recent inquiries
(E) urge readers to adopt a new strategy for dealing with dilemmas

9. Which of the following rhetorical devices is used in this passage?

(A) Visual description
(B) Extended analogy
(C) Collective voice
(D) Appeal to emotion
(E) Anthropological jargon

GO ON TO THE NEXT PAGE

Practice Test 8

Questions 10-18 are based on the following passage.

This passage is adapted from a 2013 essay about the terminology that Shakespeare used in his plays.

Shakespeare enjoyed the use of alliterative phrases. One such phrase, "miching mallecho," comes from a scene in *Hamlet* and defines Hamlet's intentions for the traveling players he has invited to
Line
5 perform at Elsinore Castle, his home. To a modern audience, neither of the two words is familiar outside this context, although the first word does still exist in certain dialects. In the North of England, "miching" refers to the stealing of small items, such as fruit
10 from an orchard, without being caught. In Wales, there is the related phrase "playing mwchms." This phrase is used to describe stealing time from school by playing hooky. In neither case is miching regarded as a serious crime: just a minor misdemeanor, nothing
15 more. In all these examples, the word contains a spirit of mockery of the accepted order of society.

The word "mallecho" is no longer used at all. At first glance, it appears to be an imported Continental European word that Shakespeare is using. Scholars
20 have searched for its derivation, and it is fairly clear that there are two root words here, presumably drawn from French or Italian: *mal*, meaning "bad," and *echo*, meaning "repetition" of some kind. It is not known for certain whether the word was actually
25 used in the English vernacular. Some historians have suggested that it may have been picked up from foreign visitors to the English court. Others believe that Shakespeare invented it himself; if the word is read in the context of the scene, it becomes clear that
30 Hamlet himself feels the need to explain the phrase:

"Miching mallecho: it means 'Mischief.'"

This elucidation would not be needed if the phrase were in general use.

Today, the word "mischief" is not regarded
35 very seriously: a mischievous act is treated with leniency. Children get up to mischief and adults smile indulgently and reminisce about the things they themselves used to do when they were young. However, in the seventeenth century, the word had
40 more serious connotations. To begin with, it was accepted that there were two kinds of mischief. On the one hand, mischief could be regarded as benevolent in intent. Prospero in *The Tempest* sends Ariel to "do that good mischief." This form
45 of mischief was present on certain days of the year when the hierarchy at court was turned on its head and a "Lord of Misrule" was appointed, a comic figure whose wishes everyone, from the highest to the lowest, had to obey. Normal conventions were
50 temporarily ignored. The rites associated with May Day also fell into this category of mischief: harmless fun.

Yet for the artists and the politicians of the Renaissance, miching mallecho was dangerous.

Some might have said it was more than dangerous,
55 a manifestation of evil where one would least expect to find it. "And some that smile have in their hearts, I fear / Millions of mischief," says Octavius Caesar in that most political drama of the Shakespeare canon, *Julius Caesar*. The fear Shakespeare's
60 contemporaries had of mischief involved never knowing to what ends it might lead. Hamlet wanted only to publish the truth about his father's death, but his actions led to the almost complete devastation of the state of Denmark. The play ends with all the
65 leading figures in Hamlet's home country dead, and only Fortinbras of Norway left to re-establish a semblance of order.

"Mischief, thou art afoot." says Mark Antony, having worked up the citizens of Rome into a confused
70 and vengeful mob. Shakespeare was not blind to the political mischief that can rile our world, but neither was he averse to pleasing us with a little verbal mischief of his own.

---

10. The primary purpose of the passage is to

(A) make an assertion about the state of contemporary linguistics
(B) explore the effect of a recently-discovered concept
(C) question Shakespeare's use of the vernacular of his era
(D) define an archaic phrase by using modern jargon
(E) discuss the widespread significance of an obscure term

11. The author explains the word "miching" (line 8) by

(A) discovering its first known usage in literature
(B) exploring its various uses in different cultures
(C) citing a definition agreed upon by scholars
(D) tracing the history of the word's modern variations
(E) determining the exact geographical scope of the term's usage

12. Ultimately, the author defines "miching" in the first paragraph as

(A) contempt for aristocratic privileges
(B) neglect of an obligation
(C) a grievous offense
(D) a behavior unique to children
(E) disregard for the accepted order of society

GO ON TO THE NEXT PAGE

2   2   2   Unauthorized copying or
reuse of any part of this
page is illegal.   2   2   2

13. In lines 17-23 ("The word . . . kind"), the author explains the word "mallecho" by

(A) quoting a famous scholar
(B) comparing cultural usages
(C) labeling it as a colloquialism
(D) discussing its etymology
(E) naming its inventor

14. The "others" mentioned in line 27 most likely believe that "miching mallecho" is a fabrication because

(A) the audience is left wondering what the phrase means
(B) Shakespeare defines it through his character's speech
(C) it is the combination of a French word and an Italian word
(D) it was appropriated by the English royalty from foreign visitors
(E) Hamlet redefined the phrase in a way that departed from its accepted meaning

15. It can be inferred from lines 32-33 ("This elucidation . . . use") that

(A) legitimate phrases are not normally defined explicitly for an audience
(B) linguists are still debating the origins of the phrase
(C) Shakespeare was not proficient in regional dialects
(D) Shakespeare's phrase is universally understood to be a concoction
(E) Shakespeare often used foreign phrases in his English scripts

16. The author suggests that mischief is "treated with leniency" (lines 35-36) today because it

(A) spurs positive change
(B) causes general confusion
(C) rarely creates real problems
(D) reminds adults of their parents
(E) induces nostalgia in adults

17. The author describes the "two kinds of mischief" (line 41) as

(A) innocent vs. blithe
(B) good-natured vs. malevolent
(C) juvenile vs. mature
(D) inoffensive vs. ubiquitous
(E) rational vs. visceral

18. The author claims that "miching mallecho was dangerous" (line 53) most likely because mischief

(A) wreaked havoc on international relations
(B) was undertaken with definite intent to harm
(C) would inspire religious disputes
(D) led to unpredictable consequences
(E) encouraged aristocrats to abandon their responsibilities

GO ON TO THE NEXT PAGE

Practice Test 8

2   2   2   Unauthorized copying or   2   2   2
                                reuse of any part of this
                                     page is illegal.

Questions 19-25 are based on the following passage.

The following essay focuses on Treasure Island, *a late nineteenth-century novel written by Robert Louis Stevenson. In this passage, the author explores pirate culture.*

When Stevenson wrote *Treasure Island*, he most
likely had no idea of the huge influence it would have
in popular culture thereafter. An adventure novel
Line published in 1883, *Treasure Island* features pirates
5 engaging in mutiny and assassination, plundering
cape towns, and causing general mayhem. Oddly
enough, the book was initially written and published
for children. A surreal tale of criminality and
wonderment, this novel gave its seafarers attributes
10 that have had a significant impact on the way pirates
are perceived today.
    Many of the plot devices in the book are based
on actual pirate lore and methodology. Consider the
black spot. In the novel, pirates use a piece of paper
15 colored on one side with a menacing black spot, on
the other with a message of what is to come for the
recipient. The recipient then does his best to flee from
his homeland, for if one ever receives a black spot,
one should never stay on to see what doom is
20 coming. This practice was not the brainchild of
Stevenson, but a modified appropriation, a custom
that was already terrible in all respects and to which
Stevenson added a horrific twist. It was already a
common practice in the Caribbean for pirates to
25 present a man with an ace of spades (traditionally a
threatening sign, as though a man were on his last
leg) to threaten him, to let him know that his
treachery and deceit would not go unnoticed. The ace
was not a death warrant, but it was a warning sign.
30   Then there are the odd traditions that Stevenson
exploited, such as the eyepatch. This feature has
become a standard of piratedom, but it was rarely
found on a pirate of the nineteenth century. In fact,
such patches were rarely found on anyone at the time,
35 and weren't unique to any one occupation. Generals,
farmers, politicians, shopkeepers: simply put, if a
person lived at the time, and happened to damage his
or her eye somehow, that person would have an
eyepatch. *But surely, at least it was only pirates who*
40 *used peg-legs, yes?* No! The same logic applies to the
peg-leg, which was used for all sorts of injuries and
was not very piratesque at all.
    And the maps! X had never marked the spot until
Stevenson sent his pirates on their little jaunt across
45 the seas to play in the sand. I suppose I'm getting
myself all riled up because Stevenson's piece of
fiction has so changed the way we think about pirates,
which were a real, and are still a very real, threat to
nations across the world. Just the other day I saw a
50 headline, "Somalian Pirates Attack International
Cruise Liner". Pirate culture is still very much alive.

And can I assure you, the guys who attacked that
cruise liner weren't sporting hooks for hands or
holding dusty burlap maps.

19. The author's primary purpose in the passage is to

(A) study the history of Somalian pirates
(B) praise the artistry of Stevenson's book
(C) demystify the image of modern day pirates
(D) compare modern day pirates to popular
    historical figures
(E) dispute the verity of assumed facts about
    pirates

20. Which of the following LEAST resembles the
"general mayhem" described in line 6?

(A) Hiding in secret coves
(B) Terrorizing port towns
(C) Sinking trade ships
(D) Blocking a marina's entrance
(E) Attacking sea vessels

21. The author describes Stevenson's "black spot"
(line 14) as a "modified appropriation" (line 21)
because

(A) the custom had already existed,
    unbeknownst to Stevenson
(B) the concept was based in reality, but
    Stevenson lessened its severity
(C) Stevenson created the idea, but many
    commentators doubt that he did
(D) Stevenson altered the intention of the spot
    for dramatic purposes
(E) Stevenson took the idea from the narratives
    of another author

22. The use of italics in lines 39-40 ("But surely . . .
yes?") serves to

(A) reference an author's work
(B) assume a reader's response
(C) call attention to a controversial argument
(D) challenge the use of a term
(E) introduce a contemporary slogan

GO ON TO THE NEXT PAGE ⟶

23. The third paragraph suggests that the peg-leg was "not very piratesque" (line 42) because

(A) it wasn't a common implement at the time
(B) both men and women had access to peg-legs
(C) only a few jobs could yield sufficient wages for buying a peg-leg
(D) peg-legs were utilized by people of all vocations
(E) pirates were normally the only individuals to use peg-legs

24. The tone of lines 43-45 ("X had . . . sand") can best be described as

(A) enigmatic
(B) passive
(C) sardonic
(D) jubilant
(E) inquisitive

25. Which best describes the shift in the author's overall tone in the passage?

(A) analytical to impassioned
(B) irreverent to tempered
(C) vitriolic to disinterested
(D) solemn to ironic
(E) nostalgic to pragmatic

STOP

If you finish before time is called, you may check your work on this section only.
Do not turn to any other section in the test.

Practice Test 8

SECTION 3
Time–20 minutes
18 Questions

Directions: For each question in this section, select the best answer from among the choices given and fill in the corresponding circle on the answer sheet.

Each sentence below has one or two blanks, each blank indicating that something has been omitted. Beneath the sentence are five words or sets of words labeled A through E. Choose the word or set of words that, when inserted in the sentence, <u>best</u> fits the meaning of the sentence as a whole.

Example:

Jimmy opened his gas station in the ------- because he wanted to be in the middle of a metropolis.

(A) country
(B) suburbs
(C) periphery
(D) environment
(E) city

---

1. Although the food critic's review was -------, frequent customers remained ------- the restaurant.

    (A) impartial . . satisfied with
    (B) laudatory . . supportive of
    (C) scathing . . loyal to
    (D) unfavorable . . wary of
    (E) analytical . . hostile to

2. Although Gretchen displayed an outwardly calm and collected manner of speech during the marketing presentation, her shaky hands ------- her inner nervousness.

    (A) ruffled   (B) belied   (C) betrayed
       (D) assuaged   (E) justified

3. It can be said that the astronomer's newest project is -------, yet the committee feels that this endeavor still lacks the ------- arguments that are essential to scientific research.

    (A) promising . . cogent
    (B) ingenious . . fallible
    (C) coherent . . seditious
    (D) synthetic . . meritorious
    (E) erroneous . . transient

4. To make it easier to ------- unhealthy eating habits, Charles recorded his daily calorie intake and forced himself to avoid the decadent chocolate soufflé that he normally ordered.

    (A) eschew   (B) balance   (C) repudiate
       (D) equivocate   (E) transcribe

5. The way in which the official status report was completed was so ------- that even seasoned statisticians committed careless factual errors while writing the document.

    (A) obstinate   (B) cavalier   (C) stringent
       (D) frenetic   (E) derisive

6. Even though the old man's rash at first seemed -------, the ------- redness of skin that gradually expanded over his neck indicated the need for immediate medical attention.

    (A) benign . . negligible
    (B) chronic . . unremitting
    (C) epidemic . . intermittent
    (D) innocuous . . flagrant
    (E) pernicious . . waning

GO ON TO THE NEXT PAGE

Practice Test 8

The two passages below are followed by questions based on their content and on the relationship between the two passages. Answer the questions on the basis of what is <u>stated</u> or <u>implied</u> in the passages and in any introductory material that may be provided.

Questions 7-18 are based on the following passages.

The following two passages discuss the continued use of nuclear power in light of recent events in Fukushima, Japan. Passage 1 is adapted from a speech given by a nuclear energy lobbyist in 2012. Passage 2 is from a report written that same year by an independent research firm.

Passage 1

In recent years, the issue of global warming has become more and more pressing. Yet there has been frustratingly little agreement among policymakers
Line regarding measures that would actually tackle the
5 problem. Fortunately, one of the best solutions has been with us for decades; it has simply been overlooked. In order for this solution to be viable once more, however, it is necessary that we address climate policy with fresh eyes and with open minds.
10 For when it comes to clean, alternative energy, the fact remains that nuclear power is still one of the safest, most effective options available.

It is understandable that, given the amount of negative press that nuclear power has suffered in
15 recent years, advocating its use might strike some as a form of sacrilege. Indeed, it is impossible to talk about nuclear energy at all without acknowledging the recent incident at Fukushima, in which an unusually large tsunami impacted four reactors at the
20 Daiichi power plant. This accident made headlines all over the globe, sparking a host of alarmist theories regarding the hazardous release of radioactive materials. In reality, the amount of radioactive material that escaped into the environment was
25 insignificant. The Nuclear and Industrial Safety Agency (NISA) estimates that just 0.16% of the reactor's total inventory was released. Also, because reactor substances have very short half-lives, these materials were reduced to one sixteenth of their
30 original activity within a month of the incident. While the accident at Fukushima certainly substantiates the idea that new reactors should be built farther inland, there is no reason to assume—because of one aberrant gasp of nature—that nuclear power is
35 unsafe. The reality is quite the opposite.

According to the World Nuclear Association, in over six decades of nuclear power, only three major accidents have ever occurred among the 435 nuclear power plants currently operational worldwide.
40 And with advances in safety technology following Fukushima, the probability of future accidents continues to decline. We should not allow a few problems to distract us from the tremendous benefits of nuclear power—namely, that it provides clean,
45 affordable energy without emitting greenhouse gases. Nuclear power deserves both our reconsideration and our reinvestment.

Passage 2

Soon after its development in the 1950s and 1960s, nuclear power was hailed by many as the
50 clean and safe energy alternative which we had long been seeking. The facts of history, however, have shown that these initial prognostications were both naïve and shortsighted. The two previous nuclear meltdowns of Three Mile Island (1979) and
55 Chernobyl (1986) notwithstanding, the most recent catastrophe at Fukushima, Japan should have forced even the most stalwart advocates of nuclear power to question their basic assumptions. Unfortunately, misinformation regarding the incident abounds,
60 largely due to questionable statistics indicating the amount of radioactive core material that was released into the atmosphere. No amount of math can change the fact that large quantities of cesium-137 were released into the air and sea on the day of the
65 Fukushima disaster; despite the best cleanup efforts of the Japanese government, it is impossible to say for certain what the full extent of radioactive contamination is, or will be, both for Japan and for the Pacific Ocean at large. While many would like to
70 convince themselves that the disaster of Fukushima has now been relegated to the past, the fact remains that we will likely be living with its effects for years, if not decades, to come.

As neuroscientist John C. Lilly once said
75 regarding nuclear power, "We're playing around with something we don't know anything about. This is the stuff of stars, not of the planet." In defiance of all the evidence to the contrary, a small cadre of diehards continues to insist that nuclear power is a clean, cost-
80 effective option—in fact, that it is the best alternative to fossil fuels that we currently have available. There is nothing clean about an environment so contaminated with radioactive waste that it is still uninhabitable two years later. Nor is there anything
85 cost-effective about $20 billion in taxpayer dollars— the cost-to-date of cleaning up after Fukushima. While it is a fact that our world requires new and alternative energy sources, the recent nuclear catastrophe at Fukushima provides indisputable
90 evidence of a risky and unsafe technology.

GO ON TO THE NEXT PAGE

7. The author of Passage 1 would agree with the author of Passage 2 that

   (A) long-term investments in nuclear power will help to reduce environmental problems
   (B) critics of nuclear power have often relied on faulty information
   (C) the hazards associated with nuclear power have received unwarranted publicity
   (D) nuclear power has frequently been construed as potentially dangerous
   (E) the scientific principles behind nuclear power cannot be comprehended by the public

8. In the first paragraph of Passage 1, the author transitions from

   (A) refuting an apparent misinterpretation to proposing new energy regulations
   (B) summarizing an unusual policy to explaining its contemporary relevance
   (C) explaining the threat of global warming to disavowing the viability of nuclear power
   (D) surveying existing research to agitating for unprecedented scientific initiatives
   (E) describing a widespread problem to endorsing an apparently divisive solution

9. In context, the author of Passage 1 suggests that the "alarmist theories" (line 21) surrounding the Fukushima incident were the result of

   (A) experiments that measured the dispersion of Fukushima reactor material
   (B) frequent complaints about the presence of the Fukushima power plant
   (C) the public's disinclination to acknowledge the benefits of nuclear energy
   (D) disagreements among policymakers that have led to conflict
   (E) the widespread negative coverage that the accident received

10. In context, the "one aberrant gasp of nature" mentioned in line 34 of Passage 1 refers to

    (A) "global warming" (line 1)
    (B) "an unusually large tsunami" (lines 18-19)
    (C) "the hazardous release of radioactive materials" (lines 22-23)
    (D) "the probability of future accidents (line 41)
    (E) "emitting greenhouse gases" (line 45)

11. The final paragraph of Passage 1 presents a contrast between

    (A) the considerable benefits and the relatively minor drawbacks that nuclear power entails
    (B) resistance to nuclear power and acceptance of other forms of alternative energy
    (C) the earlier acceptance and the current disparagement of nuclear energy
    (D) the wide influence of nuclear power and the limited reach of other energy sources
    (E) the rarity of nuclear power accidents and the enormous scope of the resulting destruction

12. In the first paragraph of Passage 2, the author refers to Chernobyl and Three Mile Island in order to

    (A) recapitulate major turning points in the regulation of nuclear power
    (B) indicate that nuclear energy is not a perfectly safe energy source
    (C) suggest that nuclear energy has been rejected by multiple national governments
    (D) define the period when the public was most approving of nuclear energy
    (E) call into question the reader's awareness of recent history

13. It can be inferred from lines 65-69 of Passage 2 ("despite the . . . large") that the Fukushima disaster

    (A) may have affected an area much more extensive than Japan alone
    (B) will have a destructive influence on ecosystems all over the globe
    (C) was not addressed in an efficient manner by the Japanese government
    (D) is likely to exacerbate the environmental problems caused by climate change
    (E) has been far more deleterious than earlier accidents related to nuclear power

14. In context, "John C. Lilly" (line 74) would most likely describe the utilization of nuclear power as

    (A) exhilarating
    (B) inevitable
    (C) inexplicable
    (D) aggressive
    (E) irresponsible

GO ON TO THE NEXT PAGE

Practice Test 8

15. The tone of the final paragraph of Passage 2 is best described as

(A) feckless
(B) cantankerous
(C) distraught
(D) disapproving
(E) importunate

16. Both passages rely on which of the following assumptions?

(A) Energy sources that contribute to pollution need to be replaced.
(B) Nuclear power will be a controversial issue well into the future.
(C) Supporters of nuclear energy tend to be more vehement than its opponents.
(D) Accident cleanup efforts are the only major expense associated with nuclear energy.
(E) The Fukushima accident will undermine new research initiatives in nuclear power.

17. The author of Passage 2 would most likely respond to the data presented in lines 25-30 of Passage 1 ("The Nuclear . . . incident") by claiming that

(A) the percentages provided cannot be verified by a reputable authority
(B) proponents of nuclear power continue to use outdated statistical methods
(C) the estimates cited obscure the real impact of the Fukushima incident
(D) the devastation caused by a plant that burns fossil fuels would have been far less severe
(E) supporters of nuclear power are unaware of the comparable accidents at Three Mile Island and Chernobyl

18. Unlike Passage 2, Passage 1 provides which of the following?

(A) A list of specific nuclear power plant meltdowns that antedated the Fukushima incident
(B) References to the presumed benefits of utilizing nuclear energy
(C) An analysis of the estimated annual cost of operating a nuclear power plant
(D) An overview of the chemicals released into the environment by the Fukushima disaster
(E) Statistical information regarding the number of nuclear power plants in existence

STOP

If you finish before time is called, you may check your work on this section only.
Do not turn to any other section in the test.

POST TEST ANALYSIS

This post test analysis is important if you want to see an improvement on your next test. Each section has a set of possible reasons for errors. Place check marks next to the ones that pertain to you, and write your own on the blank lines provided. Use this form to better analyze your performance. **If you don't understand why you made errors, there is no way you can correct them!**

1. **SENTENCE COMPLETION:**

    Problems with the sentence:
    - ❑ Wasn't familiar with phrases, idioms, or words in the sentence
    - ❑ Missed the clues or tones
    - ❑ Put your OWN word in the blank rather than one from the sentence
    - ❑ Completely avoided marking
    - ❑ Other: _____

    _____

    Problems with the answers:
    - ❑ Did not use process of elimination
    - ❑ Did not ignore unknown words
    - ❑ Did not use prefix/root/suffix knowledge to figure out the meaning of the unknown words
    - ❑ Did not match the clues and tones of the answer with those of the sentence
    - ❑ Did not recognize vocabulary words
    - ❑ Did not check answer to see if it fit
    - ❑ Other: _____

    _____

    Leaving questions unanswered:
    - ❑ Did not try
    - ❑ Did not fill in the blank(s) with words
    - ❑ Ran out of time
    - ❑ Other: _____

    _____

2. **SHORT READING COMPREHENSION:**
    - ❑ Did not read entire paragraph
    - ❑ Did not see more than one point
    - ❑ Missed contrast clues
    - ❑ Did not pinpoint thesis
    - ❑ Did not identify similarities and differences in Double Short Reading Comp
    - ❑ Other: _____

    _____

3. **LONG READING COMPREHENSION:**
    - ❑ Did not understand the question, line reference, or answers
    - ❑ Spent too much time reading the passages
    - ❑ Did not underline the line reference
    - ❑ Read too much or too little
    - ❑ Did not answer the specific question; instead analyzed its main idea
    - ❑ Did not do process of elimination based on facts in the passage
    - ❑ Couldn't find the false words
    - ❑ Couldn't choose between two possible answers
    - ❑ Did not use tone to help eliminate answers
    - ❑ When stuck at 2 guessed instead of pulling additional fact
    - ❑ Couldn't finish in time
    - ❑ Other: _____

    _____

ANSWER KEY

TEST 8

SECTION 1

#	Answer	LEVEL		#	Answer	LEVEL		#	Answer	LEVEL		#	Answer	LEVEL
1	A	(1)		7	C	(5)		13	A	(4)		19	E	(2)
2	E	(3)		8	A	(5)		14	D	(3)		20	D	(3)
3	D	(3)		9	C	(4)		15	B	(3)		21	A	(5)
4	D	(3)		10	B	(3)		16	A	(3)		22	A	(5)
5	E	(5)		11	D	(2)		17	C	(4)		23	A	(4)
6	B	(4)		12	E	(4)		18	E	(3)		24	A	(2)

SECTION 2

#	Answer	LEVEL		#	Answer	LEVEL		#	Answer	LEVEL		#	Answer	LEVEL
1	E	(1)		7	B	(3)		13	D	(5)		19	E	(1)
2	B	(2)		8	D	(4)		14	B	(2)		20	A	(2)
3	E	(3)		9	C	(2)		15	A	(3)		21	D	(3)
4	D	(4)		10	E	(3)		16	E	(3)		22	B	(4)
5	C	(5)		11	B	(2)		17	B	(3)		23	D	(2)
6	D	(3)		12	E	(2)		18	D	(3)		24	C	(3)
												25	A	(5)

SECTION 3

#	Answer	LEVEL		#	Answer	LEVEL		#	Answer	LEVEL		#	Answer	LEVEL
1	C	(2)		6	D	(5)		11	A	(3)		16	A	(5)
2	C	(3)		7	D	(1)		12	B	(2)		17	C	(3)
3	A	(3)		8	E	(3)		13	A	(3)		18	E	(4)
4	A	(4)		9	E	(3)		14	E	(3)				
5	B	(4)		10	B	(2)		15	D	(3)				

Difficulty levels range from 1 - 5 with 1 being the easiest and 5 being the hardest.
For answer explanations please visit www.ies2400.com/criticalreading

PRACTICE TEST 9

SECTION 1
Time–25 minutes
24 Questions

Directions: For each question in this section, select the best answer from among the choices given and fill in the corresponding circle on the answer sheet.

Each sentence below has one or two blanks, each blank indicating that something has been omitted. Beneath the sentence are five words or sets of words labeled A through E. Choose the word or set of words that, when inserted in the sentence, <u>best</u> fits the meaning of the sentence as a whole.

Example:

Jimmy opened his gas station in the ------- because he wanted to be in the middle of a metropolis.

(A) country
(B) suburbs
(C) periphery
(D) environment
(E) city   Ⓐ Ⓑ Ⓒ Ⓓ ●

---

1. Facultative bacteria are considered the most ------- because they have the ability to modify their metabolic activities to suit their environments.

   (A) numerous   (B) adaptive   (C) expansive
     (D) threatening   (E) profound

2. The suspect sought to ------- any appearance of guilt by answering the investigator's questions in a lucid and forthright manner.

   (A) forgive   (B) betray   (C) propagate
     (D) dispel   (E) solidify

3. In contrast to most scholars, who are ------- in their approach to research, Alice Earle ------- the conservation of the marine life that she studies.

   (A) biased . . promotes
   (B) neutral . . disregards
   (C) detached . . champions
   (D) professional . . publishes
   (E) meticulous . . conceptualizes

4. In an effort to ------- its reputation for serving unhealthy and artificial food, the company created ads that depicted active children, thriving expanses of farmland, and other ------- imagery.

   (A) mend . . depraved
   (B) solidify . . profitable
   (C) enhance . . salubrious
   (D) erode . . fabricated
   (E) counteract . . appealing

5. Once an ingredient favored only by health food devotees and idiosyncratic chefs, kale has become a ------- of the culinary industry in the course of the last several years.

   (A) specimen   (B) paragon   (C) luminary
     (D) mainstay   (E) verity

GO ON TO THE NEXT PAGE

The passages below are followed by questions based on their content. Answer the questions on the basis of what is <u>stated</u> or <u>implied</u> in the passages and in any introductory material that may be provided.

Questions 6-7 are based on the following passage.

"Don't go west, young man," he said to me, after hearing my plea about wanting to start a band in Los Angeles. I had explained to him the intimate details,
Line how two boys I had grown up with had settled there
5 recently. "They're already playing music together," I said. "They're pretty good, I know it!" But the whole time, he just looked at me with doleful eyes. He must have had a story of his own; I wondered if I could goad him into telling me. Eventually, he just said to
10 me, "Don't go west. Never go west. There's nothing good past Kansas."

6. The word "intimate" in line 3 most nearly means

(A) clandestine
(B) specific
(C) familiar
(D) collaborative
(E) surreptitious

7. The man's final statement in lines 10-11 ("There's nothing . . . Kansas") is best characterized as

(A) a conviction
(B) a prevarication
(C) a hesitation
(D) a resignation
(E) an exaggeration

Questions 8-9 are based on the following passage.

Nonlinear storytelling, as seen in Quentin Tarantino's films, has now become rather popular among film buffs. Traditionally, most movies
Line follow a three-act structure in which events occur
5 chronologically, with the occasional flashback here or there. Yet in Tarantino's films, the hodgepodge of events is calculated and deliberate, elevating nonlinear storytelling to a fulfilling cerebral experience. At each film's end, we must ask ourselves why the filmmaker
10 arranged the events in such a way. Was there something to be learned from placing the beginning at the end, or vice versa? Perhaps we will never know clearly. There is, however, a measure of comfort in this notion: a nonlinear story perpetually engages us to "get
15 it," always leaving more to be discovered.

8. The author refers to "Quentin Tarantino" (lines 1-2) in order to

(A) depict a director who promoted the necessity of nonlinear films
(B) point out a pivotal figure in nonlinear storytelling's rise in popularity
(C) exonerate the film industry for producing controversial movies
(D) foster the impression that Tarantino is a nontraditional thinker
(E) provide an example of a filmmaker who uses nonlinear storytelling

9. The passage suggests that nonlinear storytelling "perpetually engages us" (line 14) because

(A) it has a very unusual structure
(B) it leaves certain issues open to inquiry
(C) it forces its audience to question reality
(D) it unites a large number of film aficionados
(E) its content leads to personal intrigue

GO ON TO THE NEXT PAGE

Questions 10-17 are based on the following passage.

This passage explores a narrator's development into a young adult through her relationship with her mother.

I clamber out of the bumble bee bus that chugs to a stop outside my house, run through the wide front door, and skid to a stop in the kitchen where
Line my mother stands waiting. She turns to me and
5 follows the age-old tradition of asking how my first day of school was. As I settle down for my afternoon snack, she begins to fill out all the school forms I've brought home—forms for emergency contact, lunch orders, PFA membership, photo censorship, medical
10 allowances, forms for individual teachers, the works.
"Mom?" I ask, wiping my chin clean of juice, "what's that blue paper for?"
She doesn't look up from her pen but replies in Chinese, "It's asking what allergies you have."
15 "I don't have any, right?"
"Right," she says and swiftly checks off a few more boxes before planting her sweeping signature on the bottom of the page.
"And this one?" I ask, peering over her shoulder.
20 "It says… 'siblings… age… school…' Are they asking about sis?"
"Mhm."
"She's in fourth grade, right? I can't wait until I'm that old!"
25 "And then you can fill out these forms by yourself," she replies, switching to English, and gives me a smile.
I still remember that day, and the many more like it, when my mother gave me a look that made
30 me wonder when I would grow up. At the time, growing up seemed like an impossibility. The future was a dip in a road obscured by mist while my mother was a more tangible presence that stood next to me. It's weird, though, how soon you reach the
35 dip and how quickly the mist disappears to reveal a new path.
I push open the front door and walk into the kitchen where my mother sits in front of her computer, her brows arched in frustration. I'm a high
40 school student now, and with routine casualness, I sling my backpack onto an empty chair and walk over to my mother.
"Back from school? Anyway, can you help me with this? I just can't understand what they're
45 asking me."
Without a word, I commandeer my mother's computer and peruse her screen; she is inspecting an online questionnaire from a hotel we've stayed at recently. "They're just asking us how our stay
50 was, mom, things like room service quality and stuff like that."
"Oh well, can you fill it out for me?"

"But it's so simple, mom, they're just asking—"
"No no, I know, but you can fill it out for me."
55 The next day she asks me to proofread an e-mail to a friend because her English grammar, in her opinion, is quite deficient. The day after that, I am called to look over her resume so that she can find another job. A week later, I help her answer questions
60 at the customs office while we get our passports approved. When I get the annual deluge of forms from school, my pen marks its way through all of them, leaving only the line at the bottom of each page for a parent's signature. And one day, I muse, I'll be
65 helping her sign that for me too.
Perhaps the gradual transition is what makes the sudden realization so sudden. The fact that I was once the one always asking for help makes the present me, who is always giving help, feel cheated.
70 Where has the strong, confident, reliable mother I had always been able to turn to gone? Since when has this vulnerable, helpless mother replaced her? My mother was always able to fill out these forms by herself when I was small, so how come she's
75 struggling now?
Sometimes I get frustrated when she asks me to write yet another e-mail for her. "It's only to your friend," I scream. "She writes to you with grammar mistakes, so why do you insist on perfect grammar
80 when you reply?" When I say things like that to her, she just gives me a smile that means she wonders when I'll grow up.
It's a Chinese tradition, though, that when children grow up they must take care of their
85 parents. It's a responsibility that grows with the children; when you are very young, you are allowed to be innocent and ignorant because you do not understand, but when you grow up and your mind widens, you must accept a series of new revelations
90 and responsibilities. My mother's brief moments of helplessness occasionally remind me of myself when I was still in grade school, but maybe they're actually signs that she is growing even older. It's a thought that I can't quite wrap my mind around yet, but I
95 know that while she grows, I grow too. That's why when she asks me for help again, I now take a deep breath and reply in English, "Sure, I can fill out those forms for you."

10. The word "planting" (line 17) most nearly means

(A) growing
(B) digging
(C) introducing
(D) placing
(E) establishing

GO ON TO THE NEXT PAGE

1   1   1   Unauthorized copying or
                            reuse of any part of this
                            page is illegal.   1   1   1

11. In the context of the passage, the mother's statement in lines 25-26 ("And then . . . yourself") can best be described as

(A) a foreshadowing
(B) a metaphor
(C) an anecdote
(D) a euphemism
(E) an admonishment

12. In context, lines 28-36 ("I still . . . path") function primarily to

(A) introduce a role reversal between the narrator and her mother
(B) indicate that the narrator was eager to grow up
(C) imply that growing up is impossibly hard for a teenager
(D) convey the narrator's frustration at the pressure her mother puts on her to grow up
(E) suggest that the road traveled is a symbol of family responsibility in Chinese tradition

13. The examples the author cites in lines 55-64 ("The next . . . signature") serve to illustrate the

(A) jobs considered impossible by some immigrant parents
(B) tasks that a parent would typically ask a teenage child to perform
(C) responsibilities that have been assumed by the narrator
(D) chores that the narrator is reluctant to undertake
(E) activities assigned to children without any real justification

14. The narrator's use of "cheated" in line 69 suggests that she is

(A) resigned to her new role as head of the family
(B) experiencing uncontrollable anger towards her mother
(C) amused by the absurdity of her circumstances
(D) horrified by the transformation in her mother
(E) having difficulty accepting a change in her lifestyle

15. The narrator poses a series of questions in lines 70-75 in order to

(A) analyze her mother's complex character
(B) highlight the urgency of her mother's condition
(C) expound a sentiment about her mother
(D) lament her family obligations
(E) introduce a new viewpoint

16. The frustration the narrator feels when she is asked to "write yet another e-mail" (line 77) for her mother is best characterized as a reaction to

(A) her new duties within her family
(B) her mother's fundamental helplessness
(C) her mother's unwillingness to learn English
(D) her perspective on Chinese tradition
(E) her mother's generous nature

17. The final paragraph suggests that the narrator views her "mother's brief moments of helplessness" (lines 90-91) as

(A) a source of contention
(B) a reminder of filial duty
(C) a sign of impending doom
(D) an inevitable outcome of aging
(E) an exaggerated cry for help

GO ON TO THE NEXT PAGE

Questions 18-25 are based on the following passage.

The author of the following passage discusses how the theater convinces us that what we see onstage is true, thus freeing us from the notion that we are watching actors in fictional roles.

We think of drama as a form of literature, which moves its audience to a recognition of the emotions and struggles that lie within the words of its
Line characters. We can all empathize with Macbeth's
5 struggle between the seditious goal that he is offered and his inherent belief in the divine appointment of kings. At some time in our lives, we have all had to consider the consequences that may follow from a conflict-inducing course of action. We have been
10 there, all of us. We know what it is like to be caught between desire and convention. Because of this recognition of a common situation, we listen to the dramatist's dialogue and we find ourselves agreeing with T. S. Eliot's definition of poetry: "Yes, that is
15 exactly what I would have said, if I had had the words." It is this moment of complete communion between the figure on the stage and ourselves that, perhaps, crystallizes the magic of theatre. We hear a new expression of the truth in our own lives.
20 Shakespeare called the theatre "a mirror to life," and for the duration of the play—and perhaps for a little while after the final curtain has fallen—we might well agree with him. However, if we think about that neat definition for a moment, we should
25 begin to realize that, in fact, a mirror does not present an exact truth. At the fair, we have all laughed at our distorted reflections in a hall of mirrors; it is a truth not quite universally acknowledged, that all mirrors distort to a greater or lesser degree. To begin with, the
30 person we see in the mirror is not the person we know: it is the person that other people see. The image of ourselves as we know ourselves has been necessarily distorted.
Whether we sit in the stalls of the theatre or are
35 perched in the topmost row of the upper balcony, we know that we are not in a real world. We know that Othello is not really strangling Desdemona. We know that the ten extras waving swords and coughing their way through the dry ice are not really fighting a
40 battle, no matter how much fake blood is smeared across their arms. We are aware of the trickery achieved with lighting and sound and screen-projection effects. Above all, we know that these characters we are watching are, as Shakespeare put it,
45 "merely players, who strut and fret their time upon the stage, and then are heard no more." How is it, then, that the playwright succeeds in making us forget all that trickery?
He does so by following the first rule of play-
50 writing. In order for the dramatist to make us believe, he must first make us "suspend our disbelief."

Shakespeare does this very often by touching on the half-hidden fears of his audience, by making us feel uneasy in the opening scenes of his plays. Some
55 begin with what we might call "civil disobedience": a rioting mob running through the streets of the city (*Julius Caesar, Coriolanus, Romeo and Juliet*). Elsewhere, Shakespeare draws on our fears and superstitions concerning the evil side of life and
60 depicts witches and ghosts (*Hamlet* or *Macbeth*). Or he draws on our fears of war (*The Histories*), or our fears of inadequacy and loss (*King Lear, As You Like It, Midsummer Night's Dream, Othello, Merchant of Venice*). We sense the uneasiness and insecurity he
65 presents and we equate these forces with what we feel in our own lives. Shakespeare makes us want to discover whether the disasters that lie just below the surfaces of all our lives can be countered, defeated, dissolved. He makes us want to know how these
70 things evolve, develop, end—all of it! It doesn't matter. We have suspended our disbelief. Is it just sleight of hand, an angling of the mirror we are looking into—or is it really magic, and have we really glimpsed the truth of life? The important thing
75 is that Shakespeare has hooked us and made us want to know what lies at the end of the play.

18. The sentiment in lines 9-10 ("We have been there, all of us") suggests that

(A) we have all at some point had to think about the possible outcomes of our decisions
(B) we have all exhibited irresponsible behavior that has fundamentally changed the course of another person's life
(C) we have all watched a performance of *Macbeth* at some point in our lives
(D) we have all questioned traditional beliefs such as the divine appointment of kings
(E) we have all hoped that a character on stage would imitate our own actions

19. The first paragraph indicates that drama appeals to us because

(A) we have a tendency to like the characters in Shakespeare's plays
(B) drama offers specific solutions to the political problems that confront society
(C) drama reminds us of everyday happenings and problems
(D) we relate to the struggles that actors face in their lives
(E) we recognize our own way of speaking in the dialogue of the characters

GO ON TO THE NEXT PAGE

1   1   1
Unauthorized copying or
reuse of any part of this
page is illegal.
1   1   1

20. The author explains why calling the theater "a mirror to life" (line 20) is problematic by

(A) calling into question our essential definitions of fantasy and actuality
(B) underscoring the limitations of a common object
(C) demonstrating how the common optical illusions produced by mirrors operate
(D) recalling a pleasant childhood memory from a local fair
(E) conjuring up an image of a place familiar to many readers

21. The purpose of the statements in lines 36-43 ("We know . . . effects") is to

(A) celebrate the tricks behind stage productions
(B) enumerate realities acknowledged by theater-goers
(C) dispel illusions that always dupe audiences
(D) criticize ill-conceived sleights-of-hand
(E) condemn the scams perpetuated by an overzealous playwright

22. In context of the final paragraph, the author lists Shakespeare's plays in lines 54-64 ("Some begin . . . *Venice*") in order to

(A) highlight the most celebrated scenes in Shakespeare's work
(B) validate a claim about how a great dramatist overcomes the skepticism of viewers
(C) prove a hypothesis about a theatrical format used only by Shakespeare
(D) reconstruct typical audience reactions to some of Shakespeare's stock characters
(E) document the role of fear in the histories of various nations

23. In context of the passage, the phrase "We have suspended our disbelief" (line 71) suggests which of the following situations?

(A) Stage managers often employ props that are so finely-crafted that they seem real.
(B) Actors who are able to mesmerize an audience are most sought after by theaters.
(C) Playwrights other than Shakespeare seldom make their audiences feel uncomfortable with the situations presented.
(D) A play makes an audience forget that the actors are not real by invoking primal emotions.
(E) Audiences are willing to believe anything directors show to them so long as it is entertaining.

24. The author poses the question in lines 71-74 ("Is it . . . life?") in order to

(A) demonstrate that many of Shakespeare's protagonists are either philosophers or magicians
(B) suggest theater's power to both captivate and disorient its audience
(C) question the validity and relevance of the dramatic arts in today's society
(D) concede that magic will always be more important than what we see
(E) cast doubt on the assertions of Shakespeare's critics

25. The author develops his main argument by

(A) quoting an authority on the subject whose hypothesis he eventually disregards
(B) developing an extended comparison involving plays by Shakespeare and T.S. Eliot
(C) showing both sides of an argument and choosing the position that is more practical
(D) evoking fear and superstition in the reader and concluding with a logical explanation
(E) discussing a general idea which the author supports by citing a specific playwright

STOP

If you finish before time is called, you may check your work on this section only.
Do not turn to any other section in the test.

2   2   2   Unauthorized copying or
reuse of any part of this
page is illegal.   2   2   2

Practice Test 9

SECTION 2
Time–25 minutes
24 Questions

Directions: For each question in this section, select the best answer from among the choices given and fill in the corresponding circle on the answer sheet.

Each sentence below has one or two blanks, each blank indicating that something has been omitted. Beneath the sentence are five words or sets of words labeled A through E. Choose the word or set of words that, when inserted in the sentence, <u>best</u> fits the meaning of the sentence as a whole.

Example:

Jimmy opened his gas station in the ------- because he wanted to be in the middle of a metropolis.

(A) country
(B) suburbs
(C) periphery
(D) environment
(E) city

1. The actress was remembered for her ------- behavior: she underhandedly compromised the integrity of other celebrities by spreading horrific rumors.

    (A) vindictive   (B) versatile   (C) amicable
       (D) docile   (E) laughable

2. Once every day, the ocean tide -------, exposing the slimy rocks that spend most of their time ------- the water.

    (A) wanes . . untouched by
    (B) retreats . . floating atop
    (C) recedes . . submerged in
    (D) advances . . immersed in
    (E) materializes . . inundated by

3. An unusual covert operations initiative, "Acoustic Kitty," involved the ------- infiltration of heavily-fortified Russian embassies by secretly implanting microphones inside cats.

    (A) surreptitious   (B) substantial   (C) valiant
       (D) inchoate   (E) acrimonious

4. When the popular party game Twister was first introduced, many adults ------- it because they believed it promoted ------- and depravity.

    (A) denounced . . licentiousness
    (B) criticized . . flexibility
    (C) lambasted . . indifference
    (D) praised . . exhilaration
    (E) exonerated . . debauchery

5. The scholarly article, though refined and well-researched, was obviously -------, leaving room for varying interpretations of its conclusions.

    (A) commendable   (B) excoriating
       (C) innocuous   (D) ambiguous
          (E) empirical

6. True stage tragedies are intended to be -------, purging negative emotions by presenting harrowing events.

    (A) cathartic   (B) bilious   (C) salient
       (D) enervating   (E) didactic

7. Despite the politician's ------- about fostering environmentally friendly policies, her posturing was ------- by her track record of voting against bills that supported wildlife preservation.

    (A) oration . . confirmed
    (B) rhetoric . . compromised
    (C) conjecture . . disproven
    (D) deliberation . . prolonged
    (E) debate . . predicated

8. Many of Nina Simone's songs inspire feelings that are surprising combinations of ------- and -------: while seemingly forlorn, these melodies can also be replete with hope.

    (A) despair . . anguish
    (B) melancholy . . buoyancy
    (C) urgency . . courage
    (D) nostalgia . . reminiscence
    (E) cheerfulness . . exuberance

GO ON TO THE NEXT PAGE

The passages below are followed by questions based on their content; questions following a pair of related passages may also be based on the relationship between the paired passages. Answer the questions on the basis of what is <u>stated</u> or <u>implied</u> in the passages and in any introductory material that may be provided.

Questions 9-12 are based on the following passages.

Passage 1

Ask a research scientist what exactly he or she does on a daily basis, and you will probably get an answer so complicated that only another scientist in the same field could understand it. It is easy to forget that
Line 5 the mass of obscure terms and intricate calculations that a scientist calls "work" often has poignantly human roots. Despite picking up a few tidbits of information while taking my kids to planetariums and science fairs, I understand nothing about astrophysics.
10 But it is possible that one of the children sitting next to me will look up at those same artificial constellations and someday dedicate a lifetime to studying the real universe. This must be where inspiration begins.

Passage 2

Everybody in my town—if you could call acres
15 upon acres of western Maryland farmland a town—belonged to one of the clubs offered by the community center. The girls mostly raised rabbits or rode horses, while the boys opted mostly for remote-control planes and model rockets. I chose rockets. Actually, "chose"
20 would be a bit of an understatement: I threw myself into the task, body and mind, heart and soul. I would spend hours putting together pre-designed models, then hours more figuring out my own fin and nose cone combinations. I would launch my rockets early
25 in the morning, on a nearby football field. I would stand there wondering what it would be like to create a rocket that could reach past the clouds, past the atmosphere.

9. In context, the last sentence in each passage can be best described as an instance of

    (A) somber bemusement
    (B) fanciful creation
    (C) reluctant acknowledgment
    (D) wry commentary
    (E) appreciative musing

10. Both passages feature which of the following?

    (A) Personal anecdote
    (B) Direct quotation
    (C) Geographic description
    (D) Scientific jargon
    (E) Allegorical reference

11. In context, lines 21-25 of Passage 2 ("I would . . . field") can best be characterized as

    (A) a synopsis of a conflict
    (B) an evocation of a turning point
    (C) a description of a process
    (D) an analysis of a misperception
    (E) an explanation of a profession

12. The author of Passage 2 would probably agree with which of the following statements about "inspiration" (line 13, Passage 1)?

    (A) It is much easier to fulfill while one is still young.
    (B) It is can be weakened by one's dedication to a task.
    (C) It can only be fostered in small collaborative settings.
    (D) It can lead to an intense and extensive time commitment.
    (E) It is often indicative of a scientifically-oriented mind.

GO ON TO THE NEXT PAGE

Questions 13-24 are based on the following passage.

This passage is adapted from a 2012 study that discusses the scientific reasoning behind the common mentalities of teenagers.

Freedom is something people inherently want. When someone drills you in this or that order, it's natural if you have the inexplicable urge to defy that order. Everyone has gone through a similar experience:
5 perhaps you were just about to clench your stomach and swallow those brussel sprouts when your mom yells across the room that if you don't eat every single sprout on your plate you're grounded, and suddenly you decide that you'd rather get grounded than eat
10 those little green bulbs. Even if it's something you already want to do, when you hear other people telling you to do it, their voices somehow twist *your* brilliant idea into *their* not-so-brilliant idea.

Another name for this reaction is called teenage
15 rebellion. It isn't that adults or young children like to listen to others any more than teenagers do, but rather that adolescents are more disposed to seek out their own choices. But what is the true cause of this rebellion that seems to plague every child entering the
20 teen years? Scientists have discovered one possible reason: even through adolescence, a teenager's mind continues to grow, but not at all the same pace. It turns out that the emotional region of the brain matures faster than the region that controls rational thought,
25 leaving the teenager with well-developed feelings but without a fully-formed capacity for control.

Thus, many teenagers have the impulse to take risks and discover their own ways of dealing with things. Just as a dog must first sniff every corner of
30 the room before feeling safe, teenagers need to try everything for themselves before they can become comfortable with their constantly changing mental and physical capabilities. Unfortunately, this explorative mentality often leads to alcohol, drugs, sexual activity,
35 bullying, and the general breaking of rules.

In response to this, many schools have increased their efforts to spread awareness of such illicit activities by enlisting speakers and organizing assemblies. Perhaps a school administration invites a group to
40 speak about bullying one month, convenes a classroom discussion about drug usage the next, and then includes more and more lectures against everything a teenager could possibly do wrong. However, if teenagers have the urge to rebel against whatever others tell them to
45 do, just how effective are these efforts?

It's almost reverse psychology. If you place a giant red button on the table and tell everyone not to touch the red button, you can practically guarantee that every single person in the room will have some degree of
50 temptation to press the red button. On the other hand, if there's just a random red button on the table and you tell people that nothing will happen if they press it, and even have a few people try it without meaningful results, then

most will eventually get the button out of their minds.
55 The same general ideas apply to teenagers. You can tell teenagers over and over again that breaking the rules will only hurt them, but the more you speak, the more they will see your words as a challenge and want to "overcome" that challenge.

60 A recent study of psychology concluded that people who are absolutely bound by a rule will be more content with it than people who believe that the rule is still provisional. When the rule has even a slim chance of being evaded, "that's just going to
65 strengthen [their] desire and [their] feeling, that's going to make [them] think, *I need to fight to win*" explains Kristin Laurin, one of the scientists who conducted the research. Drugs have a *high chance* of critically harming you, sexual activity has made *many*
70 *children* drop out of school, bullies will *almost* always be caught, as we tell the teens, but the statistics aren't one hundred percent in support of these trends. For teens, this amounts to saying that they will *probably* end up on the wrong path if they break these rules, but
75 that anyone who is special enough can still prevail.

What, then, can schools do to help their students? It doesn't take science to prove that experiencing something firsthand leaves a stronger impression than hearing the story from someone else. In recent
80 efforts to lower the bullying trend, many awareness organizations have brought innovative ideas to schools: these organizations simulate a bullying environment and twist the situation until each student in the group has had a taste of what it feels like to be bullied. Within
85 the groups, more select groups form and naturally dominate the rest of the kids. The experts conducting the activity are able to push the situation so that each of the teenagers is hurt in some way. When the simulation finally ends, each student is left with a vivid impression
90 of what being bullied feels like, producing a higher likelihood that the students will not exhibit bullying behaviors in the future.

These are but a few cases in which reiterating the same mantra over and over again will actually produce
95 the opposite effect. Moreover, giving teenagers a long list of things they shouldn't do may instead give them ideas that they never would have devised independently. Of course, schools can't just stand to the side while their students experiment in all the
100 wrong fields, but trying to tell them "you'll regret this in the future" may not produce the desired results. What adolescents' split minds tell them is to discover society for themselves without asking the adults for directions. Teens want to test the boundaries of their
105 abilities without irritating spoilers or tired adages. The more you try to contain this energy, the more teens yearn for the green grass on the other side. Why not let them taste the grass for themselves and come to their own conclusions? If the grass is poisonous, they'll
110 naturally come back to where it's safe, even without your telling them.

GO ON TO THE NEXT PAGE

13. The first two sentences of the passage (lines 1-4) suggest that

    (A) freedom is an ideal that can never really be attained
    (B) humans instinctively disobey authority in order to maintain a sense of autonomy
    (C) it is always wise to disregard strict orders from others
    (D) freedom can only result from following well-established social structures
    (E) teenagers are naturally more rebellious than people in other age groups

14. Lines 10-13 ("Even if . . . idea") imply that people

    (A) demand that their ideas be followed
    (B) tend to rebel as a form of retaliation
    (C) habitually seek approval from others
    (D) prefer to make their own choices
    (E) reject ideas inconsistent with their beliefs

15. In lines 12-13, the words "*your*" and "*their*" are italicized in order to

    (A) question the relevance of certain terms to contemporary psychological debates
    (B) create philosophical uncertainty about the origins of a yearning
    (C) endorse the ultimate ambiguity of a concept
    (D) highlight a logical incongruity concerning the content of an procedure
    (E) emphasize an undesirable change in the origin of an idea

16. In lines 14-18 ("Another name . . . choices"), the author defines teenage rebellion as an adolescent's

    (A) propensity to shun advice when making decisions
    (B) irrational behavior before reaching maturity
    (C) loss of self-control when overwhelmed with emotion
    (D) violent reaction to expectations of conformity
    (E) bad decision-making when disobeying his or her parents

17. According to the information presented in the second paragraph, "teenage rebellion" (lines 14-15) is most likely attributable to

    (A) a teenager's ability to learn and thus grow from changes in mood
    (B) abnormalities affecting brain function that disappear over time
    (C) the disparity between a teenager's logical development and emotional development
    (D) the emotional fragility that accompanies a lack of life experience
    (E) a teenager's general distrust of adults and all those who hold authority

18. In context of the third paragraph, the analogy of the "dog" (line 29) is used to illustrate that

    (A) teenagers feel most comfortable in settings known to them from childhood
    (B) dogs are just as impulsive and quick to make bad decisions as teenagers
    (C) teenagers consistently disregard the advice they are given
    (D) the negative consequences of an action are usually sufficient to quiet a rebellious teen
    (E) teenagers need to explore their limitations before they can feel secure

19. The question posed in lines 43-45 ("However, if . . . efforts?") suggests that

    (A) the measures that schools are taking in order to prevent negative behavior are ultimately promoting that same behavior
    (B) a variety of efforts to stop rebellious behavior will only succeed if these measures are endorsed by established authorities
    (C) teenagers can change their negative behaviors if they are subjected to strict psychological tests
    (D) the protocols that schools adopt to combat negative behavior effectively address the primary causes of teenage rebellion
    (E) it is important for schools to lecture teenagers against both bullying in particular and wrong-doing in general

GO ON TO THE NEXT PAGE

20. According to lines 60-75 ("A recent . . . prevail"), teenagers believe that they "can still prevail" (line 75) because

(A) they understand that most statistics relating to bad experiences are inflated to persuade skeptics
(B) they know that even if they get caught, they will most likely not get in serious trouble
(C) they realize that most rules are definite, but they yearn to find the loopholes and exceptions
(D) they are aware that they are special and that they are impervious to danger
(E) there exists the slightest chance that they can avoid the negative outcomes of their actions

21. According to the author, the "awareness organizations" (line 80) treat the epidemic of bullying by

(A) allowing the most timid and vulnerable students special privileges
(B) creating a situation in which the bullies feel the effects of bullying
(C) dictating harsher consequences for any child caught bullying another
(D) calming teenagers through a series of meditation workshops
(E) implementing new rules that allow bullied children to take legal action

22. The "schools" in line 36 would most likely find the author's answer to the problem of teenage rebellion in lines 104-110 ("The more . . . them") to be

(A) contentious
(B) esoteric
(C) counterintuitive
(D) elucidating
(E) laudable

23. Which of the following situations, if true, would most likely undermine the validity of the author's solution in lines 104-110 ("The more . . . them")?

(A) A teenage girl drinks alcohol at a party and decides she doesn't like it.
(B) A bully finds himself the butt of a joke and decides that he should be kinder.
(C) An advocacy group starts a lecture series on the evils of drinking alcohol.
(D) A lifelong addict has been abusing drugs since he first tried them in high school.
(E) A boy's sister gets in trouble so often that the boy avoids bad behavior.

24. The tone of the last sentence of the passage can best be described as

(A) resigned
(B) vacillating
(C) confident
(D) scholarly
(E) pompous

STOP

If you finish before time is called, you may check your work on this section only.
Do not turn to any other section in the test.

SECTION 3
Time–20 minutes
19 Questions

Directions: For each question in this section, select the best answer from among the choices given and fill in the corresponding circle on the answer sheet.

Each sentence below has one or two blanks, each blank indicating that something has been omitted. Beneath the sentence are five words or sets of words labeled A through E. Choose the word or set of words that, when inserted in the sentence, <u>best</u> fits the meaning of the sentence as a whole.

Example:

Jimmy opened his gas station in the ------- because he wanted to be in the middle of a metropolis.

(A) country
(B) suburbs
(C) periphery
(D) environment
(E) city

1. The professor's remarks were both outwardly ------- and cleverly -------, seemingly arrogant but actually informed by veiled kindness.

   (A) manipulative . . boorish
   (B) crude . . unreliable
   (C) flippant . . furtive
   (D) bombastic . . reassuring
   (E) haughty . . solicitous

2. In order to ------- the excessively competitive nature of her students, Ms. Jones often repeated the maxim, "This is not a contest; it is just a test."

   (A) hobble (B) expedite (C) nourish
      (D) accelerate (E) galvanize

3. The clients ------- the renovation budget to such an extent that the interior decorator felt that their professional relationship would ultimately be -------.

   (A) altered . . callow
   (B) wavered on . . paradoxical
   (C) renounced . . promising
   (D) dithered on . . unsatisfactory
   (E) perpetuated . . lucrative

4. In an instance of extremely ------- behavior, the students demonstrated egregious disrespect for the guest speaker by consistently interrupting his lecture.

   (A) cynical (B) maladroit (C) shrewd
      (D) insolent (E) manipulative

5. Instead of being ------- when addressing police officers, you should recognize them as authority figures and, accordingly, treat them with -------.

   (A) refractory . . truculence
   (B) discourteous . . reticence
   (C) impudent . . deference
   (D) obsequious . . respect
   (E) rebellious . . insouciance

6. The unending debate only served to ------- further controversy; in the absence of a solid resolution, new altercations would continue to arise.

   (A) gerrymander (B) diminish (C) engender
      (D) reprimand (E) obfuscate

GO ON TO THE NEXT PAGE

3   3   3   3   3   3

Unauthorized copying or
reuse of any part of this
page is illegal.

The two passages below are followed by questions based on their content and on the relationship between the two passages. Answer the questions on the basis of what is <u>stated</u> or <u>implied</u> in the passages and in any introductory material that may be provided.

Questions 7-18 are based on the following passages.

The following passages offer two perspectives on the idea of selfishness. The first passage is adapted from a book by a contemporary philosopher, while the second passage is excerpted from an article by a genetic biologist.

Passage 1

The word "egoism" comes from the Latin personal pronoun meaning "I." Egoism is therefore simply a word used by intellectuals to mean
Line selfishness. We live in a society that would rather
5 define issues than resolve them, so it is unsurprising to discover that there appear to be many forms of egoism. Ethical egoism postulates that individuals ought to do whatever is in their self-interest. Rational egoism posits that it is only reasonable to act in
10 one's self-interest. Psychological egoism decrees that individuals are always motivated by self-interest. There are many other forms, apparently.

Nor are contemporary intellectuals the only ones who have been preoccupied with egoism; indeed,
15 it was Thomas Jefferson who wrote: "Self-interest, or rather self-love, or egoism, has been plausibly substituted as the basis of morality. But I consider our relations with others as constituting the boundaries of morality . . . Self-love, therefore, is no part of
20 morality." Despite Jefferson's warnings against egoism's influence, egoism remains a pervasive force—in life and, yes, in how we respond to morality.

Selfishness is a part of all forms of creation. All
25 forms of life are born, eat, procreate, and die. Every form of life has to interact not only with those of its own type but also with other forms of life in order to survive. Plants grow in areas where other organisms can aid them and thus can help to ensure their
30 survival. Animals adapt to their surroundings and to one another, attesting that other forms of life are necessary for their own existence. If a species ignores such interrelations, then sooner or later such a species will die out. This is not egoism, but common sense,
35 an acceptance of the structure of life—whatever "life" may mean to us. We, humans, are the only species that possesses the arrogance to claim that we are above such mundane strictures. We call the results of such a claim "civilization," and it is this belief that
40 encourages many human beings to feel "superior" to the members of all other species—and to quite a few members of their own.

And yet, the very fact that we try to define "egoism" suggests that we are dissatisfied with
45 ourselves. It is not a new thing. The people of the Middle Ages believed that within man there are two combatants: the body and the spirit. The spirit suggests what we are capable of; the body demands immediate satisfaction. We have lost the sense of
50 balance between the two—lost our morality, as Jefferson might say. Morality is the right word to use, for there is a balance between what we *would* and what we *are*.

Passage 2

Egoism is what underlies human common-sense
55 morality. For an action to be morally right, it is essential that the action maximize one's own self-interest. Friedrich Nietzche proclaimed in *Beyond Good and Evil* that "egoism belongs to the essence of a noble soul" and that "the noble soul accepts the fact
60 of his egoism without question . . . as something that may have its basis in the primary law of things." We are creatures dictated by our genetics and our most basic self-interest: to continue being replicated. Our evolution does not operate on the level of a social
65 group. Our evolution operates on the basis of what lingers in our genetic identities.

Take for example, the hypothetical case of a mother bear and her cub preparing for winter hibernation. In the months prior, the mother bear will
70 consume as much sustenance as she needs to double her weight. However, should she not achieve the required weight by eating animals of other species, a mother bear will often eat her own cub in order to fulfill her nutritional needs. Unpleasant indeed, yet
75 the mother bear is acting in the interest of her own survival. It seems that a parent ought to protect its offspring to secure reproduction, but if the entire bloodline of the organism is at stake, biological imperatives take over.

80 Some may argue that this form of selfishness is not relevant to humans. On the contrary, it is the basis of all human interaction. Examine the physical makeup of a newborn baby. Proportionately, its head is significantly larger than the rest of its body.
85 There are several reasons for this, but one reason in particular is most important: brain development. Over time, babies have developed larger craniums that have been genetically modified to sustain larger brains, but this requirement (along with decreased
90 mobility) renders a human babies helpless for a long

GO ON TO THE NEXT PAGE

3   3   3   Unauthorized copying or   3   3   3
                                  reuse of any part of this
                                  page is illegal.

period of time. To offset this need for extensive care, larger heads were accompanied by larger eyes to elicit parental connection to the baby. Genetically speaking, such a trait combats a human mother's
95 possible urge to abandon her young, as humanity's innate love of visual stimulation counteracts an instinct that may otherwise be considered "natural."

   Those who rail against "egoism" are simply following a genetic predisposition. One contemplates
100 such issues not—as many are fooled into believing— from an explicit "sense of superiority." Rather, these contemplations are the by-products of forces that we are often powerless to discern.

7. The authors of both passages would most likely agree that egoism is

   (A) diametrically opposed to morality
   (B) controlled by hereditary factors
   (C) the sole basis of survival
   (D) not an exclusively modern concept
   (E) the foundation of ethics

8. In context, lines 7-12 ("Ethical egoism . . . apparently") serve to

   (A) prove that egoism cannot be discussed without attention to its many forms and varieties
   (B) celebrate the large number of perspectives that have influenced discussions of egoism
   (C) serve to differentiate between traditional and contemporary responses to an idea
   (D) present a few specialized uses of a term that is broadly defined earlier in the passage
   (E) demonstrate that an understanding of egoism requires adherence to a well-formulated theory

9. The "interrelations" mentioned in line 33 refer to

   (A) bonds between members of a family
   (B) levels of hierarchy in an ecosystem
   (C) purposeful cooperation across species
   (D) foundations of advanced civilization
   (E) interactions between different forms of life

10. According to the author of Passage 1, human beings feel "superior" (line 40) because they

   (A) have proven to be more civilized than other animal species
   (B) have made technological strides that other mammals have not matched
   (C) think that they possess a unique form of sophistication
   (D) continually examine universal biological and genetic processes
   (E) consider and contemplate such concepts as egoism and morality

11. In lines 45-49 ("The people . . . satisfaction"), the author establishes a relationship between

   (A) past and present
   (B) capacity and gratification
   (C) morality and necessity
   (D) frustration and satisfaction
   (E) reality and imagination

12. The author of Passage 2 quotes Friedrich Nietzsche in lines 58-61 most likely in order to

   (A) substantiate a claim
   (B) undermine a theory
   (C) signal a suspect line of reasoning
   (D) concede a point in another argument
   (E) explain a pervasive paradox

13. The statements in lines 63-66 ("Our evolution . . . identities") are notable for their use of

   (A) scientific speculation
   (B) historical research
   (C) parallel structure
   (D) extended metaphor
   (E) ironic understatement

14. The primary purpose of the statements in lines 80-81 ("Some may . . . humans") is to

   (A) acknowledge a counterargument
   (B) make an unexpected admission
   (C) illustrate a biological concept
   (D) refute a common formulation
   (E) account for disturbing fact

GO ON TO THE NEXT PAGE

15. In the final paragraph of Passage 2, the author indicates that "those who rail against" egoism (line 98) are

    (A) often unconscious of the actual sources of their behavior
    (B) committed to a worldview that values rationality over instinct
    (C) uncomfortable with the findings of modern genetic science
    (D) determined to increase public awareness of the dangers of egoism
    (E) unable to reconcile their declared beliefs with their true values

16. The "case of a mother bear" (lines 67-68) described in Passage 2 is presented as an example of

    (A) "basic self-interest" (line 63)
    (B) "a social group" (lines 64-65)
    (C) "need for extensive care" (line 91)
    (D) "parental connection to the baby" (line 93)
    (E) "innate love" (line 96)

17. The author of Passage 2 would most likely view Thomas Jefferson's definition of morality (lines 15-20) as

    (A) veracious
    (B) admirable
    (C) puzzling
    (D) inaccurate
    (E) grievous

18. The author of Passage 2 would assert that the phenomenon of human beings feeling "superior" (line 40, Passage 1) is

    (A) imperative
    (B) incidental
    (C) consequential
    (D) detrimental
    (E) profitable

STOP

If you finish before time is called, you may check your work on this section only.
Do not turn to any other section in the test.

POST TEST ANALYSIS

This post test analysis is important if you want to see an improvement on your next test. Each section has a set of possible reasons for errors. Place check marks next to the ones that pertain to you, and write your own on the blank lines provided. Use this form to better analyze your performance. **If you don't understand why you made errors, there is no way you can correct them!**

1. **SENTENCE COMPLETION:**

   Problems with the sentence:
   - ❑ Wasn't familiar with phrases, idioms, or words in the sentence
   - ❑ Missed the clues or tones
   - ❑ Put your OWN word in the blank rather than one from the sentence
   - ❑ Completely avoided marking
   - ❑ Other: _____

   _____

   Problems with the answers:
   - ❑ Did not use process of elimination
   - ❑ Did not ignore unknown words
   - ❑ Did not use prefix/root/suffix knowledge to figure out the meaning of the unknown words
   - ❑ Did not match the clues and tones of the answer with those of the sentence
   - ❑ Did not recognize vocabulary words
   - ❑ Did not check answer to see if it fit
   - ❑ Other: _____

   _____

   Leaving questions unanswered:
   - ❑ Did not try
   - ❑ Did not fill in the blank(s) with words
   - ❑ Ran out of time
   - ❑ Other: _____

   _____

2. **SHORT READING COMPREHENSION:**
   - ❑ Did not read entire paragraph
   - ❑ Did not see more than one point
   - ❑ Missed contrast clues
   - ❑ Did not pinpoint thesis
   - ❑ Did not identify similarities and differences in Double Short Reading Comp
   - ❑ Other: _____

   _____

3. **LONG READING COMPREHENSION:**
   - ❑ Did not understand the question, line reference, or answers
   - ❑ Spent too much time reading the passages
   - ❑ Did not underline the line reference
   - ❑ Read too much or too little
   - ❑ Did not answer the specific question; instead analyzed its main idea
   - ❑ Did not do process of elimination based on facts in the passage
   - ❑ Couldn't find the false words
   - ❑ Couldn't choose between two possible answers
   - ❑ Did not use tone to help eliminate answers
   - ❑ When stuck at 2 guessed instead of pulling additional fact
   - ❑ Couldn't finish in time
   - ❑ Other: _____

   _____

ANSWER KEY

TEST 9

SECTION 1

#	Answer	LEVEL
1	B	(1)
2	D	(2)
3	C	(3)
4	E	(4)
5	D	(5)
6	B	(3)
7	A	(4)
8	E	(2)
9	B	(4)
10	D	(3)
11	A	(3)
12	A	(3)
13	C	(2)
14	E	(2)
15	C	(3)
16	A	(2)
17	B	(4)
18	A	(3)
19	C	(3)
20	B	(4)
21	B	(3)
22	B	(3)
23	D	(3)
24	B	(2)
25	E	(4)

SECTION 2

#	Answer	LEVEL
1	A	(2)
2	C	(2)
3	A	(3)
4	A	(3)
5	D	(3)
6	A	(4)
7	B	(4)
8	B	(5)
9	E	(3)
10	A	(3)
11	C	(2)
12	D	(2)
13	B	(2)
14	D	(3)
15	E	(3)
16	A	(2)
17	C	(3)
18	E	(4)
19	A	(2)
20	E	(3)
21	B	(3)
22	C	(3)
23	D	(5)
24	C	(4)

SECTION 3

#	Answer	LEVEL
1	E	(2)
2	A	(1)
3	D	(3)
4	D	(4)
5	C	(4)
6	C	(3)
7	D	(4)
8	D	(3)
9	E	(2)
10	C	(3)
11	B	(3)
12	A	(2)
13	C	(3)
14	A	(3)
15	A	(4)
16	A	(4)
17	D	(4)
18	B	(5)

Difficulty levels range from 1 - 5 with 1 being the easiest and 5 being the hardest.
For answer explanations please visit www.ies2400.com/criticalreading

PRACTICE TEST 10

1   1   1   Unauthorized copying or
reuse of any part of this
page is illegal.   1   1   1

SECTION 1
Time–25 minutes
25 Questions

Directions: For each question in this section, select the best answer from among the choices given and fill in the corresponding circle on the answer sheet.

Each sentence below has one or two blanks, each blank indicating that something has been omitted. Beneath the sentence are five words or sets of words labeled A through E. Choose the word or set of words that, when inserted in the sentence, <u>best</u> fits the meaning of the sentence as a whole.

Example:

Jimmy opened his gas station in the ------- because he wanted to be in the middle of a metropolis.

(A) country
(B) suburbs
(C) periphery
(D) environment
(E) city

---

1. Afraid that her son would ------- his earlier, uncaring attitude to his studies, Mrs. Rose hired a series of tutors in subjects such as geometry, chemistry, and history.

    (A) speculate about   (B) abscond from
       (C) evolve from   (D) regress to
          (E) benefit from

2. George is a kind man, though not a garrulous one; unfortunately, his neighbors mistake his ------- for -------.

    (A) candor . . inflexibility
    (B) effusiveness . . antagonism
    (C) contentment . . expansiveness
    (D) reticence . . hostility
    (E) gratuity . . aggravation

3. The candidate's audition was both ------- and -------; though short, it was original.

    (A) succinct . . nascent
    (B) laconic . . valiant
    (C) pithy . . unprecedented
    (D) interminable . . impromptu
    (E) impulsive . . cavalier

4. The novels of Thomas Mann regularly depict characters who have abjured the demands of steady careers and instead give themselves over to lives of -------.

    (A) dilettantism   (B) acerbity   (C) vapidity
       (D) euphoria   (E) mawkishness

5. Sean has a tendency to ------- the little authority that he wields, yet it is well known that his superiors at the law firm regard him as little more than their -------.

    (A) broadcast . . lout
    (B) downplay . . sycophant
    (C) enhance . . curmudgeon
    (D) utilize . . mentor
    (E) flaunt . . lackey

GO ON TO THE NEXT PAGE

Practice Test 10

The passages below are followed by questions based on their content; questions following a pair of related passages may also be based on the relationship between the paired passages. Answer the questions on the basis of what is stated or implied in the passages and in any introductory material that may be provided.

Questions 6-9 are based on the following passages.

Passage 1

Why would anyone go to a coffee shop to write? The gurgle of the drip coffee, the violent hiss of the latte—every distraction possible! Even worse are
Line
5　the patrons: other would-be writers blogging about the latest fashion craze. I can envision their thought bubbles: "black and white are so in this season," as opposed to all those other seasons, when black and white clearly meant fashion suicide. Then there are the supposed "prolific" novelists who pilfer bits of
10　dialogue from the myriad conversations around them. They snatch hold of the lives of others (these poor, unknowing victims of narrative vampirism) retelling stolen stories and never bothering with real creativity, all the while sipping their cups of decaf free trade
15　brew—with soy milk of course.

Passage 2

J.K. Rowling frequented her local coffee shop while conceiving and writing the *Harry Potter* series. It was there that she imagined and envisioned her magical world, possibly pulling inspiration from the
20　daily operations of the café and the coffee lovers walking in and sitting near her. The people at the café were not people at all, but prototypes of the characters that she would eventually bring to life on the page. While some may argue that writing today has become
25　merely a means of appropriating a stranger's life, who really cares? Writing is not the espousal of another's experiences; it is the dramatization and reimagining of that life as a story so specific that it inadvertently becomes universal.

6.　Both passages discuss how

(A) novelists abstain from utilizing everyday circumstances
(B) immediate surroundings can influence written work
(C) café life is dramatized by very different kinds of novelists
(D) creative and reassuring episodes emerge in a hectic atmosphere
(E) successful writers observe and falsify the lives of strangers

7.　The author of Passage 2 would most likely answer the question in line 1 of Passage 1 by suggesting that

(A) humdrum surroundings often force a writer to be innovative
(B) certain locations can be very lucrative for amateur novelists
(C) cafés are some of the only places where a writer can find narrative models
(D) a particular setting can be used to create unique imagined worlds
(E) matters of environment can rob a writer of innate creativity

8.　The author of Passage 2 would most likely react to the concept of "narrative vampirism" (line 12, Passage 1) with

(A) dispassion, since it does not have any effect on authors themselves
(B) scorn, because its application is insignificant in fabricating written work
(C) ambivalence, since its usage would depend on the content of the work
(D) support, as it is a popular and lucrative element of fiction writing
(E) indifference, because writers have the license to interpret the world as they see fit

9.　Unlike the author of Passage 2, the author of Passage 1 uses which of the following?

(A) Extended analogy
(B) Rhetorical question
(C) Purposeful sarcasm
(D) Literary allusion
(E) Ironic exaggeration

GO ON TO THE NEXT PAGE

Questions 10-18 are based on the following passage.

In this passage, the author discusses the Saturday morning movies that he frequented as a young boy.

As a child growing up just after the Second World War, I loved going to "the pictures." It was a long time before I was allowed to go on my own, and only
Line then if my parents deemed the film suitable. Westerns
5   were my favorite, especially if the Apache were on the warpath, which they usually were. Personally, I rooted for them every time, but neither their superiority in numbers, nor the fact that they were defending their own land, helped them to win a single victory.
10   On Saturday mornings, the local cinema offered a program for children, a kind of exclusive club: no adults allowed, apart from the cinema staff. I pleaded to join and, eventually, my parents gave in. At ten o'clock every Saturday morning, I joined the
15   squirming line of small boys in short gray trousers and wrinkled socks, each jostling to be the first to enter and race down to the front rows. Behind us sat older boys, accompanied by some very superior, older girls whom we younger boys didn't like much
20   —some of these girls wore lipstick and most seemed little interested in the program. The noise in the cinema was intense, and a couple of disciplinarian dragon ladies, armed with torches, stalked the aisles, admonishing the rowdy and threatening the
25   insubordinate. The lights dimmed. The whole cinema roared and cheered.

The program always began with a short informative film about something encouraging for a country not long out of a war. We scorned this
30   segment, unless it was about steam trains or breaking land speed records. This was followed by a sort of morality tale, full of rather wooden actors speaking English in the BBC accents rarely heard in the streets of East Yorkshire, and at which we snickered. Relief
35   was at hand: a comic short from America, hopefully Laurel and Hardy with another "fine mess" they had gotten themselves into. We laughed till the tears came! The lights came up for a small break, for advertisements and the ice cream lady, who was
40   making her way up the aisle. She was besieged.

But soon the noise grew. Thunderously, we stamped our impatience on the wooden floor. The usherettes moved, swiftly and unavailingly, to quiet us. The lights dimmed again, the screen lit up. We
45   roared approval. The second half of the program was what we had come for. It began as usual, with a western, without the Apache but with Gene Autry (groan from all, because he always spent five minutes singing to a bored girl) or with Roy Rogers, who
50   didn't always sing, who was slimmer and fitter and quicker than Gene with a gun or a lariat; plus, Rogers had a great horse, Trigger. In fact, Autry or Rogers, it made no difference: in less than forty minutes, the

baddies were thwarted. Good triumphed efficiently.
55   Finally, the climax of the morning's entertainment arrived: the latest installment of the series! Often, it was Flash Gordon. Each week, with courage, resourcefulness, and daring, he battled and thwarted Ming the Merciless. Occasionally, it was
60   Zorro, who upheld justice for the poorer inhabitants of California. Each week, fairness and freedom were threatened, seemingly doomed. Our hero was left in dire peril and we had to wait until the next week to discover that he had escaped and that liberty was
65   allowed to survive . . . until the next threat came along. Flash, Zorro, even the Lone Ranger: we believed in them all.

Yet, for me, only one superhero meant anything: Nyoka, Jungle Girl. She was a sort of female Tarzan,
70   although she spoke better English. She lived in the jungle, through which she ran barefoot, repelling lions and grappling with giant crocodiles and highly venomous snakes. She rescued poor natives from being tyrannized by crooked hunters greedy for
75   the gold and rare jewels hidden in King Solomon's mines. She was resourceful, tough and intelligent: no problem discouraged her for long. Every week she was left facing a dilemma that was seemingly impossible to escape; by the following week, she
80   had come up with a solution and was on her way again. I admired her without restraint. After an hour with her, I felt I could do anything, even take on those stern and powerful usherettes—although I did not actually put the theory to the test.
85   Nowadays, I laugh at the naïveté of those Saturday morning films. Yet they achieved their purpose. Nyoka reminded us children of the necessity of resilience in life. Our parents did not need to be reminded of that: they had just lived through five
90   years of war and they wanted the world to be less fraught for us than it had been for them. Nyoka was a glorious symbol of that hope, and I have never forgotten her. And, if ever I find myself in the jungle, before me a lake covered in burning oil, behind me
95   native hordes with poisoned spears, I shall know exactly what to do.

GO ON TO THE NEXT PAGE

10. The primary purpose of the passage is to

(A) analyze the societal pressures that eventually led to the creation of the first fully modern cinema house
(B) consider a branch of culture that shaped the author's childhood
(C) document the author's least pleasant childhood experiences at the movie theater
(D) imply that England was at the forefront of modern cinematic techniques
(E) speculate about the importance of British cinema in a post-war political context

11. The atmosphere of the movie theater described in the second and third paragraphs can best be characterized as

(A) exclusive
(B) threatening
(C) composed
(D) rambunctious
(E) educational

12. An example of the "dragon ladies" (line 23) would most likely be the

(A) "older girls" (line 19)
(B) "wooden actors" (line 32)
(C) "ice cream lady" (line 39)
(D) "female Tarzan" (line 69)
(E) "powerful usherettes" (line 83)

13. The "short informative film" mentioned in lines 27-28 was shown primarily to

(A) waste time before the main event
(B) raise the morale of a weary society
(C) educate British children about culture
(D) introduce the historical background of the feature film
(E) entertain the audience with a contemporary comedy

14. The reaction to Gene Autry's "singing" (line 49) implies that

(A) the children thought five minutes was too short for full enjoyment of the music
(B) the audience was frustrated by this segment of the entertainment program
(C) the children would have preferred Roy Rogers as the singer
(D) the audience was angry with the girl for expressing boredom
(E) the children in the audience were waiting to hear a duet

15. According to the information in the fifth paragraph, the format of the serial relies on which of the following to maintain interest?

(A) Morality
(B) Subterfuge
(C) Satire
(D) Suspense
(E) Triumph

16. The author's fascination with "Nyoka, Jungle Girl" (line 69) most likely stemmed from

(A) her superior eloquence
(B) her attractive looks
(C) her indomitable nature
(D) her tractable demeanor
(E) her wild upbringing

17. The tone of the last sentence of the passage ("And, if . . . do") can best be described as one of

(A) sarcasm
(B) pessimism
(C) empathy
(D) belligerence
(E) levity

18. Which of the following describes the overall structure of the passage?

(A) Academic analysis followed by personal commentary
(B) A sociological generalization supported by specific examples
(C) An account of a problem followed by a suggested solution
(D) Reminiscence followed by a present-day perspective
(E) A discussion of opposing viewpoints followed by an attempt to reconcile them

GO ON TO THE NEXT PAGE

Questions 19-25 are based on the following passage.

The following passage was written by scientist whose specialty is animal behavior.

Dogs have been domesticated 9,000 years longer than cats have, yet this fact is not necessarily a guarantee that our affinity for dogs is stronger.
Line Oxytocin, the hormone responsible for the initiation of
5 maternal instincts in humans, is found in high levels in postpartum women and contributes to the emotional bond between mother and child. The same hormone is found in comparable amounts in both cats and dogs, and in their respective owners, indicating that the
10 emotional connection between man and pet stems from a deep biological foundation. This bond may even explain why dogs are used not only as companions but also as participants in human-led group endeavors such as hunting and police activity.
15   Over time, the dog has developed unique capabilities that have enhanced its symbiotic relationship with humanity. Dogs are able to use left-side bias facial recognition, an advanced interpretation and communication tool, to detect
20 human emotions. Imagine splitting your face in half, mirroring the left side and the right side individually, and merging together the two resulting left sides and the two resulting right sides; because no face is perfectly symmetrical, you will find that the left-side
25 merger is quite unlike the right-side merger. Dogs are profoundly aware of this discrepancy and use only the left halves of human visages to determine the subtle changes that directly relate to human feelings. You may express calmness with relaxed lips, or
30 apprehension with widened eyes, yet these facial tics mostly go unnoticed among people. Dogs, however, register these changes.
   Through extensive testing, researchers have proven that dogs are the only non-humanoid species
35 capable of responding accurately and consistently to pointing. One could only presume that these traits have their origins in the hunter-retriever alliance; in this relationship, the submissive beast locates the rewards of the hunt in exchange for food and shelter, with body
40 language serving as the sole means of communication. Since our ancestors couldn't ask the wolf, "Could you please fetch me that rabbit?" how else could this trust between wild animal and human establish itself?
   In an experiment that pinpointed the
45 developmental aspects of domestication, Russian geneticist Dmitry Bleyaev set out to do with a few generations of silver foxes what it had taken other dog domesticators thousands of years to accomplish. Bleyaev's endeavor consisted of housing 3,000
50 wild silver foxes to observe their range of emotions, including (but not limited to) fear, aggression, and timidity. Only those animals that exhibited neutral to positive interactions (inquisitiveness, friendliness, playfulness) were allowed to reproduce. The next

55 generation of foxes exhibited more of these particular traits; repeating this procedure over and over produced a majority of silver foxes suited to harmonious and productive interactions with humans. Scientists, indeed, have determined a direct correlation between
60 an animal's genetic makeup and its ability to be tamed.
   To see if these personality traits could be a matter of learned behavior as well as genetic makeup, Bleyaev and his fellow researchers placed aggressive kits and fearful young foxes with den mothers who
65 sought out human interaction. The younger animals did not become more susceptible to domestication, and thus never learned to trust humans. The results of this research revealed that taming is the result of selective breeding: those personality attributes that are most
70 compatible with human lifestyles and needs are singled out and passed on. Despite the results of Bleyaev's study, some skeptics believe that taming is solely a conditioned response, though it is forbiddingly hard to fault Bleyaev's methods.

19. The first paragraph of the passage is best characterized as

(A) an comparative analysis of the maternal instincts of different species
(B) a scientific explanation of a wide-ranging phenomenon
(C) a chronology of humanity's relationship with cats and dogs
(D) an edifying description of an often-neglected chemical imbalance
(E) a validation of the argument that dogs are more trustworthy than cats

20. The passage indicates that "left-side bias facial recognition" (line 18) is

(A) seldom used by canines that have not been domesticated
(B) utilized by humans only in research and experimental settings
(C) employed by dogs to discern nuances of human emotion
(D) well understood by many pet owners and dog trainers
(E) exhibited by only a handful of non-humanoid animals

GO ON TO THE NEXT PAGE

Practice Test 10

21. In lines 36-40 ("One could . . . communication") the author implies that a dog's ability to respond to pointing stems from

(A) enmity
(B) scarcity
(C) empathy
(D) necessity
(E) similarity

22. Lines 44-48 ("In an . . . accomplish") suggest that Bleyaev's goal was

(A) ostentatious
(B) erudite
(C) subversive
(D) honorable
(E) ambitious

23. Which of the following, if true, would most effectively undermine Bleyaev's conclusion about "learned behavior" (line 62)?

(A) A baby polar bear with calm parents nonetheless becomes vicious.
(B) A traumatized kitten grows up to be hostile to strangers.
(C) A carefully bred Pomeranian enjoys the company of humans.
(D) A group of prairie dogs is trained to dig holes that have conical shapes.
(E) An aggressive chimpanzee becomes friendly after contact with docile apes.

24. In line 73, "forbiddingly" most nearly means

(A) chillingly
(B) ominously
(C) unapproachably
(D) deleteriously
(E) extremely

25. The overall tone of the passage is

(A) optimistic
(B) colloquial
(C) informative
(D) skeptical
(E) maudlin

STOP

If you finish before time is called, you may check your work on this section only.
Do not turn to any other section in the test.

Practice Test 10

SECTION 2
Time–25 minutes
24 Questions

> **Directions:** For each question in this section, select the best answer from among the choices given and fill in the corresponding circle on the answer sheet.

Each sentence below has one or two blanks, each blank indicating that something has been omitted. Beneath the sentence are five words or sets of words labeled A through E. Choose the word or set of words that, when inserted in the sentence, <u>best</u> fits the meaning of the sentence as a whole.

Example:

Jimmy opened his gas station in the ------- because he wanted to be in the middle of a metropolis.

(A) country
(B) suburbs
(C) periphery
(D) environment
(E) city   Ⓐ Ⓑ Ⓒ Ⓓ ●

---

1. Anna Wintour often encourages fashion designers to be both ------- and -------, hoping that they will create new and exciting aesthetics that are also profitable.

   (A) visionary . . commonplace
   (B) innovative . . practical
   (C) reactionary . . remunerative
   (D) groundbreaking . . immense
   (E) eager . . demure

2. Although Francis was thought to be very -------, his speech at the video game convention revealed a ------- side of his personality that even his closest friends had never witnessed.

   (A) paranoid . . pompous
   (B) timorous . . prudent
   (C) diffident . . confident
   (D) delusional . . querulous
   (E) flamboyant . . histrionic

3. A review of a play must be an evenhanded assessment that depicts both the ------- of the playwright and his creative shortcomings, never giving way to extremely biased opinions.

   (A) satires   (B) inadequacies   (C) mentalities
      (D) faculties   (E) drawbacks

4. Instead of settling for ------- interpretations of the assigned essay, the philosophy professor urged his students to ------- the text for deeper meanings.

   (A) superficial . . plumb
   (B) facile . . reveal
   (C) insignificant . . edit
   (D) regressive . . examine
   (E) fortuitous . . explicate

5. Independent screenwriters typically attempt to avoid -------, yet studio movies must often resort to timeworn formulas because they are ------- storytelling devices.

   (A) clichés . . popular
   (B) foreshadowing . . compelling
   (C) flashbacks . . invaluable
   (D) quips . . unsubstantiated
   (E) platitudes . . ineffectual

6. The writer's contributions can be considered far from -------, since he only pens one or two articles each month for a publication that demands weekly, if not daily, submissions.

   (A) voluntary   (B) prosaic   (C) prolific
      (D) economical   (E) disproportionate

7. Clint Mansell's film scores are widely deemed ------- on account of their unconventionally cacophonous melodies.

   (A) nihilistic   (B) iconoclastic   (C) absurd
      (D) misguided   (E) bucolic

8. We were put off by the ------- look of the dressmaker's most recent collection; for reasons that remained unclear, she had chosen cuts and patterns that had gone out of fashion decades earlier.

   (A) sordid   (B) classic   (C) superannuated
      (D) hallowed   (E) timeless

GO ON TO THE NEXT PAGE

The passages below are followed by questions based on their content; questions following a pair of related passages may also be based on the relationship between the paired passages. Answer the questions on the basis of what is <u>stated</u> or <u>implied</u> in the passages and in any introductory material that may be provided.

Questions 9-10 are based on the following passage.

A debate has raged in recent years as to whether we should apply business practices to government entities. Proponents of such measures believe that the
Line public's best interests are served by limiting spending
5 and slashing budgets, but these partisans seem to have forgotten what the proper purpose of government is. The government's job is not to produce goods, but to protect and serve its citizens. It is impossible to focus on the health and safety of the populace when
10 an organization is constantly worried about whether its funding will be, like the proverbial rug, pulled out from under its feet.

9. In the passage, the author's attitude towards the "partisans" (line 5) can best be described as

   (A) antagonistic
   (B) evenhanded
   (C) duplicitous
   (D) pragmatic
   (E) apathetic

10. The sentence in lines 7-8 ("The government's . . . citizens") functions primarily to

   (A) suggest a controversial comparison
   (B) assert a meaningful distinction
   (C) examine an undisputed fact
   (D) contradict a widely accepted notion
   (E) introduce a surprising digression

Questions 11-12 are based on the following passage.

Nowadays, it is commonly believed that any play or film with a tragic ending can be labeled a "tragedy." This is a blatant misconception, since most seeming
Line tragedies are actually dramas with a few dark or dire
5 themes. Classical Greek tragedy involves a protagonist who begins at one emotional state, such as euphoria and jubilation, but completes his emotional arc at the opposite end of the spectrum. He often suffers a major downfall through a personal tragic flaw, such as the
10 arrogance that undoes the title character of *Oedipus Rex*. But tragedy's structure can also be the inverse. Fundamentally, a tragic play must involve a cathartic experience, allowing the audience to run the emotional gamut and therefore be purged of fear and anxiety.
15 However, current attempts all miss the basic crux of this form and misattribute the term "tragedy" to works that are really "serious dramas."

11. The author cites "*Oedipus Rex*" (lines 10-11) in order to

   (A) curtail the use of a common misnomer
   (B) support his claim that all tragedies are flawed
   (C) discuss a modern depiction of tragedy
   (D) shift the focus from tragedy to drama
   (E) offer an example of a particular form of playwriting

12. The passage is primarily concerned with

   (A) defining a term that is commonly misused
   (B) delineating an obsolete application of a word
   (C) providing a new perspective on a forgotten genre
   (D) supporting a modern reconception of a term
   (E) promoting the adoption of a theatrical genre in film

GO ON TO THE NEXT PAGE

Practice Test 10

Questions 13-24 are based on the following passages.

Edward Hopper (1882-1967) was an American painter known for his realistic portrayals of isolated individuals. In the passages that follow, two authors consider Hopper's accomplishments and legacy.

Passage 1

The work of one of America's finest twentieth-century artists, Edward Hopper, has been subjected to much critical discussion by art aficionados—
Line although, significantly, not by the general public by
5 whom he has always been venerated. Hopper himself rarely discussed his work publicly. However, he did once remark that, "The whole answer is there on the canvas."
This suggests that he took to heart a maxim given
10 to him by Robert Henri, one of his teachers in the New York School of Art: "It isn't the subject [of a painting] that counts, but what you feel about it." Henri may well have been referring to matters of artistic inspiration: Hopper seems to have taken this advice
15 to be equally applicable to anyone who wanders into an art gallery. Hopper's paintings create within the observer a feeling of instant recognition not only of what is clearly presented in the depiction, but also of all the implications and questions that lie behind what
20 is actually shown.
Automat (1927) depicts a woman sitting alone at a small table, on which is a cup of coffee. However, the power of the picture comes from the viewer's gradual assimilation of details: the woman's clothing suggests
25 a certain smartness, and an empty plate sits beside the coffee cup. On the shelf behind the woman—perhaps significantly—is a small bowl of colorful fruit. Its presence contrasts with that of the precisely depicted brown radiator standing against the wall nearby. The
30 more one explores the picture, the more one unearths new questions and considerations. Is the painting a comment on urban isolation, or does it simply record a moment of solitude and reflection within the busy levels of a city? These ambiguities of recognition
35 are what hold the attention and, eventually, the involvement of the onlooker.
Above all else, in every one of Hopper's paintings, the contrast between darkness and illumination forces us to consider the truth of his
40 pictures. Sometimes—as in his most popular picture, *Nighthawks* (1942)—the darkness is all-encompassing, and makes us aware of the gulf between our personal life voyages and those of others. At other times—as in one of his last pictures, *Office in a Small City* (1953)—
45 Hopper reverses this motif. The picture blazes with the stark light of office windows and a cerulean sky: through one office window we see a man sitting at a bare desk, gazing through a second window just across the way. Is this a room with a view, or a view with

50 hidden insights? Remember Henri's words: "What you feel" is what counts.

Passage 2

In 1946, painter and illustrator Ad Reinhardt created a cartoon entitled "How to Look at Modern Art in America". This now-famous and often clever
55 image depicts the totality of modern art as a gigantic family tree: the roots and trunk bear the names of the European painters who inspired the American avant-garde, while each leaf in the foliage up above bears the name of a prominent American painter or
60 sculptor. Some of these named leaves sprout from healthy branches, some from rotting and soon-to-break boughs. A leaf with the name "Hopper" can be seen on a branch that is ready to crack, pulled down by a grim black weight that bears the words "Subject Matter."
65 I have always found Reinhardt's response to Edward Hopper to be too dismissive. Subject matter or no subject matter, Hopper is one of the finest painters of mass and light and shade that America has ever produced. Look at the indigo shadows in his interior
70 scenes, the pale, blistering yellows of his afternoon landscapes. Each one is a small miracle. And yet, even as a lifelong admirer of Hopper and his art, I have always felt that there is a kernel of truth in Reinhardt's offhanded depiction. With their lonely office workers
75 and astonishing twilight hues, Hopper's paintings offer one picture-perfect representation after another. But what else do they offer? No shock, no revelation, no terror. They would have made sense—maybe—in a small New England town in 1910. After the horrors of
80 two world wars, the rise of totalitarianism, the advent of the atom bomb, Hopper's works make almost no sense at all.
Compare this to Reinhardt. There isn't, to be honest, much pleasure to be gained from Reinhardt's
85 paintings—many of them forbidding and threatening black-on-black abstract canvases. But there is meaning in these. With paintings so uncomfortable and so unconventional, Reinhardt acknowledged that we have entered a discomforting, disorienting stretch of history.
90 America could never be the same after so much social and political trauma, and neither could its art. Hopper, in contrast, was a fine scene painter to the end—even though the world of progressive art had less and less use for scene painters as the tumultuous 1940s, and
95 then the transformative 1950s, rocked American aesthetics. He offered cool comfort to an age that had already lost its innocence; today, it is possible to look back and wonder why he was so alert to grass greens and sunset oranges and so many other brilliant turns of
100 depiction, and so oblivious to so much else.

GO ON TO THE NEXT PAGE

13. The word "venerated" in line 5 of Passage 1 most nearly means

(A) sanctified
(B) dignified
(C) revered
(D) rewarded
(E) vindicated

14. The quotation "The whole . . . canvas" at the end of the first paragraph in Passage 1 functions primarily to

(A) summarize two prevailing views
(B) downplay a popular criticism
(C) undermine a controversial stance
(D) provide an important exception
(E) clarify a unique intuition

15. It can be reasonably inferred from the statement "Henri may . . . gallery" (lines 12-16, Passage 1) that Hopper intended to

(A) encourage the need for subjectivity while viewing art
(B) distinguish his artistic inspirations from those of his mentor
(C) provoke specific and unequivocal expressions in viewers of art
(D) attribute credit for his innovations to his former teacher
(E) choose his artistic subjects in response to sanctioned tastes

16. The author of Passage 1 would most likely answer the question "But what . . . offer?" (lines 76-77, Passage 2) by asserting that Hopper's paintings

(A) avoid monopolizing the viewer's attention by using contrasting elements
(B) encourage the viewer to appreciate quotidian subject matter
(C) suggest subtle solutions to conflicts and struggles that normally cause despair
(D) provoke thought from the viewer by cultivating meaningful uncertainty
(E) programatically frustrate the viewer's assumptions about fine art

17. The primary purpose of Passage 1 is to

(A) account for the contemporary influence of Edward Hopper's masterpieces
(B) theorize about the historic origins of a polarizing painter
(C) encourage the reader to understand an artist from an uncommon perspective
(D) reveal the lesser-known aspects of a painter's motivations
(E) consider the ways in which a viewer may respond to a renowned painter's works

18. The author of Passage 2 would most likely view "these ambiguities" (line 34, Passage 1) as

(A) enticing
(B) indispensable
(C) incidental
(D) perplexing
(E) temporal

19. The description of the cartoon in the first paragraph of Passage 2 functions as

(A) an introduction to a claim presented later in the passage
(B) a hypothetical example intended to balance a partial view
(C) an illustration of opinions that still prevail among many art critics
(D) a concession to the preeminent artistic ideology of Hopper's era
(E) a consideration of historical facts that are eventually refuted

20. It can be inferred that the author of Passage 2 considers "picture-perfect" art (line 76) to be

(A) inane
(B) provocative
(C) comprehensive
(D) wanting
(E) sentimental

21. The tone of the statement "They would . . . 1910" (lines 78-79, Passage 2) can be best characterized as

(A) dismissive
(B) pedantic
(C) objective
(D) accusatory
(E) solemn

GO ON TO THE NEXT PAGE

Practice Test 10

22. The author of Passage 2 would most likely view the painting *Office in a Small City*, described in the final paragraph of Passage 1, as

    (A) uninteresting, because the subject matter is over-used

    (B) revolutionary, because it deviates from Hopper's typical style

    (C) limited, because it does not offer a response to social upheavals

    (D) amateurish, because it fails to employ realistic representation techniques

    (E) practical, because it allows the viewer various options for interpretation

23. In the final paragraph of Passage 2, the author suggests that Ad Reinhardt's paintings are

    (A) oppressive, because of their allusions to specific crises

    (B) revelatory, since they foreshadowed even greater breakthroughs in art technique

    (C) transformative, because they redefined the role of the artist in society

    (D) expressive despite their austere and daunting appearances

    (E) symptomatic of a hopelessly grim political outlook

24. The authors of both passages would most likely agree on which of the following statements about Edward Hopper?

    (A) His color choices were striking and memorable.

    (B) His paintings communicate his irritation with abstract art.

    (C) His enigmatic subject matter was intriguing.

    (D) His humble scenes reflected a troubled modern world.

    (E) His pleasing forms and hues successfully offer escape from bleak realities.

STOP

If you finish before time is called, you may check your work on this section only.
Do not turn to any other section in the test.

SECTION 3
Time–20 minutes
18 Questions

Directions: For each question in this section, select the best answer from among the choices given and fill in the corresponding circle on the answer sheet.

Each sentence below has one or two blanks, each blank indicating that something has been omitted. Beneath the sentence are five words or sets of words labeled A through E. Choose the word or set of words that, when inserted in the sentence, <u>best</u> fits the meaning of the sentence as a whole.

Example:

Jimmy opened his gas station in the ------- because he wanted to be in the middle of a metropolis.

(A) country
(B) suburbs
(C) periphery
(D) environment
(E) city

1. Undeterred by the ------- of his colleagues, the head of the laboratory continued to use small and confined groups of test subjects, rather than the ------- samplings favored by the scientific community, in his research.

   (A) admonitions . . broad
   (B) warnings . . overbearing
   (C) caveats . . minuscule
   (D) collaboration . . variegated
   (E) liberality . . diversified

2. The ------- response from Mr. Peabody seemed uncharacteristic; under normal circumstances, he is known to be ------- and easygoing.

   (A) insouciant . . rambling
   (B) terse . . apprehensive
   (C) edgy . . imperturbable
   (D) blithe . . tranquil
   (E) eccentric . . unflappable

3. At present, the Plate Tectonic Theory leaves nothing to be disputed: geologists unanimously agree that arguments against this idea should be considered ------- at best.

   (A) equivocal   (B) halcyon   (C) parsimonious
       (D) erroneous   (E) transient

4. Daniel's father was remarkably ------- and uninvolved when dealing with his son's needs, often ------- Daniel's mother to address any matters that should arise.

   (A) solicitous . . relying on
   (B) retroactive . . forbidding
   (C) indifferent . . deferring to
   (D) irascible . . persuading
   (E) lax . . supplicating

5. Determined to ------- information on preventive safety measures, the medical staff took to social media to promulgate the facts at its disposal.

   (A) disseminate   (B) isolate   (C) conceal
       (D) diffract   (E) substantiate

6. The physician's dire error was considered ------- by the hospital administrator, whose ------- evaluation included a thorough investigation of all procedures.

   (A) pernicious . . cosmopolitan
   (B) venial . . covert
   (C) insular . . vigilant
   (D) heinous . . casual
   (E) egregious . . scrupulous

GO ON TO THE NEXT PAGE

The passage below is followed by questions based on its content. Answer the questions on the basis of what is <u>stated</u> or <u>implied</u> in the passage and in any introductory material that may be provided.

Questions 7-18 are based on the following passage.

This passage was written by a teacher who worked for many years in British colleges and public schools. The author here recounts a memorable episode from his first teaching job.

It was 1960. I was a young man of twenty-one, just out of college and ready to try my hand at teaching in a vocational school. At the North
Line   Monmouthshire College of Commercial Training
5   in Wales, Mr. Walby was the head of the English Department and my very first boss.

Mr. Walby was a man of great girth. In fact, he was the fattest man I had ever seen. He had jowly cheeks and his small eyes were hidden behind
10   thick-rimmed spectacles. His sparse hair was spread flat and thin against the top of his head, and his dark moustache drooped a little at each end. When he walked, he lumbered at a sedate yet stately pace, although he rarely moved from his office when he
15   was actually present in the college. Looking rather like a walrus at ease, he leaned back in his straining leather chair, clasped his vast pudgy hands at the nape of his neck, and stared, in supreme content, at the opposite wall. On this wall was framed his one
20   great achievement of each year: the timetable for his department.

The timetable was his pride and joy. Once it was completed, it was absolutely inviolable. In fact, in the five years that I was at the college, the timetable
25   never changed. A lesson in any of the subjects that came under Mr. Walby's loving care lasted one hour. Each subject was allotted ten hours a week. Thus, each class received a double lesson, in each subject, at the same time, every day for five school
30   days. In Mr. Walby's eyes, this was the perfect timetable. The teachers were less impressed, and the college inspectors, when they made their biennial visit, critically demanded that Mr. Walby revise his system. Mr. Walby nodded his head in grave
35   agreement with the inspectors' commands and, once the uncomprehending outsiders had left, continued to pass his day, gazing at what he had wrought. A slight twitch of his moustache, and the memory of the invaders became no more.
40   From the very start, I was in awe of him. He was imperturbable and ironic. He was no fool. He understood how organizations work—not theoretically, but practically, as they do in the real world, full of unpredictable bluster and the narrow
45   avoidance of chaos. He was adept at divining what makes individuals tick; as a result, he realized and relished the fundamental absurdity of people in

authority. He quietly worked to puncture pomposity and to prick the paltry pride of the college principal,
50   taking particular delight in waging this quiet, constant offensive. He took one look at me and had me summed up correctly, as floundering, inoffensive, and innocent. I thought he probably liked the idea of having his very own idle gentleman in the
55   department.

I was to teach students literature and essay writing. "There are about thirty girls in the class," Mr. Walby told me. "On average they are about seventeen years-old, training to be secretaries. They'll regard
60   you as quite a perk." He cast a knowing glance away from the timetable and in my direction.

"Are they all girls?" My voice had taken on a trembling, timid sound.

"Well, I don't know about England, but here in
65   Wales the secretaries tend to be feminine. The men tend to go for the steel works, or maybe the coal mines. Beer and rugby down the club Saturdays." He chuckled. "Bit of a change for you, I expect. You'll be fine. You are twenty-one. You come from London.
70   You speak proper, like the newsreader on the BBC. What more could they ask for? The Welsh quite like foreigners." He held a beat. "Well, all foreigners except Germans, of course."

"But the war's been over for nearly twenty
75   years."

He gave me a stern look. "Not in the valleys," he replied evenly. "Did the office give you a register and a mark book?"

I shook my head in the negative. He pulled open
80   a drawer in his desk and picked out a thin, cardboard-backed folder and held it out to me. I moved forward to take it. As he closed the drawer, I caught a glimpse of a framed black-and-white photo of a slim young man in uniform, leaning against a low wall; behind
85   the young man was a sun-flecked sea. He was jauntily smiling into the camera.

Mr. Walby pushed his chair back and stood up; the furniture of his office seemed dwarfed. I stood aside as he proceeded to the door. He held it open and
90   turned to me.

"You've seen the staff room?"

I nodded.

"I'll take you to the classroom and introduce you to your class."
95   Mr. Walby moved past me and into the corridor. As he did so, he put his hand on my shoulder. "You'll manage," he said, gently and quietly.

GO ON TO THE NEXT PAGE

7. The passage is best described as

    (A) an ambivalent discussion of outdated and
        unusual educational practices
    (B) an explanation of the social forces that
        would eventually modernize Wales
    (C) an account of an individual who is both
        amusing and admirable
    (D) a summary of the typical benefits and
        drawbacks of a college teaching career
    (E) a satiric portrait of an educator with few
        redeeming qualities

8. The first paragraph primarily serves to

    (A) advocate a particular course of action
    (B) provide background information
    (C) describe an idiosyncratic setting
    (D) highlight an educational procedure
    (E) dramatize an unexpected event

9. According to the description in lines 7-21
    ("Mr. Walby . . . department"), Mr. Walby's most
    striking characteristics are

    (A) his immense size and his placid demeanor
    (B) his unconventional appearance and his
        buffoonish personality
    (C) his negligent attitude and his contempt
        for tradition
    (D) his evident industriousness and his
        reputation as a shrewd negotiator
    (E) his corpulence and his indifference to
        administrative matters

10. The "timetable" (line 22) is notable because it is

    (A) subject to yearly revision
    (B) based on incomprehensible principles
    (C) universally regarded as inefficient
    (D) not open to negotiation
    (E) thoroughly respected by the narrator

11. Mr. Walby's behavior toward the "college
    inspectors" (line 32) is best described as

    (A) raucous defiance
    (B) affable compliance
    (C) genuine impartiality
    (D) inauthentic appeasement
    (E) vociferous protest

12. In context, the word "divining" (line 45) is best
    understood to mean

    (A) warning
    (B) consecrating
    (C) discovering
    (D) representing
    (E) inspiring

13. The description in lines 40-53 ("He was . . .
    innocent") indicates that Mr. Walby

    (A) is extremely perceptive and is not easily
        intimidated by authority
    (B) has a lively sense of humor and plays pranks
        on the college principal
    (C) believes that the narrator is hopelessly out of
        place at the vocational school
    (D) has contributed to the college's decline with
        his irresponsible mentality
    (E) supports seditious ideas that nobody else
        in Wales endorses

14. The narrator's reference to his own "voice"
    (line 62) primarily serves to

    (A) clarify an essential element of the narrator's
        personal background
    (B) convey his apprehension about the
        circumstances he will face at the college
    (C) add a moment of everyday humor to an
        unpleasant discussion
    (D) indicate the low likelihood that the narrator
        will ever teach male students
    (E) suggest the narrator's insufficient
        preparation for his teaching stint

15. In context, Mr. Walby's statement that "The
    Welsh quite like foreigners" (lines 71-72)
    suggests that

    (A) the narrator has not traveled broadly
        enough to satisfy the students' curiosity
        about distant countries
    (B) Welsh students occasionally travel beyond
        Europe as part of their education
    (C) inhabitants of Wales are generally more
        gregarious than denizens of London
    (D) the narrator will be attractive to his students
        on account of his non-native status
    (E) the narrator has resided in countries that the
        students at the college know little about

GO ON TO THE NEXT PAGE

3   3   3   Unauthorized copying or
reuse of any part of this   3   3   3
page is illegal.

16. In line 77, the word "evenly" is closest in meaning to

(A) peacefully
(B) blandly
(C) firmly
(D) exhaustedly
(E) marginally

17. The observation that the furniture "seemed dwarfed" (line 88) suggests that

(A) Mr. Walby's noteworthy mass dominates the room
(B) the school cannot afford normally-sized office furniture
(C) the narrator is grappling with events that make him feel estranged and upset
(D) Mr. Walby is reminiscent of a figure from the narrator's childhood
(E) Mr. Walby finds compact and unobtrusive furniture pleasing

18. In the final paragraph, Mr. Walby puts his hand on the narrator's shoulder and remarks that "You'll manage" (lines 96-97) most likely in order to

(A) prepare the narrator for an unexpected piece of news
(B) show how much the narrator's approbation means to him
(C) initiate a much more intense conversation about educational principles
(D) temper his harsh manner of speaking with a more conciliatory tone
(E) offer encouragement and express his trust in the narrator

STOP

If you finish before time is called, you may check your work on this section only.
Do not turn to any other section in the test.

POST TEST ANALYSIS

This post test analysis is important if you want to see an improvement on your next test. Each section has a set of possible reasons for errors. Place check marks next to the ones that pertain to you, and write your own on the blank lines provided. Use this form to better analyze your performance. **If you don't understand why you made errors, there is no way you can correct them!**

1. **SENTENCE COMPLETION:**

   Problems with the sentence:
   ❑ Wasn't familiar with phrases, idioms, or words in the sentence
   ❑ Missed the clues or tones
   ❑ Put your OWN word in the blank rather than one from the sentence
   ❑ Completely avoided marking
   ❑ Other: _____

   _____

   Problems with the answers:
   ❑ Did not use process of elimination
   ❑ Did not ignore unknown words
   ❑ Did not use prefix/root/suffix knowledge to figure out the meaning of the unknown words
   ❑ Did not match the clues and tones of the answer with those of the sentence
   ❑ Did not recognize vocabulary words
   ❑ Did not check answer to see if it fit
   ❑ Other: _____

   _____

   Leaving questions unanswered:
   ❑ Did not try
   ❑ Did not fill in the blank(s) with words
   ❑ Ran out of time
   ❑ Other: _____

   _____

2. **SHORT READING COMPREHENSION:**

   ❑ Did not read entire paragraph
   ❑ Did not see more than one point
   ❑ Missed contrast clues
   ❑ Did not pinpoint thesis
   ❑ Did not identify similarities and differences in Double Short Reading Comp
   ❑ Other: _____

   _____

3. **LONG READING COMPREHENSION:**

   ❑ Did not understand the question, line reference, or answers
   ❑ Spent too much time reading the passages
   ❑ Did not underline the line reference
   ❑ Read too much or too little
   ❑ Did not answer the specific question; instead analyzed its main idea
   ❑ Did not do process of elimination based on facts in the passage
   ❑ Couldn't find the false words
   ❑ Couldn't choose between two possible answers
   ❑ Did not use tone to help eliminate answers
   ❑ When stuck at 2 guessed instead of pulling additional fact
   ❑ Couldn't finish in time
   ❑ Other: _____

   _____

ANSWER KEY

TEST 10

SECTION 1

#	Answer	Level
1	D	(2)
2	D	(2)
3	C	(4)
4	A	(5)
5	E	(4)
6	B	(3)
7	D	(3)
8	E	(4)
9	C	(4)
10	B	(1)
11	D	(3)
12	E	(3)
13	B	(4)
14	B	(3)
15	D	(4)
16	C	(5)
17	E	(4)
18	D	(2)
19	B	(5)
20	C	(3)
21	D	(3)
22	E	(2)
23	E	(3)
24	E	(2)
25	C	(1)

SECTION 2

#	Answer	Level
1	B	(2)
2	C	(2)
3	D	(3)
4	A	(4)
5	A	(3)
6	C	(4)
7	B	(3)
8	C	(5)
9	A	(1)
10	B	(3)
11	E	(1)
12	A	(2)
13	C	(2)
14	D	(3)
15	A	(3)
16	D	(3)
17	E	(4)
18	C	(4)
19	A	(4)
20	D	(5)
21	A	(4)
22	C	(4)
23	D	(4)
24	A	(2)

SECTION 3

#	Answer	Level
1	A	(1)
2	C	(2)
3	D	(2)
4	C	(3)
5	A	(4)
6	E	(5)
7	C	(2)
8	B	(1)
9	A	(3)
10	D	(3)
11	D	(4)
12	C	(3)
13	A	(3)
14	B	(4)
15	D	(3)
16	C	(3)
17	A	(2)
18	E	(2)

Difficulty levels range from 1 - 5 with 1 being the easiest and 5 being the hardest.
For answer explanations please visit www.ies2400.com/criticalreading

TEST 1

SECTION 1

1 Ⓐ Ⓑ Ⓒ Ⓓ Ⓔ
2 Ⓐ Ⓑ Ⓒ Ⓓ Ⓔ
3 Ⓐ Ⓑ Ⓒ Ⓓ Ⓔ
4 Ⓐ Ⓑ Ⓒ Ⓓ Ⓔ
5 Ⓐ Ⓑ Ⓒ Ⓓ Ⓔ
6 Ⓐ Ⓑ Ⓒ Ⓓ Ⓔ

7 Ⓐ Ⓑ Ⓒ Ⓓ Ⓔ
8 Ⓐ Ⓑ Ⓒ Ⓓ Ⓔ
9 Ⓐ Ⓑ Ⓒ Ⓓ Ⓔ
10 Ⓐ Ⓑ Ⓒ Ⓓ Ⓔ
11 Ⓐ Ⓑ Ⓒ Ⓓ Ⓔ
12 Ⓐ Ⓑ Ⓒ Ⓓ Ⓔ

13 Ⓐ Ⓑ Ⓒ Ⓓ Ⓔ
14 Ⓐ Ⓑ Ⓒ Ⓓ Ⓔ
15 Ⓐ Ⓑ Ⓒ Ⓓ Ⓔ
16 Ⓐ Ⓑ Ⓒ Ⓓ Ⓔ
17 Ⓐ Ⓑ Ⓒ Ⓓ Ⓔ
18 Ⓐ Ⓑ Ⓒ Ⓓ Ⓔ

19 Ⓐ Ⓑ Ⓒ Ⓓ Ⓔ
20 Ⓐ Ⓑ Ⓒ Ⓓ Ⓔ
21 Ⓐ Ⓑ Ⓒ Ⓓ Ⓔ
22 Ⓐ Ⓑ Ⓒ Ⓓ Ⓔ
23 Ⓐ Ⓑ Ⓒ Ⓓ Ⓔ
24 Ⓐ Ⓑ Ⓒ Ⓓ Ⓔ

SECTION 2

1 Ⓐ Ⓑ Ⓒ Ⓓ Ⓔ
2 Ⓐ Ⓑ Ⓒ Ⓓ Ⓔ
3 Ⓐ Ⓑ Ⓒ Ⓓ Ⓔ
4 Ⓐ Ⓑ Ⓒ Ⓓ Ⓔ
5 Ⓐ Ⓑ Ⓒ Ⓓ Ⓔ
6 Ⓐ Ⓑ Ⓒ Ⓓ Ⓔ

7 Ⓐ Ⓑ Ⓒ Ⓓ Ⓔ
8 Ⓐ Ⓑ Ⓒ Ⓓ Ⓔ
9 Ⓐ Ⓑ Ⓒ Ⓓ Ⓔ
10 Ⓐ Ⓑ Ⓒ Ⓓ Ⓔ
11 Ⓐ Ⓑ Ⓒ Ⓓ Ⓔ
12 Ⓐ Ⓑ Ⓒ Ⓓ Ⓔ

13 Ⓐ Ⓑ Ⓒ Ⓓ Ⓔ
14 Ⓐ Ⓑ Ⓒ Ⓓ Ⓔ
15 Ⓐ Ⓑ Ⓒ Ⓓ Ⓔ
16 Ⓐ Ⓑ Ⓒ Ⓓ Ⓔ
17 Ⓐ Ⓑ Ⓒ Ⓓ Ⓔ
18 Ⓐ Ⓑ Ⓒ Ⓓ Ⓔ

19 Ⓐ Ⓑ Ⓒ Ⓓ Ⓔ
20 Ⓐ Ⓑ Ⓒ Ⓓ Ⓔ
21 Ⓐ Ⓑ Ⓒ Ⓓ Ⓔ
22 Ⓐ Ⓑ Ⓒ Ⓓ Ⓔ
23 Ⓐ Ⓑ Ⓒ Ⓓ Ⓔ
24 Ⓐ Ⓑ Ⓒ Ⓓ Ⓔ

SECTION 3

1 Ⓐ Ⓑ Ⓒ Ⓓ Ⓔ
2 Ⓐ Ⓑ Ⓒ Ⓓ Ⓔ
3 Ⓐ Ⓑ Ⓒ Ⓓ Ⓔ
4 Ⓐ Ⓑ Ⓒ Ⓓ Ⓔ
5 Ⓐ Ⓑ Ⓒ Ⓓ Ⓔ

6 Ⓐ Ⓑ Ⓒ Ⓓ Ⓔ
7 Ⓐ Ⓑ Ⓒ Ⓓ Ⓔ
8 Ⓐ Ⓑ Ⓒ Ⓓ Ⓔ
9 Ⓐ Ⓑ Ⓒ Ⓓ Ⓔ
10 Ⓐ Ⓑ Ⓒ Ⓓ Ⓔ

11 Ⓐ Ⓑ Ⓒ Ⓓ Ⓔ
12 Ⓐ Ⓑ Ⓒ Ⓓ Ⓔ
13 Ⓐ Ⓑ Ⓒ Ⓓ Ⓔ
14 Ⓐ Ⓑ Ⓒ Ⓓ Ⓔ
15 Ⓐ Ⓑ Ⓒ Ⓓ Ⓔ

16 Ⓐ Ⓑ Ⓒ Ⓓ Ⓔ
17 Ⓐ Ⓑ Ⓒ Ⓓ Ⓔ
18 Ⓐ Ⓑ Ⓒ Ⓓ Ⓔ
19 Ⓐ Ⓑ Ⓒ Ⓓ Ⓔ

SCORING YOUR TEST

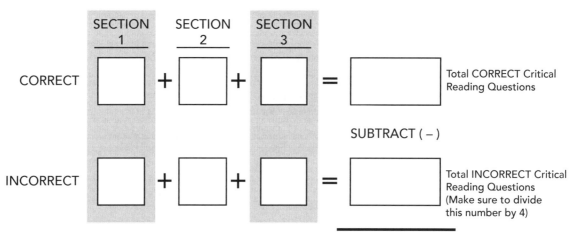

CORRECT

SECTION 1 + SECTION 2 + SECTION 3 = [ ] Total CORRECT Critical Reading Questions

SUBTRACT (−)

INCORRECT

SECTION 1 + SECTION 2 + SECTION 3 = [ ] Total INCORRECT Critical Reading Questions (Make sure to divide this number by 4)

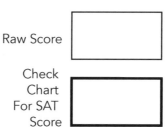

Raw Score [ ]

Check Chart For SAT Score [ ]

How to Score Your SAT

1. Subtotal the number of CORRECT answers for each section of the practice test. Put this number in the Total CORRECT box.

2. Subtotal the number of INCORRECT answers for each section of the practice test. Divide the subtotal by 4. Put this number in the Total INCORRECT box.

3. Subtract the second number from the first. This is your Raw Score.

4. Look up your Raw Score number in the SAT Scoring Chart. This is your scaled score.

SAT SCORING CHART

RAW SCORE	SCALED SCORE	RAW SCORE	SCALED SCORE	RAW SCORE	SCALED SCORE	RAW SCORE	SCALED SCORE
67	800	47	600-640	27	460-500	7	300-340
66	770-800	46	590-630	26	450-490	6	300-340
65	750-790	45	580-620	25	450-490	5	290-330
64	740-780	44	580-620	24	440-480	4	280-320
63	740-780	43	570-610	23	430-470	3	270-310
62	730-770	42	570-610	22	420-460	2	260-300
61	720-760	41	560-600	21	420-460	1	230-270
60	710-750	40	550-590	20	410-450	0	200-240
59	700-740	39	550-590	19	400-440	-1	200-230
58	690-730	38	540-580	18	400-440	-2	200-220
57	680-720	37	530-570	17	390-430	-3	200-210
56	670-710	36	530-570	16	380-420		
55	670-710	35	520-560	15	380-420		
54	660-700	34	510-550	14	370-410		
53	650-690	33	500-540	13	360-400		
52	640-680	32	500-540	12	350-390		
51	630-670	31	490-530	11	350-390		
50	620-660	30	480-520	10	340-380		
49	610-650	29	470-510	9	330-370		
48	600-640	28	470-510	8	310-350		

TEST
2

SECTION 1

1 Ⓐ Ⓑ Ⓒ Ⓓ Ⓔ
2 Ⓐ Ⓑ Ⓒ Ⓓ Ⓔ
3 Ⓐ Ⓑ Ⓒ Ⓓ Ⓔ
4 Ⓐ Ⓑ Ⓒ Ⓓ Ⓔ
5 Ⓐ Ⓑ Ⓒ Ⓓ Ⓔ
6 Ⓐ Ⓑ Ⓒ Ⓓ Ⓔ

7 Ⓐ Ⓑ Ⓒ Ⓓ Ⓔ
8 Ⓐ Ⓑ Ⓒ Ⓓ Ⓔ
9 Ⓐ Ⓑ Ⓒ Ⓓ Ⓔ
10 Ⓐ Ⓑ Ⓒ Ⓓ Ⓔ
11 Ⓐ Ⓑ Ⓒ Ⓓ Ⓔ
12 Ⓐ Ⓑ Ⓒ Ⓓ Ⓔ

13 Ⓐ Ⓑ Ⓒ Ⓓ Ⓔ
14 Ⓐ Ⓑ Ⓒ Ⓓ Ⓔ
15 Ⓐ Ⓑ Ⓒ Ⓓ Ⓔ
16 Ⓐ Ⓑ Ⓒ Ⓓ Ⓔ
17 Ⓐ Ⓑ Ⓒ Ⓓ Ⓔ
18 Ⓐ Ⓑ Ⓒ Ⓓ Ⓔ

19 Ⓐ Ⓑ Ⓒ Ⓓ Ⓔ
20 Ⓐ Ⓑ Ⓒ Ⓓ Ⓔ
21 Ⓐ Ⓑ Ⓒ Ⓓ Ⓔ
22 Ⓐ Ⓑ Ⓒ Ⓓ Ⓔ
23 Ⓐ Ⓑ Ⓒ Ⓓ Ⓔ
24 Ⓐ Ⓑ Ⓒ Ⓓ Ⓔ

SECTION 2

1 Ⓐ Ⓑ Ⓒ Ⓓ Ⓔ
2 Ⓐ Ⓑ Ⓒ Ⓓ Ⓔ
3 Ⓐ Ⓑ Ⓒ Ⓓ Ⓔ
4 Ⓐ Ⓑ Ⓒ Ⓓ Ⓔ
5 Ⓐ Ⓑ Ⓒ Ⓓ Ⓔ
6 Ⓐ Ⓑ Ⓒ Ⓓ Ⓔ

7 Ⓐ Ⓑ Ⓒ Ⓓ Ⓔ
8 Ⓐ Ⓑ Ⓒ Ⓓ Ⓔ
9 Ⓐ Ⓑ Ⓒ Ⓓ Ⓔ
10 Ⓐ Ⓑ Ⓒ Ⓓ Ⓔ
11 Ⓐ Ⓑ Ⓒ Ⓓ Ⓔ
12 Ⓐ Ⓑ Ⓒ Ⓓ Ⓔ

13 Ⓐ Ⓑ Ⓒ Ⓓ Ⓔ
14 Ⓐ Ⓑ Ⓒ Ⓓ Ⓔ
15 Ⓐ Ⓑ Ⓒ Ⓓ Ⓔ
16 Ⓐ Ⓑ Ⓒ Ⓓ Ⓔ
17 Ⓐ Ⓑ Ⓒ Ⓓ Ⓔ
18 Ⓐ Ⓑ Ⓒ Ⓓ Ⓔ

19 Ⓐ Ⓑ Ⓒ Ⓓ Ⓔ
20 Ⓐ Ⓑ Ⓒ Ⓓ Ⓔ
21 Ⓐ Ⓑ Ⓒ Ⓓ Ⓔ
22 Ⓐ Ⓑ Ⓒ Ⓓ Ⓔ
23 Ⓐ Ⓑ Ⓒ Ⓓ Ⓔ
24 Ⓐ Ⓑ Ⓒ Ⓓ Ⓔ

SECTION 3

1 Ⓐ Ⓑ Ⓒ Ⓓ Ⓔ
2 Ⓐ Ⓑ Ⓒ Ⓓ Ⓔ
3 Ⓐ Ⓑ Ⓒ Ⓓ Ⓔ
4 Ⓐ Ⓑ Ⓒ Ⓓ Ⓔ
5 Ⓐ Ⓑ Ⓒ Ⓓ Ⓔ

6 Ⓐ Ⓑ Ⓒ Ⓓ Ⓔ
7 Ⓐ Ⓑ Ⓒ Ⓓ Ⓔ
8 Ⓐ Ⓑ Ⓒ Ⓓ Ⓔ
9 Ⓐ Ⓑ Ⓒ Ⓓ Ⓔ
10 Ⓐ Ⓑ Ⓒ Ⓓ Ⓔ

11 Ⓐ Ⓑ Ⓒ Ⓓ Ⓔ
12 Ⓐ Ⓑ Ⓒ Ⓓ Ⓔ
13 Ⓐ Ⓑ Ⓒ Ⓓ Ⓔ
14 Ⓐ Ⓑ Ⓒ Ⓓ Ⓔ
15 Ⓐ Ⓑ Ⓒ Ⓓ Ⓔ

16 Ⓐ Ⓑ Ⓒ Ⓓ Ⓔ
17 Ⓐ Ⓑ Ⓒ Ⓓ Ⓔ
18 Ⓐ Ⓑ Ⓒ Ⓓ Ⓔ
19 Ⓐ Ⓑ Ⓒ Ⓓ Ⓔ

SCORING YOUR TEST

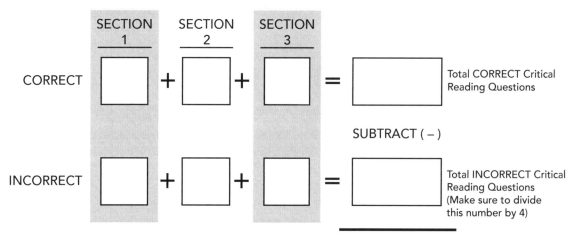

CORRECT $\qquad$ SECTION 1 $\square$ + SECTION 2 $\square$ + SECTION 3 $\square$ = $\square$ Total CORRECT Critical Reading Questions

SUBTRACT (−)

INCORRECT $\square$ + $\square$ + $\square$ = $\square$ Total INCORRECT Critical Reading Questions (Make sure to divide this number by 4)

Raw Score $\square$

Check Chart For SAT Score $\square$

How to Score Your SAT

1. Subtotal the number of CORRECT answers for each section of the practice test. Put this number in the Total CORRECT box.

2. Subtotal the number of INCORRECT answers for each section of the practice test. Divide the subtotal by 4. Put this number in the Total INCORRECT box.

3. Subtract the second number from the first. This is your Raw Score.

4. Look up your Raw Score number in the SAT Scoring Chart. This is your scaled score.

SAT SCORING CHART

RAW SCORE	SCALED SCORE	RAW SCORE	SCALED SCORE	RAW SCORE	SCALED SCORE	RAW SCORE	SCALED SCORE
67	800	47	600-640	27	460-500	7	300-340
66	770-800	46	590-630	26	450-490	6	300-340
65	750-790	45	580-620	25	450-490	5	290-330
64	740-780	44	580-620	24	440-480	4	280-320
63	740-780	43	570-610	23	430-470	3	270-310
62	730-770	42	570-610	22	420-460	2	260-300
61	720-760	41	560-600	21	420-460	1	230-270
60	710-750	40	550-590	20	410-450	0	200-240
59	700-740	39	550-590	19	400-440	-1	200-230
58	690-730	38	540-580	18	400-440	-2	200-220
57	680-720	37	530-570	17	390-430	-3	200-210
56	670-710	36	530-570	16	380-420		
55	670-710	35	520-560	15	380-420		
54	660-700	34	510-550	14	370-410		
53	650-690	33	500-540	13	360-400		
52	640-680	32	500-540	12	350-390		
51	630-670	31	490-530	11	350-390		
50	620-660	30	480-520	10	340-380		
49	610-650	29	470-510	9	330-370		
48	600-640	28	470-510	8	310-350		

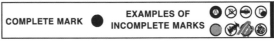
TEST 3

SECTION 1

1 Ⓐ Ⓑ Ⓒ Ⓓ Ⓔ	7 Ⓐ Ⓑ Ⓒ Ⓓ Ⓔ	13 Ⓐ Ⓑ Ⓒ Ⓓ Ⓔ	19 Ⓐ Ⓑ Ⓒ Ⓓ Ⓔ
2 Ⓐ Ⓑ Ⓒ Ⓓ Ⓔ	8 Ⓐ Ⓑ Ⓒ Ⓓ Ⓔ	14 Ⓐ Ⓑ Ⓒ Ⓓ Ⓔ	20 Ⓐ Ⓑ Ⓒ Ⓓ Ⓔ
3 Ⓐ Ⓑ Ⓒ Ⓓ Ⓔ	9 Ⓐ Ⓑ Ⓒ Ⓓ Ⓔ	15 Ⓐ Ⓑ Ⓒ Ⓓ Ⓔ	21 Ⓐ Ⓑ Ⓒ Ⓓ Ⓔ
4 Ⓐ Ⓑ Ⓒ Ⓓ Ⓔ	10 Ⓐ Ⓑ Ⓒ Ⓓ Ⓔ	16 Ⓐ Ⓑ Ⓒ Ⓓ Ⓔ	22 Ⓐ Ⓑ Ⓒ Ⓓ Ⓔ
5 Ⓐ Ⓑ Ⓒ Ⓓ Ⓔ	11 Ⓐ Ⓑ Ⓒ Ⓓ Ⓔ	17 Ⓐ Ⓑ Ⓒ Ⓓ Ⓔ	23 Ⓐ Ⓑ Ⓒ Ⓓ Ⓔ
6 Ⓐ Ⓑ Ⓒ Ⓓ Ⓔ	12 Ⓐ Ⓑ Ⓒ Ⓓ Ⓔ	18 Ⓐ Ⓑ Ⓒ Ⓓ Ⓔ	24 Ⓐ Ⓑ Ⓒ Ⓓ Ⓔ
			25 Ⓐ Ⓑ Ⓒ Ⓓ Ⓔ

SECTION 2

1 Ⓐ Ⓑ Ⓒ Ⓓ Ⓔ	7 Ⓐ Ⓑ Ⓒ Ⓓ Ⓔ	13 Ⓐ Ⓑ Ⓒ Ⓓ Ⓔ	19 Ⓐ Ⓑ Ⓒ Ⓓ Ⓔ
2 Ⓐ Ⓑ Ⓒ Ⓓ Ⓔ	8 Ⓐ Ⓑ Ⓒ Ⓓ Ⓔ	14 Ⓐ Ⓑ Ⓒ Ⓓ Ⓔ	20 Ⓐ Ⓑ Ⓒ Ⓓ Ⓔ
3 Ⓐ Ⓑ Ⓒ Ⓓ Ⓔ	9 Ⓐ Ⓑ Ⓒ Ⓓ Ⓔ	15 Ⓐ Ⓑ Ⓒ Ⓓ Ⓔ	21 Ⓐ Ⓑ Ⓒ Ⓓ Ⓔ
4 Ⓐ Ⓑ Ⓒ Ⓓ Ⓔ	10 Ⓐ Ⓑ Ⓒ Ⓓ Ⓔ	16 Ⓐ Ⓑ Ⓒ Ⓓ Ⓔ	22 Ⓐ Ⓑ Ⓒ Ⓓ Ⓔ
5 Ⓐ Ⓑ Ⓒ Ⓓ Ⓔ	11 Ⓐ Ⓑ Ⓒ Ⓓ Ⓔ	17 Ⓐ Ⓑ Ⓒ Ⓓ Ⓔ	23 Ⓐ Ⓑ Ⓒ Ⓓ Ⓔ
6 Ⓐ Ⓑ Ⓒ Ⓓ Ⓔ	12 Ⓐ Ⓑ Ⓒ Ⓓ Ⓔ	18 Ⓐ Ⓑ Ⓒ Ⓓ Ⓔ	24 Ⓐ Ⓑ Ⓒ Ⓓ Ⓔ

SECTION 3

1 Ⓐ Ⓑ Ⓒ Ⓓ Ⓔ	6 Ⓐ Ⓑ Ⓒ Ⓓ Ⓔ	11 Ⓐ Ⓑ Ⓒ Ⓓ Ⓔ	16 Ⓐ Ⓑ Ⓒ Ⓓ Ⓔ
2 Ⓐ Ⓑ Ⓒ Ⓓ Ⓔ	7 Ⓐ Ⓑ Ⓒ Ⓓ Ⓔ	12 Ⓐ Ⓑ Ⓒ Ⓓ Ⓔ	17 Ⓐ Ⓑ Ⓒ Ⓓ Ⓔ
3 Ⓐ Ⓑ Ⓒ Ⓓ Ⓔ	8 Ⓐ Ⓑ Ⓒ Ⓓ Ⓔ	13 Ⓐ Ⓑ Ⓒ Ⓓ Ⓔ	18 Ⓐ Ⓑ Ⓒ Ⓓ Ⓔ
4 Ⓐ Ⓑ Ⓒ Ⓓ Ⓔ	9 Ⓐ Ⓑ Ⓒ Ⓓ Ⓔ	14 Ⓐ Ⓑ Ⓒ Ⓓ Ⓔ	
5 Ⓐ Ⓑ Ⓒ Ⓓ Ⓔ	10 Ⓐ Ⓑ Ⓒ Ⓓ Ⓔ	15 Ⓐ Ⓑ Ⓒ Ⓓ Ⓔ	

Cut out this page and make copies so you can take each test multiple times.

189

SCORING YOUR TEST

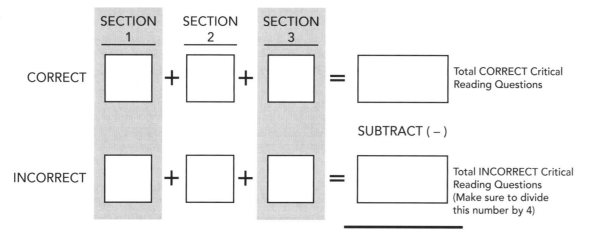

	SECTION 1		SECTION 2		SECTION 3			
CORRECT	☐	+	☐	+	☐	=	☐	Total CORRECT Critical Reading Questions

SUBTRACT (−)

	SECTION 1		SECTION 2		SECTION 3			
INCORRECT	☐	+	☐	+	☐	=	☐	Total INCORRECT Critical Reading Questions (Make sure to divide this number by 4)

Raw Score ☐

Check Chart For SAT Score ☐

How to Score Your SAT

1. Subtotal the number of CORRECT answers for each section of the practice test. Put this number in the Total CORRECT box.

2. Subtotal the number of INCORRECT answers for each section of the practice test. Divide the subtotal by 4. Put this number in the Total INCORRECT box.

3. Subtract the second number from the first. This is your Raw Score.

4. Look up your Raw Score number in the SAT Scoring Chart. This is your scaled score.

SAT SCORING CHART

RAW SCORE	SCALED SCORE	RAW SCORE	SCALED SCORE	RAW SCORE	SCALED SCORE	RAW SCORE	SCALED SCORE
67	800	47	600-640	27	460-500	7	300-340
66	770-800	46	590-630	26	450-490	6	300-340
65	750-790	45	580-620	25	450-490	5	290-330
64	740-780	44	580-620	24	440-480	4	280-320
63	740-780	43	570-610	23	430-470	3	270-310
62	730-770	42	570-610	22	420-460	2	260-300
61	720-760	41	560-600	21	420-460	1	230-270
60	710-750	40	550-590	20	410-450	0	200-240
59	700-740	39	550-590	19	400-440	-1	200-230
58	690-730	38	540-580	18	400-440	-2	200-220
57	680-720	37	530-570	17	390-430	-3	200-210
56	670-710	36	530-570	16	380-420		
55	670-710	35	520-560	15	380-420		
54	660-700	34	510-550	14	370-410		
53	650-690	33	500-540	13	360-400		
52	640-680	32	500-540	12	350-390		
51	630-670	31	490-530	11	350-390		
50	620-660	30	480-520	10	340-380		
49	610-650	29	470-510	9	330-370		
48	600-640	28	470-510	8	310-350		

TEST

4

SECTION 1

1	Ⓐ Ⓑ Ⓒ Ⓓ Ⓔ	7	Ⓐ Ⓑ Ⓒ Ⓓ Ⓔ	13	Ⓐ Ⓑ Ⓒ Ⓓ Ⓔ	19	Ⓐ Ⓑ Ⓒ Ⓓ Ⓔ
2	Ⓐ Ⓑ Ⓒ Ⓓ Ⓔ	8	Ⓐ Ⓑ Ⓒ Ⓓ Ⓔ	14	Ⓐ Ⓑ Ⓒ Ⓓ Ⓔ	20	Ⓐ Ⓑ Ⓒ Ⓓ Ⓔ
3	Ⓐ Ⓑ Ⓒ Ⓓ Ⓔ	9	Ⓐ Ⓑ Ⓒ Ⓓ Ⓔ	15	Ⓐ Ⓑ Ⓒ Ⓓ Ⓔ	21	Ⓐ Ⓑ Ⓒ Ⓓ Ⓔ
4	Ⓐ Ⓑ Ⓒ Ⓓ Ⓔ	10	Ⓐ Ⓑ Ⓒ Ⓓ Ⓔ	16	Ⓐ Ⓑ Ⓒ Ⓓ Ⓔ	22	Ⓐ Ⓑ Ⓒ Ⓓ Ⓔ
5	Ⓐ Ⓑ Ⓒ Ⓓ Ⓔ	11	Ⓐ Ⓑ Ⓒ Ⓓ Ⓔ	17	Ⓐ Ⓑ Ⓒ Ⓓ Ⓔ	23	Ⓐ Ⓑ Ⓒ Ⓓ Ⓔ
6	Ⓐ Ⓑ Ⓒ Ⓓ Ⓔ	12	Ⓐ Ⓑ Ⓒ Ⓓ Ⓔ	18	Ⓐ Ⓑ Ⓒ Ⓓ Ⓔ	24	Ⓐ Ⓑ Ⓒ Ⓓ Ⓔ

SECTION 2

1	Ⓐ Ⓑ Ⓒ Ⓓ Ⓔ	7	Ⓐ Ⓑ Ⓒ Ⓓ Ⓔ	13	Ⓐ Ⓑ Ⓒ Ⓓ Ⓔ	19	Ⓐ Ⓑ Ⓒ Ⓓ Ⓔ
2	Ⓐ Ⓑ Ⓒ Ⓓ Ⓔ	8	Ⓐ Ⓑ Ⓒ Ⓓ Ⓔ	14	Ⓐ Ⓑ Ⓒ Ⓓ Ⓔ	20	Ⓐ Ⓑ Ⓒ Ⓓ Ⓔ
3	Ⓐ Ⓑ Ⓒ Ⓓ Ⓔ	9	Ⓐ Ⓑ Ⓒ Ⓓ Ⓔ	15	Ⓐ Ⓑ Ⓒ Ⓓ Ⓔ	21	Ⓐ Ⓑ Ⓒ Ⓓ Ⓔ
4	Ⓐ Ⓑ Ⓒ Ⓓ Ⓔ	10	Ⓐ Ⓑ Ⓒ Ⓓ Ⓔ	16	Ⓐ Ⓑ Ⓒ Ⓓ Ⓔ	22	Ⓐ Ⓑ Ⓒ Ⓓ Ⓔ
5	Ⓐ Ⓑ Ⓒ Ⓓ Ⓔ	11	Ⓐ Ⓑ Ⓒ Ⓓ Ⓔ	17	Ⓐ Ⓑ Ⓒ Ⓓ Ⓔ	23	Ⓐ Ⓑ Ⓒ Ⓓ Ⓔ
6	Ⓐ Ⓑ Ⓒ Ⓓ Ⓔ	12	Ⓐ Ⓑ Ⓒ Ⓓ Ⓔ	18	Ⓐ Ⓑ Ⓒ Ⓓ Ⓔ	24	Ⓐ Ⓑ Ⓒ Ⓓ Ⓔ

SECTION 3

1	Ⓐ Ⓑ Ⓒ Ⓓ Ⓔ	6	Ⓐ Ⓑ Ⓒ Ⓓ Ⓔ	11	Ⓐ Ⓑ Ⓒ Ⓓ Ⓔ	16	Ⓐ Ⓑ Ⓒ Ⓓ Ⓔ
2	Ⓐ Ⓑ Ⓒ Ⓓ Ⓔ	7	Ⓐ Ⓑ Ⓒ Ⓓ Ⓔ	12	Ⓐ Ⓑ Ⓒ Ⓓ Ⓔ	17	Ⓐ Ⓑ Ⓒ Ⓓ Ⓔ
3	Ⓐ Ⓑ Ⓒ Ⓓ Ⓔ	8	Ⓐ Ⓑ Ⓒ Ⓓ Ⓔ	13	Ⓐ Ⓑ Ⓒ Ⓓ Ⓔ	18	Ⓐ Ⓑ Ⓒ Ⓓ Ⓔ
4	Ⓐ Ⓑ Ⓒ Ⓓ Ⓔ	9	Ⓐ Ⓑ Ⓒ Ⓓ Ⓔ	14	Ⓐ Ⓑ Ⓒ Ⓓ Ⓔ	19	Ⓐ Ⓑ Ⓒ Ⓓ Ⓔ
5	Ⓐ Ⓑ Ⓒ Ⓓ Ⓔ	10	Ⓐ Ⓑ Ⓒ Ⓓ Ⓔ	15	Ⓐ Ⓑ Ⓒ Ⓓ Ⓔ		

SCORING YOUR TEST

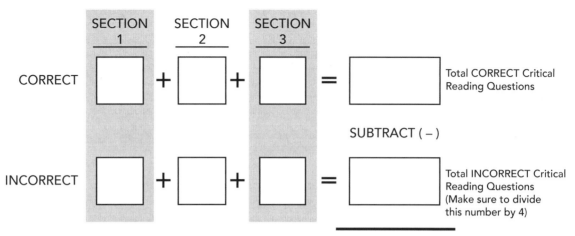

	SECTION 1		SECTION 2		SECTION 3			
CORRECT	☐	+	☐	+	☐	=	☐	Total CORRECT Critical Reading Questions

SUBTRACT (–)

	SECTION 1		SECTION 2		SECTION 3			
INCORRECT	☐	+	☐	+	☐	=	☐	Total INCORRECT Critical Reading Questions (Make sure to divide this number by 4)

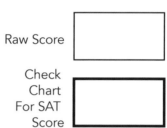

Raw Score ☐

Check Chart For SAT Score ☐

How to Score Your SAT

1. Subtotal the number of CORRECT answers for each section of the practice test. Put this number in the Total CORRECT box.

2. Subtotal the number of INCORRECT answers for each section of the practice test. Divide the subtotal by 4. Put this number in the Total INCORRECT box.

3. Subtract the second number from the first. This is your Raw Score.

4. Look up your Raw Score number in the SAT Scoring Chart. This is your scaled score.

SAT SCORING CHART

RAW SCORE	SCALED SCORE	RAW SCORE	SCALED SCORE	RAW SCORE	SCALED SCORE	RAW SCORE	SCALED SCORE
67	800	47	600-640	27	460-500	7	300-340
66	770-800	46	590-630	26	450-490	6	300-340
65	750-790	45	580-620	25	450-490	5	290-330
64	740-780	44	580-620	24	440-480	4	280-320
63	740-780	43	570-610	23	430-470	3	270-310
62	730-770	42	570-610	22	420-460	2	260-300
61	720-760	41	560-600	21	420-460	1	230-270
60	710-750	40	550-590	20	410-450	0	200-240
59	700-740	39	550-590	19	400-440	-1	200-230
58	690-730	38	540-580	18	400-440	-2	200-220
57	680-720	37	530-570	17	390-430	-3	200-210
56	670-710	36	530-570	16	380-420		
55	670-710	35	520-560	15	380-420		
54	660-700	34	510-550	14	370-410		
53	650-690	33	500-540	13	360-400		
52	640-680	32	500-540	12	350-390		
51	630-670	31	490-530	11	350-390		
50	620-660	30	480-520	10	340-380		
49	610-650	29	470-510	9	330-370		
48	600-640	28	470-510	8	310-350		

TEST 5

SECTION 1

1 Ⓐ Ⓑ Ⓒ Ⓓ Ⓔ
2 Ⓐ Ⓑ Ⓒ Ⓓ Ⓔ
3 Ⓐ Ⓑ Ⓒ Ⓓ Ⓔ
4 Ⓐ Ⓑ Ⓒ Ⓓ Ⓔ
5 Ⓐ Ⓑ Ⓒ Ⓓ Ⓔ
6 Ⓐ Ⓑ Ⓒ Ⓓ Ⓔ

7 Ⓐ Ⓑ Ⓒ Ⓓ Ⓔ
8 Ⓐ Ⓑ Ⓒ Ⓓ Ⓔ
9 Ⓐ Ⓑ Ⓒ Ⓓ Ⓔ
10 Ⓐ Ⓑ Ⓒ Ⓓ Ⓔ
11 Ⓐ Ⓑ Ⓒ Ⓓ Ⓔ
12 Ⓐ Ⓑ Ⓒ Ⓓ Ⓔ

13 Ⓐ Ⓑ Ⓒ Ⓓ Ⓔ
14 Ⓐ Ⓑ Ⓒ Ⓓ Ⓔ
15 Ⓐ Ⓑ Ⓒ Ⓓ Ⓔ
16 Ⓐ Ⓑ Ⓒ Ⓓ Ⓔ
17 Ⓐ Ⓑ Ⓒ Ⓓ Ⓔ
18 Ⓐ Ⓑ Ⓒ Ⓓ Ⓔ

19 Ⓐ Ⓑ Ⓒ Ⓓ Ⓔ
20 Ⓐ Ⓑ Ⓒ Ⓓ Ⓔ
21 Ⓐ Ⓑ Ⓒ Ⓓ Ⓔ
22 Ⓐ Ⓑ Ⓒ Ⓓ Ⓔ
23 Ⓐ Ⓑ Ⓒ Ⓓ Ⓔ
24 Ⓐ Ⓑ Ⓒ Ⓓ Ⓔ

SECTION 2

1 Ⓐ Ⓑ Ⓒ Ⓓ Ⓔ
2 Ⓐ Ⓑ Ⓒ Ⓓ Ⓔ
3 Ⓐ Ⓑ Ⓒ Ⓓ Ⓔ
4 Ⓐ Ⓑ Ⓒ Ⓓ Ⓔ
5 Ⓐ Ⓑ Ⓒ Ⓓ Ⓔ
6 Ⓐ Ⓑ Ⓒ Ⓓ Ⓔ

7 Ⓐ Ⓑ Ⓒ Ⓓ Ⓔ
8 Ⓐ Ⓑ Ⓒ Ⓓ Ⓔ
9 Ⓐ Ⓑ Ⓒ Ⓓ Ⓔ
10 Ⓐ Ⓑ Ⓒ Ⓓ Ⓔ
11 Ⓐ Ⓑ Ⓒ Ⓓ Ⓔ
12 Ⓐ Ⓑ Ⓒ Ⓓ Ⓔ

13 Ⓐ Ⓑ Ⓒ Ⓓ Ⓔ
14 Ⓐ Ⓑ Ⓒ Ⓓ Ⓔ
15 Ⓐ Ⓑ Ⓒ Ⓓ Ⓔ
16 Ⓐ Ⓑ Ⓒ Ⓓ Ⓔ
17 Ⓐ Ⓑ Ⓒ Ⓓ Ⓔ
18 Ⓐ Ⓑ Ⓒ Ⓓ Ⓔ

19 Ⓐ Ⓑ Ⓒ Ⓓ Ⓔ
20 Ⓐ Ⓑ Ⓒ Ⓓ Ⓔ
21 Ⓐ Ⓑ Ⓒ Ⓓ Ⓔ
22 Ⓐ Ⓑ Ⓒ Ⓓ Ⓔ
23 Ⓐ Ⓑ Ⓒ Ⓓ Ⓔ
24 Ⓐ Ⓑ Ⓒ Ⓓ Ⓔ

SECTION 3

1 Ⓐ Ⓑ Ⓒ Ⓓ Ⓔ
2 Ⓐ Ⓑ Ⓒ Ⓓ Ⓔ
3 Ⓐ Ⓑ Ⓒ Ⓓ Ⓔ
4 Ⓐ Ⓑ Ⓒ Ⓓ Ⓔ
5 Ⓐ Ⓑ Ⓒ Ⓓ Ⓔ

6 Ⓐ Ⓑ Ⓒ Ⓓ Ⓔ
7 Ⓐ Ⓑ Ⓒ Ⓓ Ⓔ
8 Ⓐ Ⓑ Ⓒ Ⓓ Ⓔ
9 Ⓐ Ⓑ Ⓒ Ⓓ Ⓔ
10 Ⓐ Ⓑ Ⓒ Ⓓ Ⓔ

11 Ⓐ Ⓑ Ⓒ Ⓓ Ⓔ
12 Ⓐ Ⓑ Ⓒ Ⓓ Ⓔ
13 Ⓐ Ⓑ Ⓒ Ⓓ Ⓔ
14 Ⓐ Ⓑ Ⓒ Ⓓ Ⓔ
15 Ⓐ Ⓑ Ⓒ Ⓓ Ⓔ

16 Ⓐ Ⓑ Ⓒ Ⓓ Ⓔ
17 Ⓐ Ⓑ Ⓒ Ⓓ Ⓔ
18 Ⓐ Ⓑ Ⓒ Ⓓ Ⓔ
19 Ⓐ Ⓑ Ⓒ Ⓓ Ⓔ

SCORING YOUR TEST

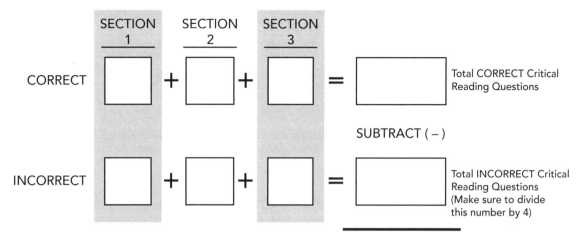

	SECTION 1	SECTION 2	SECTION 3		
CORRECT	☐	+ ☐	+ ☐	= ☐	Total CORRECT Critical Reading Questions

SUBTRACT (–)

	SECTION 1	SECTION 2	SECTION 3		
INCORRECT	☐	+ ☐	+ ☐	= ☐	Total INCORRECT Critical Reading Questions (Make sure to divide this number by 4)

Raw Score ☐

Check Chart For SAT Score ☐

How to Score Your SAT

1. Subtotal the number of CORRECT answers for each section of the practice test. Put this number in the Total CORRECT box.

2. Subtotal the number of INCORRECT answers for each section of the practice test. Divide the subtotal by 4. Put this number in the Total INCORRECT box.

3. Subtract the second number from the first. This is your Raw Score.

4. Look up your Raw Score number in the SAT Scoring Chart. This is your scaled score.

SAT SCORING CHART

RAW SCORE	SCALED SCORE	RAW SCORE	SCALED SCORE	RAW SCORE	SCALED SCORE	RAW SCORE	SCALED SCORE
67	800	47	600-640	27	460-500	7	300-340
66	770-800	46	590-630	26	450-490	6	300-340
65	750-790	45	580-620	25	450-490	5	290-330
64	740-780	44	580-620	24	440-480	4	280-320
63	740-780	43	570-610	23	430-470	3	270-310
62	730-770	42	570-610	22	420-460	2	260-300
61	720-760	41	560-600	21	420-460	1	230-270
60	710-750	40	550-590	20	410-450	0	200-240
59	700-740	39	550-590	19	400-440	-1	200-230
58	690-730	38	540-580	18	400-440	-2	200-220
57	680-720	37	530-570	17	390-430	-3	200-210
56	670-710	36	530-570	16	380-420		
55	670-710	35	520-560	15	380-420		
54	660-700	34	510-550	14	370-410		
53	650-690	33	500-540	13	360-400		
52	640-680	32	500-540	12	350-390		
51	630-670	31	490-530	11	350-390		
50	620-660	30	480-520	10	340-380		
49	610-650	29	470-510	9	330-370		
48	600-640	28	470-510	8	310-350		

TEST 6

SECTION 1

1 Ⓐ Ⓑ Ⓒ Ⓓ Ⓔ	7 Ⓐ Ⓑ Ⓒ Ⓓ Ⓔ	13 Ⓐ Ⓑ Ⓒ Ⓓ Ⓔ	19 Ⓐ Ⓑ Ⓒ Ⓓ Ⓔ
2 Ⓐ Ⓑ Ⓒ Ⓓ Ⓔ	8 Ⓐ Ⓑ Ⓒ Ⓓ Ⓔ	14 Ⓐ Ⓑ Ⓒ Ⓓ Ⓔ	20 Ⓐ Ⓑ Ⓒ Ⓓ Ⓔ
3 Ⓐ Ⓑ Ⓒ Ⓓ Ⓔ	9 Ⓐ Ⓑ Ⓒ Ⓓ Ⓔ	15 Ⓐ Ⓑ Ⓒ Ⓓ Ⓔ	21 Ⓐ Ⓑ Ⓒ Ⓓ Ⓔ
4 Ⓐ Ⓑ Ⓒ Ⓓ Ⓔ	10 Ⓐ Ⓑ Ⓒ Ⓓ Ⓔ	16 Ⓐ Ⓑ Ⓒ Ⓓ Ⓔ	22 Ⓐ Ⓑ Ⓒ Ⓓ Ⓔ
5 Ⓐ Ⓑ Ⓒ Ⓓ Ⓔ	11 Ⓐ Ⓑ Ⓒ Ⓓ Ⓔ	17 Ⓐ Ⓑ Ⓒ Ⓓ Ⓔ	23 Ⓐ Ⓑ Ⓒ Ⓓ Ⓔ
6 Ⓐ Ⓑ Ⓒ Ⓓ Ⓔ	12 Ⓐ Ⓑ Ⓒ Ⓓ Ⓔ	18 Ⓐ Ⓑ Ⓒ Ⓓ Ⓔ	24 Ⓐ Ⓑ Ⓒ Ⓓ Ⓔ

SECTION 2

1 Ⓐ Ⓑ Ⓒ Ⓓ Ⓔ	7 Ⓐ Ⓑ Ⓒ Ⓓ Ⓔ	13 Ⓐ Ⓑ Ⓒ Ⓓ Ⓔ	19 Ⓐ Ⓑ Ⓒ Ⓓ Ⓔ
2 Ⓐ Ⓑ Ⓒ Ⓓ Ⓔ	8 Ⓐ Ⓑ Ⓒ Ⓓ Ⓔ	14 Ⓐ Ⓑ Ⓒ Ⓓ Ⓔ	20 Ⓐ Ⓑ Ⓒ Ⓓ Ⓔ
3 Ⓐ Ⓑ Ⓒ Ⓓ Ⓔ	9 Ⓐ Ⓑ Ⓒ Ⓓ Ⓔ	15 Ⓐ Ⓑ Ⓒ Ⓓ Ⓔ	21 Ⓐ Ⓑ Ⓒ Ⓓ Ⓔ
4 Ⓐ Ⓑ Ⓒ Ⓓ Ⓔ	10 Ⓐ Ⓑ Ⓒ Ⓓ Ⓔ	16 Ⓐ Ⓑ Ⓒ Ⓓ Ⓔ	22 Ⓐ Ⓑ Ⓒ Ⓓ Ⓔ
5 Ⓐ Ⓑ Ⓒ Ⓓ Ⓔ	11 Ⓐ Ⓑ Ⓒ Ⓓ Ⓔ	17 Ⓐ Ⓑ Ⓒ Ⓓ Ⓔ	23 Ⓐ Ⓑ Ⓒ Ⓓ Ⓔ
6 Ⓐ Ⓑ Ⓒ Ⓓ Ⓔ	12 Ⓐ Ⓑ Ⓒ Ⓓ Ⓔ	18 Ⓐ Ⓑ Ⓒ Ⓓ Ⓔ	24 Ⓐ Ⓑ Ⓒ Ⓓ Ⓔ
			25 Ⓐ Ⓑ Ⓒ Ⓓ Ⓔ

SECTION 3

1 Ⓐ Ⓑ Ⓒ Ⓓ Ⓔ	6 Ⓐ Ⓑ Ⓒ Ⓓ Ⓔ	11 Ⓐ Ⓑ Ⓒ Ⓓ Ⓔ	16 Ⓐ Ⓑ Ⓒ Ⓓ Ⓔ
2 Ⓐ Ⓑ Ⓒ Ⓓ Ⓔ	7 Ⓐ Ⓑ Ⓒ Ⓓ Ⓔ	12 Ⓐ Ⓑ Ⓒ Ⓓ Ⓔ	17 Ⓐ Ⓑ Ⓒ Ⓓ Ⓔ
3 Ⓐ Ⓑ Ⓒ Ⓓ Ⓔ	8 Ⓐ Ⓑ Ⓒ Ⓓ Ⓔ	13 Ⓐ Ⓑ Ⓒ Ⓓ Ⓔ	18 Ⓐ Ⓑ Ⓒ Ⓓ Ⓔ
4 Ⓐ Ⓑ Ⓒ Ⓓ Ⓔ	9 Ⓐ Ⓑ Ⓒ Ⓓ Ⓔ	14 Ⓐ Ⓑ Ⓒ Ⓓ Ⓔ	
5 Ⓐ Ⓑ Ⓒ Ⓓ Ⓔ	10 Ⓐ Ⓑ Ⓒ Ⓓ Ⓔ	15 Ⓐ Ⓑ Ⓒ Ⓓ Ⓔ	

SCORING YOUR TEST

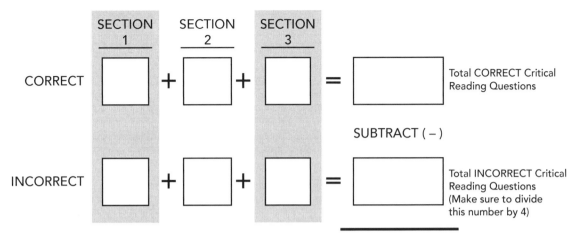

	SECTION 1		SECTION 2		SECTION 3			
CORRECT	☐	+	☐	+	☐	=	☐	Total CORRECT Critical Reading Questions
INCORRECT	☐	+	☐	+	☐	=	☐	Total INCORRECT Critical Reading Questions (Make sure to divide this number by 4)

SUBTRACT (−)

Raw Score ☐

Check Chart For SAT Score ☐

How to Score Your SAT

1. Subtotal the number of CORRECT answers for each section of the practice test. Put this number in the Total CORRECT box.

2. Subtotal the number of INCORRECT answers for each section of the practice test. Divide the subtotal by 4. Put this number in the Total INCORRECT box.

3. Subtract the second number from the first. This is your Raw Score.

4. Look up your Raw Score number in the SAT Scoring Chart. This is your scaled score.

SAT SCORING CHART

RAW SCORE	SCALED SCORE	RAW SCORE	SCALED SCORE	RAW SCORE	SCALED SCORE	RAW SCORE	SCALED SCORE
67	800	47	600-640	27	460-500	7	300-340
66	770-800	46	590-630	26	450-490	6	300-340
65	750-790	45	580-620	25	450-490	5	290-330
64	740-780	44	580-620	24	440-480	4	280-320
63	740-780	43	570-610	23	430-470	3	270-310
62	730-770	42	570-610	22	420-460	2	260-300
61	720-760	41	560-600	21	420-460	1	230-270
60	710-750	40	550-590	20	410-450	0	200-240
59	700-740	39	550-590	19	400-440	-1	200-230
58	690-730	38	540-580	18	400-440	-2	200-220
57	680-720	37	530-570	17	390-430	-3	200-210
56	670-710	36	530-570	16	380-420		
55	670-710	35	520-560	15	380-420		
54	660-700	34	510-550	14	370-410		
53	650-690	33	500-540	13	360-400		
52	640-680	32	500-540	12	350-390		
51	630-670	31	490-530	11	350-390		
50	620-660	30	480-520	10	340-380		
49	610-650	29	470-510	9	330-370		
48	600-640	28	470-510	8	310-350		

TEST 7

SECTION 1

1 Ⓐ Ⓑ Ⓒ Ⓓ Ⓔ
2 Ⓐ Ⓑ Ⓒ Ⓓ Ⓔ
3 Ⓐ Ⓑ Ⓒ Ⓓ Ⓔ
4 Ⓐ Ⓑ Ⓒ Ⓓ Ⓔ
5 Ⓐ Ⓑ Ⓒ Ⓓ Ⓔ
6 Ⓐ Ⓑ Ⓒ Ⓓ Ⓔ

7 Ⓐ Ⓑ Ⓒ Ⓓ Ⓔ
8 Ⓐ Ⓑ Ⓒ Ⓓ Ⓔ
9 Ⓐ Ⓑ Ⓒ Ⓓ Ⓔ
10 Ⓐ Ⓑ Ⓒ Ⓓ Ⓔ
11 Ⓐ Ⓑ Ⓒ Ⓓ Ⓔ
12 Ⓐ Ⓑ Ⓒ Ⓓ Ⓔ

13 Ⓐ Ⓑ Ⓒ Ⓓ Ⓔ
14 Ⓐ Ⓑ Ⓒ Ⓓ Ⓔ
15 Ⓐ Ⓑ Ⓒ Ⓓ Ⓔ
16 Ⓐ Ⓑ Ⓒ Ⓓ Ⓔ
17 Ⓐ Ⓑ Ⓒ Ⓓ Ⓔ
18 Ⓐ Ⓑ Ⓒ Ⓓ Ⓔ

19 Ⓐ Ⓑ Ⓒ Ⓓ Ⓔ
20 Ⓐ Ⓑ Ⓒ Ⓓ Ⓔ
21 Ⓐ Ⓑ Ⓒ Ⓓ Ⓔ
22 Ⓐ Ⓑ Ⓒ Ⓓ Ⓔ
23 Ⓐ Ⓑ Ⓒ Ⓓ Ⓔ
24 Ⓐ Ⓑ Ⓒ Ⓓ Ⓔ

SECTION 2

1 Ⓐ Ⓑ Ⓒ Ⓓ Ⓔ
2 Ⓐ Ⓑ Ⓒ Ⓓ Ⓔ
3 Ⓐ Ⓑ Ⓒ Ⓓ Ⓔ
4 Ⓐ Ⓑ Ⓒ Ⓓ Ⓔ
5 Ⓐ Ⓑ Ⓒ Ⓓ Ⓔ
6 Ⓐ Ⓑ Ⓒ Ⓓ Ⓔ

7 Ⓐ Ⓑ Ⓒ Ⓓ Ⓔ
8 Ⓐ Ⓑ Ⓒ Ⓓ Ⓔ
9 Ⓐ Ⓑ Ⓒ Ⓓ Ⓔ
10 Ⓐ Ⓑ Ⓒ Ⓓ Ⓔ
11 Ⓐ Ⓑ Ⓒ Ⓓ Ⓔ
12 Ⓐ Ⓑ Ⓒ Ⓓ Ⓔ

13 Ⓐ Ⓑ Ⓒ Ⓓ Ⓔ
14 Ⓐ Ⓑ Ⓒ Ⓓ Ⓔ
15 Ⓐ Ⓑ Ⓒ Ⓓ Ⓔ
16 Ⓐ Ⓑ Ⓒ Ⓓ Ⓔ
17 Ⓐ Ⓑ Ⓒ Ⓓ Ⓔ
18 Ⓐ Ⓑ Ⓒ Ⓓ Ⓔ

19 Ⓐ Ⓑ Ⓒ Ⓓ Ⓔ
20 Ⓐ Ⓑ Ⓒ Ⓓ Ⓔ
21 Ⓐ Ⓑ Ⓒ Ⓓ Ⓔ
22 Ⓐ Ⓑ Ⓒ Ⓓ Ⓔ
23 Ⓐ Ⓑ Ⓒ Ⓓ Ⓔ
24 Ⓐ Ⓑ Ⓒ Ⓓ Ⓔ
25 Ⓐ Ⓑ Ⓒ Ⓓ Ⓔ

SECTION 3

1 Ⓐ Ⓑ Ⓒ Ⓓ Ⓔ
2 Ⓐ Ⓑ Ⓒ Ⓓ Ⓔ
3 Ⓐ Ⓑ Ⓒ Ⓓ Ⓔ
4 Ⓐ Ⓑ Ⓒ Ⓓ Ⓔ
5 Ⓐ Ⓑ Ⓒ Ⓓ Ⓔ

6 Ⓐ Ⓑ Ⓒ Ⓓ Ⓔ
7 Ⓐ Ⓑ Ⓒ Ⓓ Ⓔ
8 Ⓐ Ⓑ Ⓒ Ⓓ Ⓔ
9 Ⓐ Ⓑ Ⓒ Ⓓ Ⓔ
10 Ⓐ Ⓑ Ⓒ Ⓓ Ⓔ

11 Ⓐ Ⓑ Ⓒ Ⓓ Ⓔ
12 Ⓐ Ⓑ Ⓒ Ⓓ Ⓔ
13 Ⓐ Ⓑ Ⓒ Ⓓ Ⓔ
14 Ⓐ Ⓑ Ⓒ Ⓓ Ⓔ
15 Ⓐ Ⓑ Ⓒ Ⓓ Ⓔ

16 Ⓐ Ⓑ Ⓒ Ⓓ Ⓔ
17 Ⓐ Ⓑ Ⓒ Ⓓ Ⓔ
18 Ⓐ Ⓑ Ⓒ Ⓓ Ⓔ

SCORING YOUR TEST

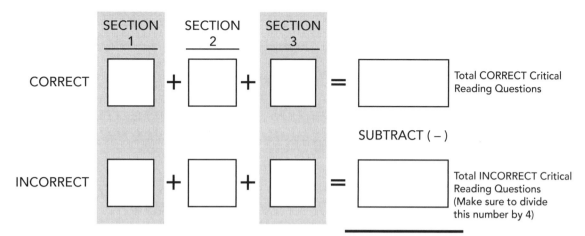

	SECTION 1		SECTION 2		SECTION 3			
CORRECT	☐	+	☐	+	☐	=	☐	Total CORRECT Critical Reading Questions
							SUBTRACT (–)	
INCORRECT	☐	+	☐	+	☐	=	☐	Total INCORRECT Critical Reading Questions (Make sure to divide this number by 4)

Raw Score ☐

Check Chart For SAT Score ☐

How to Score Your SAT

1. Subtotal the number of CORRECT answers for each section of the practice test. Put this number in the Total CORRECT box.

2. Subtotal the number of INCORRECT answers for each section of the practice test. Divide the subtotal by 4. Put this number in the Total INCORRECT box.

3. Subtract the second number from the first. This is your Raw Score.

4. Look up your Raw Score number in the SAT Scoring Chart. This is your scaled score.

SAT SCORING CHART

RAW SCORE	SCALED SCORE	RAW SCORE	SCALED SCORE	RAW SCORE	SCALED SCORE	RAW SCORE	SCALED SCORE
67	800	47	600-640	27	460-500	7	300-340
66	770-800	46	590-630	26	450-490	6	300-340
65	750-790	45	580-620	25	450-490	5	290-330
64	740-780	44	580-620	24	440-480	4	280-320
63	740-780	43	570-610	23	430-470	3	270-310
62	730-770	42	570-610	22	420-460	2	260-300
61	720-760	41	560-600	21	420-460	1	230-270
60	710-750	40	550-590	20	410-450	0	200-240
59	700-740	39	550-590	19	400-440	-1	200-230
58	690-730	38	540-580	18	400-440	-2	200-220
57	680-720	37	530-570	17	390-430	-3	200-210
56	670-710	36	530-570	16	380-420		
55	670-710	35	520-560	15	380-420		
54	660-700	34	510-550	14	370-410		
53	650-690	33	500-540	13	360-400		
52	640-680	32	500-540	12	350-390		
51	630-670	31	490-530	11	350-390		
50	620-660	30	480-520	10	340-380		
49	610-650	29	470-510	9	330-370		
48	600-640	28	470-510	8	310-350		

COMPLETE MARK ●	EXAMPLES OF INCOMPLETE MARKS	You must use a No. 2 pencil and marks must be complete. Do not use a mechanical pencil. It is very important that you fill in the entire circle darkly and completely. If you change your response, erase as completely as possible. Incomplete marks or erasures may affect your score.

TEST 8

SECTION 1

1 Ⓐ Ⓑ Ⓒ Ⓓ Ⓔ	7 Ⓐ Ⓑ Ⓒ Ⓓ Ⓔ	13 Ⓐ Ⓑ Ⓒ Ⓓ Ⓔ	19 Ⓐ Ⓑ Ⓒ Ⓓ Ⓔ
2 Ⓐ Ⓑ Ⓒ Ⓓ Ⓔ	8 Ⓐ Ⓑ Ⓒ Ⓓ Ⓔ	14 Ⓐ Ⓑ Ⓒ Ⓓ Ⓔ	20 Ⓐ Ⓑ Ⓒ Ⓓ Ⓔ
3 Ⓐ Ⓑ Ⓒ Ⓓ Ⓔ	9 Ⓐ Ⓑ Ⓒ Ⓓ Ⓔ	15 Ⓐ Ⓑ Ⓒ Ⓓ Ⓔ	21 Ⓐ Ⓑ Ⓒ Ⓓ Ⓔ
4 Ⓐ Ⓑ Ⓒ Ⓓ Ⓔ	10 Ⓐ Ⓑ Ⓒ Ⓓ Ⓔ	16 Ⓐ Ⓑ Ⓒ Ⓓ Ⓔ	22 Ⓐ Ⓑ Ⓒ Ⓓ Ⓔ
5 Ⓐ Ⓑ Ⓒ Ⓓ Ⓔ	11 Ⓐ Ⓑ Ⓒ Ⓓ Ⓔ	17 Ⓐ Ⓑ Ⓒ Ⓓ Ⓔ	23 Ⓐ Ⓑ Ⓒ Ⓓ Ⓔ
6 Ⓐ Ⓑ Ⓒ Ⓓ Ⓔ	12 Ⓐ Ⓑ Ⓒ Ⓓ Ⓔ	18 Ⓐ Ⓑ Ⓒ Ⓓ Ⓔ	24 Ⓐ Ⓑ Ⓒ Ⓓ Ⓔ

SECTION 2

1 Ⓐ Ⓑ Ⓒ Ⓓ Ⓔ	7 Ⓐ Ⓑ Ⓒ Ⓓ Ⓔ	13 Ⓐ Ⓑ Ⓒ Ⓓ Ⓔ	19 Ⓐ Ⓑ Ⓒ Ⓓ Ⓔ
2 Ⓐ Ⓑ Ⓒ Ⓓ Ⓔ	8 Ⓐ Ⓑ Ⓒ Ⓓ Ⓔ	14 Ⓐ Ⓑ Ⓒ Ⓓ Ⓔ	20 Ⓐ Ⓑ Ⓒ Ⓓ Ⓔ
3 Ⓐ Ⓑ Ⓒ Ⓓ Ⓔ	9 Ⓐ Ⓑ Ⓒ Ⓓ Ⓔ	15 Ⓐ Ⓑ Ⓒ Ⓓ Ⓔ	21 Ⓐ Ⓑ Ⓒ Ⓓ Ⓔ
4 Ⓐ Ⓑ Ⓒ Ⓓ Ⓔ	10 Ⓐ Ⓑ Ⓒ Ⓓ Ⓔ	16 Ⓐ Ⓑ Ⓒ Ⓓ Ⓔ	22 Ⓐ Ⓑ Ⓒ Ⓓ Ⓔ
5 Ⓐ Ⓑ Ⓒ Ⓓ Ⓔ	11 Ⓐ Ⓑ Ⓒ Ⓓ Ⓔ	17 Ⓐ Ⓑ Ⓒ Ⓓ Ⓔ	23 Ⓐ Ⓑ Ⓒ Ⓓ Ⓔ
6 Ⓐ Ⓑ Ⓒ Ⓓ Ⓔ	12 Ⓐ Ⓑ Ⓒ Ⓓ Ⓔ	18 Ⓐ Ⓑ Ⓒ Ⓓ Ⓔ	24 Ⓐ Ⓑ Ⓒ Ⓓ Ⓔ
			25 Ⓐ Ⓑ Ⓒ Ⓓ Ⓔ

SECTION 3

1 Ⓐ Ⓑ Ⓒ Ⓓ Ⓔ	6 Ⓐ Ⓑ Ⓒ Ⓓ Ⓔ	11 Ⓐ Ⓑ Ⓒ Ⓓ Ⓔ	16 Ⓐ Ⓑ Ⓒ Ⓓ Ⓔ
2 Ⓐ Ⓑ Ⓒ Ⓓ Ⓔ	7 Ⓐ Ⓑ Ⓒ Ⓓ Ⓔ	12 Ⓐ Ⓑ Ⓒ Ⓓ Ⓔ	17 Ⓐ Ⓑ Ⓒ Ⓓ Ⓔ
3 Ⓐ Ⓑ Ⓒ Ⓓ Ⓔ	8 Ⓐ Ⓑ Ⓒ Ⓓ Ⓔ	13 Ⓐ Ⓑ Ⓒ Ⓓ Ⓔ	18 Ⓐ Ⓑ Ⓒ Ⓓ Ⓔ
4 Ⓐ Ⓑ Ⓒ Ⓓ Ⓔ	9 Ⓐ Ⓑ Ⓒ Ⓓ Ⓔ	14 Ⓐ Ⓑ Ⓒ Ⓓ Ⓔ	
5 Ⓐ Ⓑ Ⓒ Ⓓ Ⓔ	10 Ⓐ Ⓑ Ⓒ Ⓓ Ⓔ	15 Ⓐ Ⓑ Ⓒ Ⓓ Ⓔ	

SCORING YOUR TEST

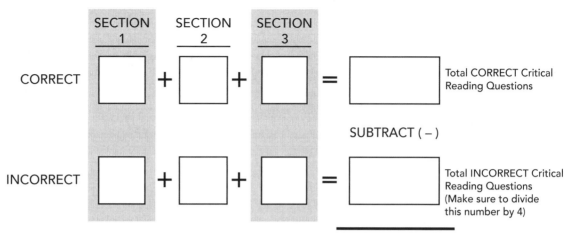

	SECTION 1		SECTION 2		SECTION 3			
CORRECT	☐	+	☐	+	☐	=	☐	Total CORRECT Critical Reading Questions

SUBTRACT (−)

INCORRECT	☐	+	☐	+	☐	=	☐	Total INCORRECT Critical Reading Questions (Make sure to divide this number by 4)

Raw Score ☐

Check Chart For SAT Score ☐

How to Score Your SAT

1. Subtotal the number of CORRECT answers for each section of the practice test. Put this number in the Total CORRECT box.
2. Subtotal the number of INCORRECT answers for each section of the practice test. Divide the subtotal by 4. Put this number in the Total INCORRECT box.
3. Subtract the second number from the first. This is your Raw Score.
4. Look up your Raw Score number in the SAT Scoring Chart. This is your scaled score.

SAT SCORING CHART

RAW SCORE	SCALED SCORE	RAW SCORE	SCALED SCORE	RAW SCORE	SCALED SCORE	RAW SCORE	SCALED SCORE
67	800	47	600-640	27	460-500	7	300-340
66	770-800	46	590-630	26	450-490	6	300-340
65	750-790	45	580-620	25	450-490	5	290-330
64	740-780	44	580-620	24	440-480	4	280-320
63	740-780	43	570-610	23	430-470	3	270-310
62	730-770	42	570-610	22	420-460	2	260-300
61	720-760	41	560-600	21	420-460	1	230-270
60	710-750	40	550-590	20	410-450	0	200-240
59	700-740	39	550-590	19	400-440	-1	200-230
58	690-730	38	540-580	18	400-440	-2	200-220
57	680-720	37	530-570	17	390-430	-3	200-210
56	670-710	36	530-570	16	380-420		
55	670-710	35	520-560	15	380-420		
54	660-700	34	510-550	14	370-410		
53	650-690	33	500-540	13	360-400		
52	640-680	32	500-540	12	350-390		
51	630-670	31	490-530	11	350-390		
50	620-660	30	480-520	10	340-380		
49	610-650	29	470-510	9	330-370		
48	600-640	28	470-510	8	310-350		

COMPLETE MARK ● EXAMPLES OF INCOMPLETE MARKS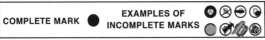

You must use a No. 2 pencil and marks must be complete. Do not use a mechanical pencil. It is very important that you fill in the entire circle darkly and completely. If you change your response, erase as completely as possible. Incomplete marks or erasures may affect your score.

TEST 9

SECTION 1

1 Ⓐ Ⓑ Ⓒ Ⓓ Ⓔ
2 Ⓐ Ⓑ Ⓒ Ⓓ Ⓔ
3 Ⓐ Ⓑ Ⓒ Ⓓ Ⓔ
4 Ⓐ Ⓑ Ⓒ Ⓓ Ⓔ
5 Ⓐ Ⓑ Ⓒ Ⓓ Ⓔ
6 Ⓐ Ⓑ Ⓒ Ⓓ Ⓔ

7 Ⓐ Ⓑ Ⓒ Ⓓ Ⓔ
8 Ⓐ Ⓑ Ⓒ Ⓓ Ⓔ
9 Ⓐ Ⓑ Ⓒ Ⓓ Ⓔ
10 Ⓐ Ⓑ Ⓒ Ⓓ Ⓔ
11 Ⓐ Ⓑ Ⓒ Ⓓ Ⓔ
12 Ⓐ Ⓑ Ⓒ Ⓓ Ⓔ

13 Ⓐ Ⓑ Ⓒ Ⓓ Ⓔ
14 Ⓐ Ⓑ Ⓒ Ⓓ Ⓔ
15 Ⓐ Ⓑ Ⓒ Ⓓ Ⓔ
16 Ⓐ Ⓑ Ⓒ Ⓓ Ⓔ
17 Ⓐ Ⓑ Ⓒ Ⓓ Ⓔ
18 Ⓐ Ⓑ Ⓒ Ⓓ Ⓔ

19 Ⓐ Ⓑ Ⓒ Ⓓ Ⓔ
20 Ⓐ Ⓑ Ⓒ Ⓓ Ⓔ
21 Ⓐ Ⓑ Ⓒ Ⓓ Ⓔ
22 Ⓐ Ⓑ Ⓒ Ⓓ Ⓔ
23 Ⓐ Ⓑ Ⓒ Ⓓ Ⓔ
24 Ⓐ Ⓑ Ⓒ Ⓓ Ⓔ
25 Ⓐ Ⓑ Ⓒ Ⓓ Ⓔ

SECTION 2

1 Ⓐ Ⓑ Ⓒ Ⓓ Ⓔ
2 Ⓐ Ⓑ Ⓒ Ⓓ Ⓔ
3 Ⓐ Ⓑ Ⓒ Ⓓ Ⓔ
4 Ⓐ Ⓑ Ⓒ Ⓓ Ⓔ
5 Ⓐ Ⓑ Ⓒ Ⓓ Ⓔ
6 Ⓐ Ⓑ Ⓒ Ⓓ Ⓔ

7 Ⓐ Ⓑ Ⓒ Ⓓ Ⓔ
8 Ⓐ Ⓑ Ⓒ Ⓓ Ⓔ
9 Ⓐ Ⓑ Ⓒ Ⓓ Ⓔ
10 Ⓐ Ⓑ Ⓒ Ⓓ Ⓔ
11 Ⓐ Ⓑ Ⓒ Ⓓ Ⓔ
12 Ⓐ Ⓑ Ⓒ Ⓓ Ⓔ

13 Ⓐ Ⓑ Ⓒ Ⓓ Ⓔ
14 Ⓐ Ⓑ Ⓒ Ⓓ Ⓔ
15 Ⓐ Ⓑ Ⓒ Ⓓ Ⓔ
16 Ⓐ Ⓑ Ⓒ Ⓓ Ⓔ
17 Ⓐ Ⓑ Ⓒ Ⓓ Ⓔ
18 Ⓐ Ⓑ Ⓒ Ⓓ Ⓔ

19 Ⓐ Ⓑ Ⓒ Ⓓ Ⓔ
20 Ⓐ Ⓑ Ⓒ Ⓓ Ⓔ
21 Ⓐ Ⓑ Ⓒ Ⓓ Ⓔ
22 Ⓐ Ⓑ Ⓒ Ⓓ Ⓔ
23 Ⓐ Ⓑ Ⓒ Ⓓ Ⓔ
24 Ⓐ Ⓑ Ⓒ Ⓓ Ⓔ

SECTION 3

1 Ⓐ Ⓑ Ⓒ Ⓓ Ⓔ
2 Ⓐ Ⓑ Ⓒ Ⓓ Ⓔ
3 Ⓐ Ⓑ Ⓒ Ⓓ Ⓔ
4 Ⓐ Ⓑ Ⓒ Ⓓ Ⓔ
5 Ⓐ Ⓑ Ⓒ Ⓓ Ⓔ

6 Ⓐ Ⓑ Ⓒ Ⓓ Ⓔ
7 Ⓐ Ⓑ Ⓒ Ⓓ Ⓔ
8 Ⓐ Ⓑ Ⓒ Ⓓ Ⓔ
9 Ⓐ Ⓑ Ⓒ Ⓓ Ⓔ
10 Ⓐ Ⓑ Ⓒ Ⓓ Ⓔ

11 Ⓐ Ⓑ Ⓒ Ⓓ Ⓔ
12 Ⓐ Ⓑ Ⓒ Ⓓ Ⓔ
13 Ⓐ Ⓑ Ⓒ Ⓓ Ⓔ
14 Ⓐ Ⓑ Ⓒ Ⓓ Ⓔ
15 Ⓐ Ⓑ Ⓒ Ⓓ Ⓔ

16 Ⓐ Ⓑ Ⓒ Ⓓ Ⓔ
17 Ⓐ Ⓑ Ⓒ Ⓓ Ⓔ
18 Ⓐ Ⓑ Ⓒ Ⓓ Ⓔ

Cut out this page and make copies so you can take each test multiple times.

201

SCORING YOUR TEST

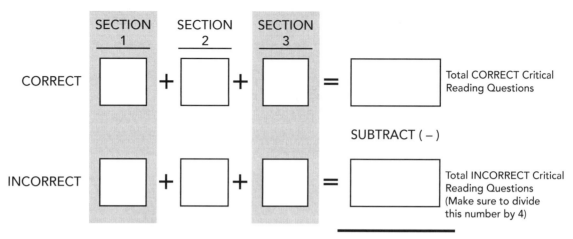

CORRECT [SECTION 1] + [SECTION 2] + [SECTION 3] = [ ] Total CORRECT Critical Reading Questions

SUBTRACT (−)

INCORRECT [SECTION 1] + [SECTION 2] + [SECTION 3] = [ ] Total INCORRECT Critical Reading Questions (Make sure to divide this number by 4)

Raw Score [ ]

Check Chart For SAT Score [ ]

How to Score Your SAT

1. Subtotal the number of CORRECT answers for each section of the practice test. Put this number in the Total CORRECT box.
2. Subtotal the number of INCORRECT answers for each section of the practice test. Divide the subtotal by 4. Put this number in the Total INCORRECT box.
3. Subtract the second number from the first. This is your Raw Score.
4. Look up your Raw Score number in the SAT Scoring Chart. This is your scaled score.

SAT SCORING CHART

RAW SCORE	SCALED SCORE	RAW SCORE	SCALED SCORE	RAW SCORE	SCALED SCORE	RAW SCORE	SCALED SCORE
67	800	47	600-640	27	460-500	7	300-340
66	770-800	46	590-630	26	450-490	6	300-340
65	750-790	45	580-620	25	450-490	5	290-330
64	740-780	44	580-620	24	440-480	4	280-320
63	740-780	43	570-610	23	430-470	3	270-310
62	730-770	42	570-610	22	420-460	2	260-300
61	720-760	41	560-600	21	420-460	1	230-270
60	710-750	40	550-590	20	410-450	0	200-240
59	700-740	39	550-590	19	400-440	-1	200-230
58	690-730	38	540-580	18	400-440	-2	200-220
57	680-720	37	530-570	17	390-430	-3	200-210
56	670-710	36	530-570	16	380-420		
55	670-710	35	520-560	15	380-420		
54	660-700	34	510-550	14	370-410		
53	650-690	33	500-540	13	360-400		
52	640-680	32	500-540	12	350-390		
51	630-670	31	490-530	11	350-390		
50	620-660	30	480-520	10	340-380		
49	610-650	29	470-510	9	330-370		
48	600-640	28	470-510	8	310-350		

COMPLETE MARK ●   **EXAMPLES OF INCOMPLETE MARKS** Ⓐ ⊗ ⊖ Ⓒ ⬤ 🖊 ✎ ⊛

TEST 10

SECTION 1

1 Ⓐ Ⓑ Ⓒ Ⓓ Ⓔ   7 Ⓐ Ⓑ Ⓒ Ⓓ Ⓔ   13 Ⓐ Ⓑ Ⓒ Ⓓ Ⓔ   19 Ⓐ Ⓑ Ⓒ Ⓓ Ⓔ
2 Ⓐ Ⓑ Ⓒ Ⓓ Ⓔ   8 Ⓐ Ⓑ Ⓒ Ⓓ Ⓔ   14 Ⓐ Ⓑ Ⓒ Ⓓ Ⓔ   20 Ⓐ Ⓑ Ⓒ Ⓓ Ⓔ
3 Ⓐ Ⓑ Ⓒ Ⓓ Ⓔ   9 Ⓐ Ⓑ Ⓒ Ⓓ Ⓔ   15 Ⓐ Ⓑ Ⓒ Ⓓ Ⓔ   21 Ⓐ Ⓑ Ⓒ Ⓓ Ⓔ
4 Ⓐ Ⓑ Ⓒ Ⓓ Ⓔ   10 Ⓐ Ⓑ Ⓒ Ⓓ Ⓔ   16 Ⓐ Ⓑ Ⓒ Ⓓ Ⓔ   22 Ⓐ Ⓑ Ⓒ Ⓓ Ⓔ
5 Ⓐ Ⓑ Ⓒ Ⓓ Ⓔ   11 Ⓐ Ⓑ Ⓒ Ⓓ Ⓔ   17 Ⓐ Ⓑ Ⓒ Ⓓ Ⓔ   23 Ⓐ Ⓑ Ⓒ Ⓓ Ⓔ
6 Ⓐ Ⓑ Ⓒ Ⓓ Ⓔ   12 Ⓐ Ⓑ Ⓒ Ⓓ Ⓔ   18 Ⓐ Ⓑ Ⓒ Ⓓ Ⓔ   24 Ⓐ Ⓑ Ⓒ Ⓓ Ⓔ
   25 Ⓐ Ⓑ Ⓒ Ⓓ Ⓔ

SECTION 2

1 Ⓐ Ⓑ Ⓒ Ⓓ Ⓔ   7 Ⓐ Ⓑ Ⓒ Ⓓ Ⓔ   13 Ⓐ Ⓑ Ⓒ Ⓓ Ⓔ   19 Ⓐ Ⓑ Ⓒ Ⓓ Ⓔ
2 Ⓐ Ⓑ Ⓒ Ⓓ Ⓔ   8 Ⓐ Ⓑ Ⓒ Ⓓ Ⓔ   14 Ⓐ Ⓑ Ⓒ Ⓓ Ⓔ   20 Ⓐ Ⓑ Ⓒ Ⓓ Ⓔ
3 Ⓐ Ⓑ Ⓒ Ⓓ Ⓔ   9 Ⓐ Ⓑ Ⓒ Ⓓ Ⓔ   15 Ⓐ Ⓑ Ⓒ Ⓓ Ⓔ   21 Ⓐ Ⓑ Ⓒ Ⓓ Ⓔ
4 Ⓐ Ⓑ Ⓒ Ⓓ Ⓔ   10 Ⓐ Ⓑ Ⓒ Ⓓ Ⓔ   16 Ⓐ Ⓑ Ⓒ Ⓓ Ⓔ   22 Ⓐ Ⓑ Ⓒ Ⓓ Ⓔ
5 Ⓐ Ⓑ Ⓒ Ⓓ Ⓔ   11 Ⓐ Ⓑ Ⓒ Ⓓ Ⓔ   17 Ⓐ Ⓑ Ⓒ Ⓓ Ⓔ   23 Ⓐ Ⓑ Ⓒ Ⓓ Ⓔ
6 Ⓐ Ⓑ Ⓒ Ⓓ Ⓔ   12 Ⓐ Ⓑ Ⓒ Ⓓ Ⓔ   18 Ⓐ Ⓑ Ⓒ Ⓓ Ⓔ   24 Ⓐ Ⓑ Ⓒ Ⓓ Ⓔ

SECTION 3

1 Ⓐ Ⓑ Ⓒ Ⓓ Ⓔ   6 Ⓐ Ⓑ Ⓒ Ⓓ Ⓔ   11 Ⓐ Ⓑ Ⓒ Ⓓ Ⓔ   16 Ⓐ Ⓑ Ⓒ Ⓓ Ⓔ
2 Ⓐ Ⓑ Ⓒ Ⓓ Ⓔ   7 Ⓐ Ⓑ Ⓒ Ⓓ Ⓔ   12 Ⓐ Ⓑ Ⓒ Ⓓ Ⓔ   17 Ⓐ Ⓑ Ⓒ Ⓓ Ⓔ
3 Ⓐ Ⓑ Ⓒ Ⓓ Ⓔ   8 Ⓐ Ⓑ Ⓒ Ⓓ Ⓔ   13 Ⓐ Ⓑ Ⓒ Ⓓ Ⓔ   18 Ⓐ Ⓑ Ⓒ Ⓓ Ⓔ
4 Ⓐ Ⓑ Ⓒ Ⓓ Ⓔ   9 Ⓐ Ⓑ Ⓒ Ⓓ Ⓔ   14 Ⓐ Ⓑ Ⓒ Ⓓ Ⓔ
5 Ⓐ Ⓑ Ⓒ Ⓓ Ⓔ   10 Ⓐ Ⓑ Ⓒ Ⓓ Ⓔ   15 Ⓐ Ⓑ Ⓒ Ⓓ Ⓔ

SCORING YOUR TEST

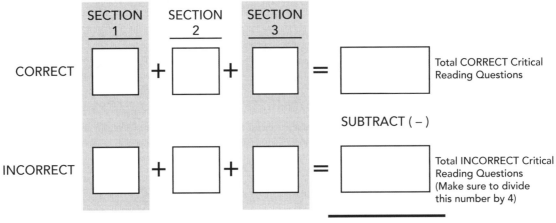

	SECTION 1		SECTION 2		SECTION 3				
CORRECT	☐	+	☐	+	☐	=	☐	Total CORRECT Critical Reading Questions	
							SUBTRACT (–)		
INCORRECT	☐	+	☐	+	☐	=	☐	Total INCORRECT Critical Reading Questions (Make sure to divide this number by 4)	

Raw Score ☐

Check Chart For SAT Score ☐

How to Score Your SAT

1. Subtotal the number of CORRECT answers for each section of the practice test. Put this number in the Total CORRECT box.

2. Subtotal the number of INCORRECT answers for each section of the practice test. Divide the subtotal by 4. Put this number in the Total INCORRECT box.

3. Subtract the second number from the first. This is your Raw Score.

4. Look up your Raw Score number in the SAT Scoring Chart. This is your scaled score.

SAT SCORING CHART

RAW SCORE	SCALED SCORE	RAW SCORE	SCALED SCORE	RAW SCORE	SCALED SCORE	RAW SCORE	SCALED SCORE
67	800	47	600-640	27	460-500	7	300-340
66	770-800	46	590-630	26	450-490	6	300-340
65	750-790	45	580-620	25	450-490	5	290-330
64	740-780	44	580-620	24	440-480	4	280-320
63	740-780	43	570-610	23	430-470	3	270-310
62	730-770	42	570-610	22	420-460	2	260-300
61	720-760	41	560-600	21	420-460	1	230-270
60	710-750	40	550-590	20	410-450	0	200-240
59	700-740	39	550-590	19	400-440	-1	200-230
58	690-730	38	540-580	18	400-440	-2	200-220
57	680-720	37	530-570	17	390-430	-3	200-210
56	670-710	36	530-570	16	380-420		
55	670-710	35	520-560	15	380-420		
54	660-700	34	510-550	14	370-410		
53	650-690	33	500-540	13	360-400		
52	640-680	32	500-540	12	350-390		
51	630-670	31	490-530	11	350-390		
50	620-660	30	480-520	10	340-380		
49	610-650	29	470-510	9	330-370		
48	600-640	28	470-510	8	310-350		

Made in the USA
Middletown, DE
28 May 2015